"Dr. Jim Osterhaus has wr [illegible] y as the coronavirus has ra [illegible] n literally reeling with the ac [illegible] h illness and death, and co [illegible] church services. Most pastors have been learning new skills, such as producing online services. Just like health-care workers and first-responders, pastors are exhausted and facing burnout. Jim Osterhaus offers practical help born out of decades of experience combining spiritual wisdom and psychological insight. I am pleased to recommend this wonderful book."

—Rt. Rev. Dr. John Howe, Senior Pastor
Lake of the Woods Church
Virginia Episcopal Bishop of Central Florida (retired)

"Ministry is a divine calling, and at the same time, it is an increasingly complex set of responses to very human needs and challenges. Through deep listening and profound wisdom, Jim Osterhaus has given us a resource that will help us not only to survive but to flourish in leadership that glorifies God and blesses our people."

—Rt. Rev. Ken Carter, Bishop
Florida Conference, The United Methodist Church

"Once on a trip through a former warzone, I came across a foreign road sign warning of a minefield ahead. Jim Osterhaus here carefully examines how to defuse or avoid destructive devices in the minefields of ministry so that we may better serve in the kingdom of God. When facing challenges, clergy often joke, 'I never learned about this in seminary,' often masking the real pain they experience as the complexities of church leadership come crashing in. Jim Osterhaus provides a clarifying overview of the ministry along with much practical advice, aiming to prevent meltdown and to increase effectiveness for the glory of God."

—Rt. Rev. Neil Lebhar, Anglican Bishop of the Gulf Atlantic

"Jim Osterhaus is a veteran consultant, counselor, and church leader. He brings together his wealth of experience and extraordinary insights in this comprehensive handbook for the local church pastor. He so helpfully emphasizes the inner life of the leader—the godly character, healthy self-definition, and humble courage needed for effective pastoral ministry. He takes the pastor from questions to ask while being considered for a position, through the early days of a new ministry, to the nitty-gritty of long-term congregational change. He teaches how to survive and thrive in church conflict, always with the goal of the transformation of both leader and congregation. *Avoiding Pastoral Pitfalls* is a rich resource, overflowing with wisdom for the growing pastor in every stage of ministry."

—Rt. Rev. John Guernsey
Anglican Bishop of the Diocese of the Mid-Atlantic

"LeBron James has a coach. Tom Brady has a coach. Serena Williams has a coach. And every coach has a playbook, a training manual, a set of principles and practices for success. In this book, uber-experienced executive coach Jim Osterhaus opens the playbook he has been using to coach executive leaders, organizational CEOs, and pastors for over three decades, focusing especially on the challenges facing pastors as leaders. This is a book you will return to over and over again. It will be coffee stained, marked up, shared with others, and memorized in places. It is an immense gift from one of the very best coaches. I should know. Jim Osterhaus was my coach for three years, and not a day goes by that I don't share with the leaders I coach what I learned from him."

—Dr. Tod Bolsinger, Executive Director, The De Pree Center Church Leadership Initiative author of *Tempered Resilience: How Leaders are Formed in the Crucible of Change*

"Very few books on pastoral ministry pack this many important topics and insights into one place. Osterhaus has spent a lifetime coaching pastors through the issues they face. His help in this volume is of utmost value."

—Dr. Jim Singleton
Associate Professor of Pastoral Leadership and Evangelism
Gordon-Conwell Theological Seminary

"Pastors have a tough job—not just because of the responsibilities and demands but because so few people understand what they do all day and what they worry about all night. Dr. Jim Osterhaus knows what pastors are facing and in *Avoiding Pastoral Pitfalls*, he provides insightful understanding that will not only help your ministry flourish but give you the tools to enjoy the journey."

—Dr. Roger Parrott, President
Belhaven University
author of *The Longview: Lasting Strategies for Rising Leaders*

"Succeeding as the pastor of a local congregation is probably one of today's most challenging vocations. Osterhaus gives a pastor all the practical wisdom and tools needed to be like Christ and to lead like Christ from the opening call to the final leave-taking. When using this book, pastors will not only survive, they should thrive."

—Dr. MaryKate Morse, Executive Dean, Portland Seminary
author of *Lifelong Leadership: Woven Together through Mentoring Communities*

"I recall as a fledgling pastor rushing to my seminary notes when the first couple came to me for marriage help. There is so much to learn on the fly in pastoral ministry. Jim Osterhaus has a store of experience as a pastoral counselor, a family systems therapist, a management consultant in sacred and secular institutions, and a coach to pastors around the country. He has even taught seminars in East Africa. He brings this lifetime of practical wisdom to bear in *Avoiding Pastoral Pitfalls*. This is a book you can turn to in specific situations and also in the larger formation of Christian eldership, shepherding the flock that is among you, exercising oversight as God would have you (1 Peter 5:2)."

—Rev. Dr. Stephen F. Noll, Vice Chancellor and President
Uganda Christian University (retired)

AVOIDING PASTORAL PITFALLS

AVOIDING PASTORAL PITFALLS

A GUIDE TO SURVIVING & THRIVING IN MINISTRY

James P. Osterhaus

Foreword by
Leighton Ford

an imprint of Hendrickson Publishing Group

Avoiding Pastoral Pitfalls: A Guide to Surviving and Thriving

Published by Hendrickson Publishers
an imprint of Hendrickson Publishing Group
Hendrickson Publishers, LLC
P. O. Box 3473
Peabody, Massachusetts 01961-3473
www.hendricksonpublishinggroup.com

ISBN 978-1-68307-370-3

Printed in the United States of America

First Printing — September 2021

Library of Congress Control Number: 2021942618

The book is dedicated to the three pastors who have been most influential in my life.

All three had keen minds and pastor's hearts.

Pastor A. W. Jackson
Dr. Butch Hardman
Dr. Leighton Ford

CONTENTS

Part Four: Negotiating Choppy Ministry Waters

Part Five: Finishing Well

ACKNOWLEDGMENTS

A book of this type, which includes many different ideas and practical suggestions, was crafted using the thinking of countless people. My calling through the years has been to talk to people, to hear their distresses, and to mine their thoughts and insights. To acknowledge all of them is, of course, impossible. But there are several who have assisted me in getting my thinking together, whom I'd like to acknowledge here specifically. These include: Tod Bolsinger, who helped me write the chapter on political considerations; John Holm, who greatly helped me with how to leave a church well; and Joe Jurkowski and Kevin Ford, partners who shaped my thinking on any number of topics. Then there is Jim Singleton, an insightful mind who has been in the trenches of ministry, in addition to teaching in the halls of academia. Rich Hurst has been a wonderful friend, a wealth of wisdom who has walked through various ministry settings. Butch Hardman, one of the three men to whom I have dedicated this book, has served as a mentor and friend for over sixty years. My dear friend Leighton Ford, who wrote the foreword to this book, has also been a friend on the journey; being near him has allowed me to experience a true man of integrity up close and personal. Then there is Steve Noll. He and I have walked and talked together for on toward fifty years. His wife, Peggy, was (as she has been on many of my writing projects) my first editor, who carefully examined the text finding and corrected my frequent mistakes.

And to all of you whom I have undoubtedly overlooked but who have contributed to my life and thought, I honor you and give you my thanks.

FOREWORD

As I write this, I have a picture in my mind of a small group gathered in a spacious home in the mountains of North Carolina. It is early spring with a chilling breeze outside as the group sits huddled by a blazing fireplace. Several younger men and women are there, and two older men. One is Jim Osterhaus. The other is me.

At this time, Jim and I had known each other since we met at a church retreat in California years before. He had been a teacher in our Arrow Leadership programs, and together we had led numerous retreats for young ministry leaders, focusing especially on the inner life of the leader. The younger ones present now were part of our various retreats before.

This time, however, is different. Jim is leading, but I am not. I am there, because I have a wounded soul. I had just come through a grueling time of conflict with some difficult people. I needed care and healing, and they were there to help.

Jim remembers that as we began, I said ruefully, "Jim, you are my psychiatrist. I am going to lie down on the couch!" Although he is not a psychiatrist, he is a gifted psychologist and counselor. There was also no couch, but around that fire I was able to open up the depths of my soul and experience.

During those hours in the mountains as we talked, I learned much about myself and about interpersonal challenges. Looking back on the situation, I can see where I had lacked wisdom and humility. We all learned from Jim about "projection"—how our critics project their own issues on others.

I have often looked back on those hours with a profound sense of gratitude for what I received and what I think the young leaders learned about themselves. I share this personal story so those who read *Avoiding Pastoral Pitfalls* will realize this book is not filled with the theories of an academic. Although these insights certainly are based on important theory and thought, what Jim has written has the mark of authenticity, because this content has been used and tested in literally hundreds of hours with hundreds of leaders who needed a gifted listener and guide.

So many times, when some younger leader I am mentoring has a difficult challenge needing help beyond what I can give, I have said, "Call Jim Osterhaus. He can help." And he has, time and time again.

I received little guidance along these lines during my ministry education. I learned a lot about Bible, theology, and church history, but not much about understanding myself and others! My friendship and partnership with Jim have helped to make up this lacuna across the years.

Now, as a gift from the Spirit, this book will guide so many of God's called servants as they in turn shepherd others from within their own hearts, souls, and minds.

Leighton Ford, Founding President
Leighton Ford Ministries
Charlotte, North Carolina

INTRODUCTION

WHAT YOU DIDN'T LEARN IN SEMINARY AND WHY IT MATTERS

In the September 2020 issue of *Christianity Today*, Kayla Stoecklein details how her husband, who had been the lead pastor of his church for five years, slowly burned out and fell into depression and anxiety. Finally, in an act of desperation, he took his own life. Kayla writes,

> Many pastors and people serving in ministry positions struggle with their mental health. And sadly, they don't always feel like there is space for them to share their struggles with their peers or congregants. Fear of losing their job, fear of losing their platform, fear of losing their voice, fear of losing respect from their peers is all a very real reality.[1]

More and more people who minister find themselves depressed. Their marriages are often in trouble. Their families are negatively affected. Often, they have few if any close friends. And, not surprisingly, a large percentage of those who enter the ministry leave it within five years. Every month, someone leaves the ministry due to moral failure, burnout, or divisiveness in their churches. Only a small percentage of pastors say they feel happy and content on a regular basis with who they are in their spiritual life, their church, or in their home.

---

1. Kayla Stoecklein, "I Was a Pastor's Wife: Suicide Made Me a Pastor's Widow," *Christianity Today* (September 2020), https://www.christianitytoday.com/pastors/2020/september-web-exclusives/pastor-suicide-wife-stoecklein-mental-health-church.html.

Over the years, I have coached and counseled hundreds of ministers from various traditions on four continents.[2] I've sat or walked and talked with ministers who have been nearly crushed by the burdens they experienced in ministry. What I have come to learn is that the average training of ministers across the globe is woefully deficient in those very areas that would allow them to avoid many of the pitfalls (or at least keep them from exacerbating those pitfalls). This book is an attempt to fill some of those voids.

WHAT I DIDN'T LEARN IN SEMINARY

Seminaries in every religious tradition have the stated objective to raise up men and women who can effectively move forward those respective traditions, while ministering to the needs—spiritual, emotional, mental, and physical—of the audiences to whom they have been called.

Over the centuries, seminaries have crafted curricula that religious leaders have judged to contain the essential elements for effective ministry: theology, hermeneutics, and homiletics. More recently, courses in human psychology, counseling, culture, and organizational processes have crept into syllabi to round out a core preparation. Even more recently, seminaries have begun to offer courses in leadership.

And yet, as I coach ministers across this country and across the traditional spectrum, I hear again and again the complaint that these pastors are ill-prepared to face the realities of day-to-day ministering. This inadequacy often appears when the newly minted minister first sits down in the church board meeting (whether it be an elder meeting, session, vestry, council, or what have you). Often the fearful thought emerges, *I'm the leader. What do I do now? What's important? What's not?* The moment conflict begins to develop, these thoughts intensify and panic often ensues when that conflict devolves on the pastor.

---

2. My mission was taken from *Lord of the Rings,* the third movie, *Return of the King.* Frodo and Sam are struggling up Mount Doom, and Frodo finally collapses under the burden of his mission. Sam picks him up and says, "I can't carry it (the ring) for you, but I can carry you." That has been my mission through the years. I was never called into ordained ministry, but I've been called to carry those who "carry the ring."

David Gortner, the director of the doctor of ministry program at Virginia Theological Seminary, conducted a fifteen-year study of students transitioning from students to pastors. He writes,

> I have found a consistent pattern among Episcopal clergy of what my colleagues and I call "talented but tenuous": highly creative people nonetheless lacking in self-confidence and decisiveness, who can come up with wonderful ideas but have neither the skill nor the will (nor feel the permission) to help communities bring ideas to fruition. They are kind, dedicated, and full of ideal visions of what the church could be; but they are also conflict-averse, uncertain how to manage their own anxiety, and unclear about the nature of human systems and organizations.[3]

Added to this idea is the fact that the vast majority of Christian churches focus ministry on the pastor rather than the community. This sets up the church in the consumer mentality, where congregants come to be "entertained," but when they feel they can get more entertainment elsewhere, they pull up stakes and move on the next location. All the while, the pastor turns into an overworked functionary who bounces from one meeting to another because, "It doesn't count if you're not there."

Let's consider several lessons that should be essential to any seminary curriculum but will undoubtedly be absent in the near future. The following are lessons I will expand on in the following chapters.

- ***You must attend to your inner life and develop disciplines that will deepen that inner life.*** We have dual citizenship (the City of God and the surrounding secular city of humankind). For most American Christians, however, these two cities have now blended into one. We don't see or understand the competing nature of the values that form a constant, ongoing tension between these two cities, but our primary citizenship and allegiance are to the City of God. We must cultivate that citizenship intentionally, realizing that our surrounding culture functions contrary to the dictates of our primary loyalties.

---

3. David Gortner, "Clergy Leadership in the 21st Century: Are We Up to the Task?," *In Trust Center for Theological Schools* (Summer 2014), http://www.intrust.org/Magazine/Issues/Summer-2014/Clergy-leadership-for-the-21st-century.

- ***You need to understand that your greatest resource is yourself.*** You may have already scanned the above points and said to yourself, *There's no way I can do these things, especially the one about conflict. I'm totally conflict-averse, and entertaining and nurturing conflict runs completely contrary to my nature.* If you thought that, then you've taken the first step to becoming more effective—that is, knowing yourself. At least at this point, you have a sense of what causes anxiety for you (conflict).

- ***Keep in mind that the threats to your ministry are not external but internal.*** It is our tendency to adapt to the surrounding immaturity we find everywhere. It is this immaturity that currently permeates our culture and virtually all its institutions that is so apparent and destructive of progress. In the church, this is expressed by those who demand, "Feed me! Nurture me! Take responsibility for me!" (What Paul addresses in the first letter he writes to the messed-up church in Corinth.) This kind of emotional climate can be dissipated only by clear, decisive, and well-defined leadership.

- ***You must understand that leadership is not a person; it's an activity.*** When people talk about "born leaders," they are typically describing a particular style of leadership that takes on a command-and-control character. People feel most comfortable when a strong leader of this genre steps up and takes responsibility to lead them in some prescribed direction. These leaders clarify direction and are good at mobilizing people to move in that direction. This activity of leadership, what we often describe as true leadership, is merely one activity that is effective in certain situations (e.g., when there is an emergency) and horrible in other situations (when the community must take responsibility to navigate tricky transitions).

- ***You must learn to wield several key leadership activities, depending on the demands of the situation.*** Most people have one mode of leading, which is effective only a fraction of the time. The other times, when other modes are required, the pastor leader becomes more and more ineffective.

- ***You must know the nature of conflict.*** Conflict is absolutely necessary to healthy church functioning, and it will always bring anxiety with it. I'm not saying that all conflict is healthy and constructive. Quite the contrary. Much of conflict is destructive. And learning the difference between healthy (Blue Zone) and unhealthy (Red Zone) conflict is critical. But understanding conflict, and how it affects and provokes issues resident within you, is key to its successful management and utilization. That brings us to the issue of self-awareness.

- ***You need to know that you grow only when you are uncomfortable.*** That's right—life is about pain, though we live in a culture that tries to avoid suffering at all costs, seeking instead the win-win happy place (which is the immature place noted above). Hopefully, this book is already making you uncomfortable as you begin to see some of your own shortcomings. That discomfort is not a bad thing (though you will experience it as anxiety and intuitively think to turn away from this book and not consider its merits).
- ***You must know that your job with the congregation (as with parenting) is to work yourself out of a job.*** This has to do with understanding the nature of power. If you are leading a consumer congregation that fully supports you for not upsetting the apple cart by raising anxiety too high, thus meeting expectations rather than recalibrating them, then you rest firmly within the majority of clergy. But you may have been reading all of that literature about how to be missional and how to see effective ministry as community-focused not pastor-focused (where often the most dependent members of your organization set the agendas, thus moving leadership toward weakness rather than strength and leveraging power to the recalcitrant, the passive-aggressive, and the most anxious members of the institution rather than toward the energetic, the visionary, the imaginative, and the most creatively motivated). These thoughts may be dangerous, for they will stimulate you to begin the transformative work of changing paradigms, which will of course raise congregational anxiety, which will provoke push-back and therefore raise your own anxiety. So why not just leave well enough alone? The congregation is content with you in the role of paid Christian who runs all over the place doing the "real" ministry, while everyone else settles back and

watches you sweat. *Well,* you say, *I just can't. This laissez-faire way of ministering doesn't seem to square with what Jesus had in mind and the way he operated.* Just remember, when the status quo is upset, people feel a sense of profound loss and dashed expectations. Then they exert inordinate amounts of pressure on the powers that be (i.e., you) to return things to the status quo. Don't forget, Jesus ended up on a cross.

- ***Pastors tend not to understand the unique culture of their church, and how that culture shapes everything that is happening within their church***. Remember Peter Drucker's words, "Culture eats strategy for breakfast." You're going to have to take a long, hard look at your culture before you set out on your well-conceived plans.
- ***Pastors by and large do not understand the complexities of the church organizational model and how this affects the unfolding ministry***. Churches are the most complex organizations in existence. I ought to know, I have consulted in many different organizational models, and churches are arguably the most complicated. If you don't begin to get a sense of how this works, it'll bite you. (It'll probably bite you anyway, but at least you'll understand where the bite came from!)
- ***Pastors usually do not understand the political realities that swirl around them—in their church, in their denomination, or in their community***. Political realities? That's right. Where two or three are gathered together, there's politics—people jockeying for position and influence (aka power) to increase their significance.
- ***Pastors don't tend to understand how to shift their congregations out of a consumer mentality, even though they may understand the critical need to do so***. If your congregation is like most in this country, then a major part of your church culture is a consumer mentality ("I'm here to be entertained and satisfied"). Changing this perception requires a great deal of strategizing.
- ***Most pastors aren't clear on how to enter their new ministry successfully, or how to leave a ministry successfully***. These

two transitions, entering a new ministry and leaving a ministry, create a great deal of anxiety for the congregation and must be handled appropriately.

- ***You absolutely cannot go it alone, even if you've been a Lone Ranger in ministry for years.*** As mentioned, I coach and have coached dozens of ministers in many different traditions around the country and in several other parts of the world. Over and over, I discover that these ministers are isolated in their ministries, and that this isolation brings with it a whole host of problems and dysfunctions. Folks, you're on the front lines and taking all manner of incoming fire! How can you possibly be effective, maintain your sanity, uphold clear boundaries, and lead effectively if you're doing this completely alone? You need the support of people who are in the same position as you. (Be advised that those who have never been in ministry have no idea what kinds of pressures you face. None!). Undoubtedly, within your communities there are minister gatherings where you can find understanding and guidance as you navigate the troubled waters of ministry. Leighton Ford is currently also setting up mentoring groups around the world for people in ministry who need to come together for mutual support (see www.leightfordministries.org).

As I said above, we'll be looking at each of these issues in the following pages. To begin with, however, I think I need to be somewhat theoretical. This will then set the foundation for all of the practical issues that we'll discuss in later chapters. So please be patient! And remember, if you're merely looking for a quick, simple, practical fix, you will undoubtedly be disappointed and thwarted in the long run. I therefore recommend reading the first few chapters in order, so the logic (hopefully, there is some obvious logic!) in the following chapters will be apparent and useful to you.

PART ONE

Who Are You as a Leader?

1

THE WELL-DEFINED LEADER

SELF-UNDERSTANDING AS THE FOUNDATION TO EFFECTIVE LEADERSHIP

Let's begin where I think it's critical for any leader to begin: with you personally as the leader. I've seen countless pastors make mistake after mistake in their leadership, but not because they lacked character or even competence. They stumbled precisely because they didn't have a firm understanding of themselves, what made them "tick," or how they came across and impacted those they tried to lead in the wider world.

Who is this leader who is able to lead effectively? They're what I call the well-defined leader. I know from Jim Collins's work that this leader is a person with two qualities: humility plus focus, a combination of character plus competence in action. But can we dig deeper than this? Can we peer inside these Level 5 leaders (as Collins denotes them) to see what actually makes them tick?

In my estimation, well-defined people are those who have a growing sense of who they are—the person God created them to be with their talents, abilities, and giftedness. They have a well-thought-through belief and value system that can be modified, but at the core is solid and mostly unchangeable. Because they have a growing sense of themselves and their uniqueness, these leaders are internally aligned (what they say is what they do). When you meet such a person, you soon note a calm presence, someone able to lead effectively. I use the term "well-defined" because when you meet these people in various situations, you always meet the same person. There are not a whole lot of variances—the situation does not define them.

Did you notice the word *alignment* in there? It's there because alignment is critical to leadership success. Those who lead, who are internally aligned with their own values (actions match words)—and thus able to build trust and align the organization around its values, mission, and vision—are the truly effective leaders. And yet, so few leaders across the organizational world, including the church world, seem to possess this essential quality, at least to the degree that they can be effective. Obviously, being well defined is not either/or. There are degrees of this in all of us. So, let's dig deeper.

INTERNALLY ALIGNED

Does getting aligned, getting your words to match your actions sound easy? It's not. In fact, our interior lives tend to be so complex and scrambled that few people have a good grasp of what actually unfolds in their brains. This means that to a greater or lesser extent, we all live in delusion—what C. S. Lewis calls "the shadows." As a result, our actions, words, and underlining values are usually out of alignment one with another. This leads our unfolding lives to be incongruent and misaligned, and thus we lose credibility with those around us. In chapter 4, we'll unpack this misalignment more as we discuss the role of anxiety in our lives.

So, what does the aligned, well-defined leader look like?

Well-Defined Leaders	Poorly-Defined Leaders
Have firm, appropriate personal boundaries	Have boundaries are too porous—or too rigid
Have self-clarity and sharply focused life goals	Have little self-clarity and fuzzy life goals
Consider themselves and their role when problems arise	Diagnose others when problems arise
Are challenged by difficult situations	Are quick to distance themselves from difficult situations
Able to hold their ground in conflict and keep their eye on the mission	Sacrifice their own position in an attempt to manage their own and others' anxiety as conflict turns personal (see chs. 2 and 17)

Well-Defined Leaders	Poorly-Defined Leaders
Focus on strengths, both for themselves and for their people	Focus on the weaknesses and pathologies in those around them
Are able to absorb a large amount of stress; can also be around other excited individuals without becoming emotionally excited, thus diffusing the situation	Are susceptible to a great deal of emotional stimulation and become personally excited, which adds to the organization's stress rather than diffuse it
They prevent anxiety and stress in the organization because their "thinking self" rules over their "emotional self"	They generate anxiety and stress in the organization because their "emotional self" rules over their "thinking self"
Demonstrate a great deal of self-awareness; pay close attention to their personal responses at every level possible, and is therefore able to develop a degree of mastery over self and relationships	Demonstrate little self-awareness, have difficulty with decision-making; because there's less separation between thinking and feeling, more of their choices are emotionally driven
Respond effectively to resistance and sabotage, seeing it as necessary and instructive	Respond poorly to resistance and sabotage, allowing it to distract them
Challenge others and encourage responsibility	Focus empathetically on helpless victims
When necessary, they're able to disappoint those dependent on them, and is therefore more likely to encourage independent, healthy relationships	Have difficulty disappointing those dependent on them, and is therefore more likely to encourage dependent, unhealthy relationships
Welcome conflict that's focused on the mission, and even introduce conflicting viewpoints	Insist on unanimity and agreement, and feel threatened when conflict arises
Seek enduring change	Seek symptom relief
Acknowledge and navigate competing values—and help others to do so	Fail to acknowledge competing values, and so default to the expedient

This well-defined leader is a wonderful idea, you might be saying to yourself, *but one that's unachievable*. I would argue that it is indeed attainable and learnable. In other words, these are not inborn traits; these are behaviors and dispositions that anyone can learn.

THE SELF-AWARE LEADER

The most effective leaders, those who are most well defined and internally aligned, are those who are the most self-aware. It's as simple as that. *Oh*, you say, *I'm not into all of the soft psych stuff.* Sufficient to say, if you aren't aware of yourself, then parts of yourself buried deep in your brain will misalign you, controlling more of your thoughts and responses than you will ever care to know. In other words, you may think that your actions are perfectly aligned with what you say and what you value, but research suggests otherwise. In fact, our brains are wired to protect ourselves from the truth of this. We stumble through life, misaligned, all the while assuming that all is perfectly well and that everyone is celebrating us the way we celebrate ourselves.

Smart people, people with all kinds of degrees from all the best places, can make terrible leaders. Not all of them, but many of them. This is because these folks, though they know all kinds of facts about many areas of life, lack any kind of self-awareness that allows them to manage themselves, which would lead to social awareness and the ability to manage relationships appropriately.

In my experience, too many leaders often have no idea how they come across to others, why people don't want to work with them, why they can't seem to get satisfactory performance out of their people, or why people are leaving the church in frustration.

If you're going to be leading, then you have to be aware of yourself so you, in turn, can help those you lead be aware of themselves. Let me give you a concrete example of two pastor leaders. Both are brilliant. Both have ministered for years. Pastor #1, Dave, is intense, task-focused, and impersonal. His tone is combative. He is a perfectionist and is rarely satisfied. And yet he's an excellent preacher, clear and logical in his sermons. Pastor #2, Sue, is also intense, but she's approachable and is said to be playful in working with her people and the surrounding community. Sue tends to draw people and build strong community with a missional orientation. Dave, on the other hand, builds a consumer mentality in his people. They come to hear the sermons but have never been given the opportunity to exercise their own gifts.

THE THREE ASPECTS OF SELF-AWARENESS

There are three aspects of self-awareness that are critical in order for a person to be well defined. The first aspect is understanding how we have been uniquely created—our particular bent, if you will. The second critical aspect is our own personal story. Each of us comes from a particular background. We grew up in a certain family. In that family, we were a particular gender and occupied a particular birth order. The third aspect is the culture that surrounds us. Let's now look at these three aspects in detail, beginning with our unique bent.

The First Aspect: Knowing Our Unique Internal "Wiring"

As we begin to figure ourselves out, it's tremendously helpful to begin focusing on the positive—our unique strengths makeup. So often, people confess they have little or no idea what they're truly good at and what they're passionate about. Obviously, if we aren't clear on our unique wiring and where our strengths and talents lie, then we won't have a clear understanding of ourselves or feel comfortable in our skin as we move about our daily lives.

To understand ourselves, there are a number of helpful tools: Enneagram, Myers-Briggs, DISC, and so on. The tool I find most helpful was developed by the Gallup organization called "StrengthsFinder." This tool assesses a person's strengths. Candace Fitzpatrick developed an enhancing tool for StrengthsFinder called "Core Clarity," which yields a profile that identifies a person's "sweet spot" (in sports, this is the best place to hit the ball)—that area of endeavor where we are most aligned with the way God made us unique.

Sufficient to say, well-defined leaders are those who spend a preponderance of their time functioning in their sweet spot. This represents that convergence of talents-turned-into-strengths where all of our faculties combine into a harmonious order. When we're functioning in our sweet spot, we're extremely focused, lost in the moment (what some people call "being in the zone"). We perform at our peak, getting caught up in the process and not noticing the passage of time. We can work for hours, and we feel actually energized rather than depleted by the experience. At these times, we're authentically centered in the true sense of ourselves—we are well defined. We pursue our sweet spot for its own sake, not worrying about the residuals that might flow from its successful prosecution. When we are in this special place we're re-creating. Although most people assume that recreation is the antithesis of work, this is true only if our work involves us doing little with our sweet spot).

Obviously, those who can combine their career with their sweet spot will be those who function at the highest levels, while at the same time maintaining a sense of accomplishment and fulfillment that unfortunately few of us realize. Those who are rarely, if ever, in their sweet spot usually find themselves depleted. These folks may also turn to artificial stimulants to produce the synthetic high that being in the sweet spot naturally produces (although these artificial means often lead to addictions and a host of associated problems).

Take Action!

If you have not already done so, take one or more of the various personal assessments. The ones I find most helpful include StrengthsFinder, Myers-Briggs Type Indicator, DISC, and Enneagram.

The Second Aspect: Knowing Your Story

You first need to understand your unique strengths makeup.[1] The next step in your journey into self-awareness and clear self-definition is to understand your personal story. Your story consists of all of the experiences that befell you since (and possibly before) your birth. These are not isolated, disconnected events, but rather unfolding narratives complete with interpretations and perspectives on life, how we should act in any given situation, and thus how we can successfully negotiate life. Your story contains a predominate theme—acceptance, competence, control, or survival—that has a tendency to emerge and

---

1. Three books helpful in understanding family dynamics from a systems point of view are Edwin H. Friedman, *Generation to Generation: Family Process in Church and Synagogue* (New York: The Guilford Press, 1985), Michael E. Kerr and Murray Bowen's *Family Evaluation: The Role of the Family as an Emotional Unit That Governs Individual Behavior and Development* (New York: W. W. Norton, 1988), and my book, *Family Tales: Rewriting the Stories That Made You Who You Are* (Downers Grove, IL: IVP, 1997).

color certain situations as anxiety arises (to be discussed more fully in chapter 17).

Let's begin with the role that anxiety plays in our lives, simply because there is nothing more disruptive in our attempts at clear self-definition than anxiety (discussed more fully in chapter 2). This begins early, in our families of origin. This initial anxiety is first generated as parents begin to impose on their children what they think their children need to be, rather than elicit from their children what their true talents and abilities are. Society, then, steps in with its demands and strictures. Let's take a look at how this operates in our lives. I'll unpack this in greater detail later in this chapter.

Take Action!

Take some time to answer the following questions:

- What's your family's story like?
- The story's authors? What were your parents/caregivers like? And how did they specifically shape who you are?
- How did your story emerge over time? What were the stepping stones of your life—those milestones that shaped who you are?
- What were the story's characters? What was your birth order? What expectations did your parents have of you? Of your siblings?
- What was the story's premise? What was the central theme around which your family story was built?
    - Competence? That you will be competent and achieve great things.
    - Acceptance? That you will be pleasing and acceptable to all who encounter you.
    - Control? That you will always be in control of the situation, taking the lead wherever possible.
    - Survival? That you won't trust many people, that you'll be eternally vigilant, making sure you survive.

- What was the story's plot? Can you come up with an unfolding story of your family as it moved through time when you were growing up?
- What was the story's dialogue? How congruent was your family's communication (people did what they said)? What were the family secrets? Who seemed to be allied with or against whom?
- What was the story's setting? What was the generation into which you were born (e.g., GI, Boomer, Gen X, Millennial)? What were the surroundings where you grew up and how did they shape you?
- To what degree are you still involved in your family of origin story?
    - You're extremely involved, planning much of your life around what your parents/siblings are doing or want you to do.
    - You're somewhat involved, interacting regularly with family members and participating in important family events.
    - You have almost no involvement, rarely seeing family members, and not seeking much information about the unfolding family stories.

The Third Aspect: Knowing Your Culture

Culture surrounds us as the context in which our lives unfold. We can look at the national culture, the local culture, and the culture that resides within every church organization. Each of these contexts exerts a strong influence on us and how we think and behave. I've been a member of a church that has two sister churches in the same denomination with similar beliefs, but all three churches are vastly different.

One of my sister churches is wealthy and has a formal worship service. Sunday mornings look like a fashion show to me. I once told the minister there that I'd come to his church, but I couldn't afford the wardrobe. The other sister church is the exact opposite of the first. With a less affluent congregation, it's relaxed with contemporary music and unstructured worship. My church is somewhere in between, with blended worship with both well-to-do and not so affluent members.

The church's region also plays a large part in its culture. For example, someone from the South will have been influenced differently than someone from New England. Someone living in Los Angeles (where image reigns) will have different pressures than someone living in Washington, DC (where power reigns). Culture also encompasses generational, gender, economic, and racial differences. A poor single mother struggling to survive will experience the world quite differently than a white middle-class male.

Each organization exerts powerful forces on those who reside within that organization. If an individual doesn't align with and conform to that culture, then strong pressures are brought to bear to either change or leave.

These three aspects of self-awareness are critical to leadership success:

1. Knowing your unique internal "wiring"
2. Knowing your story
3. Knowing your culture

Let's now turn our attention to the role that anxiety plays in each of our lives.

2

THE ROLE OF ANXIETY IN OUR LIVES

Anxiety is the unseen yet powerful influence on how we live. It's also a powerful influencer on our path to healthy self-definition—and those in ministry should pay particular heed to the role they allow it to play in their lives.

Among other factors, anxiety can be seen as an internal fuel that drives us—an unsettled fear about what might happen in the future. There's the everyday anxiety all of us experience as the happenstances of life unfold. Then there's the more insidious chronic anxiety that lurks in the background that has been programed into us by our initial interactions with our earliest caregivers.

The response to the perception of threat (realistic or unrealistic) is to be fearful or anxious. This threat might be nothing more than, *I've got to get up this morning and go to work, or I'll lose my job and have no money*. The more easily people are threatened, the more anxiety they suffer. Anxiety is automatic and usually operates out of our awareness. As we will see below, anxiety is often tied to two huge concerns: (1) am I safe and (2) am I significant?

Advertisers and politicians know the power of anxiety. Both groups exploit what they know to be people's worries to further their own ends. The advertiser says, "Buy room spray so your friends won't be offended and think less of you." And the politician says, "Vote for me because I'll keep you safe from all the terrible people out there that surround our nation."

Anxiety emerges in those regions of our brain where reason is fuzzy at best. As a result, what creates the sense of threat that generates anxiety more often than not is markedly unreasonable.

Though usually thought of as negative, anxiety does have a positive side. We need moderate amounts of it to get up in the morning and get things done. Anxiety, of course, is part of the human condition; there's no escaping it. It's doubtful anyone would want to live a totally anxiety-free life, or could live such a life for that matter.

Anxiety comes in many forms:

- It can be acute and short term), as in a crisis; or it can be chronic, lasting years or even generations.
- It can be intense (though we usually label our response to a real threatening event as fear), when we anticipate a negative event (e.g., an approaching hurricane).
- It can be a semiconscious unsettledness (e.g., when the in-laws are coming for dinner!).

Anxiety resides in individuals, but it also exists in relationships and organizations. A primary arena for anxiety exists in our families, where two fundamental urges reside: the need to belong, and the need to be a separate individual. Some families insist on togetherness, condemning any deviation from the established norms of thinking, feeling, or behaving.

People raised in these families are prone to be more bound to relationships, and their behavior and outlook are overly dependent on those relationships. They grow up with strong pressure to adjust their thinking and acting to other people. Their lives become strongly governed by emotional processes rather than reasoning. They quickly sense the feelings and moods of those around them and adjust their own thinking and behaving accordingly.

Those who grow up in these contexts tend to conform to group norms and have difficulty understanding and stating what they themselves believe, wish for, or endorse. Or they go to the other extreme, becoming overly rigid in their beliefs and allowing no room for deviation. In a society where the majority has moved away from kingdom understandings and behaviors, those who are oriented toward the collective experience great difficulty going against what those around them believe and endorse. In other words, they have boundary problems (as we will discuss below).

Keep in mind that the urge to belong and the urge to be a separate individual reside, to a greater or lesser degree, in all individuals and organizations. These urges determine the long-term direction of our lives and our organizations, whether or not we acknowledge these forces. Arguably, the well-defined person has a strong sense of self (how God made me) with the equal capacity to enter strong collective relationships without sacrificing that strong sense of self.

Personal boundaries obviously come into play here. Those who live more as separate individuals may often find they have boundaries that are too sturdy, while those who have a more robust need to belong may have boundaries that are too weak. This will be discussed more fully in the next chapter.

Poorly-defined people tend to connect with other poorly-defined people (in marriage, churches, and other organizational settings). The anxiety experienced by each person within the organization infects the entire organization. Many churches are comprised of poorly-defined people and are often led by a poorly-defined minister. The signature theme of these churches is anxiety, which courses through the whole organization. When one congregant becomes alarmed, for whatever reason, that anxiety then resonates throughout the church, and symptoms begin to emerge (within the ruling board, or the children's ministry, or the choir, or what have you).[1]

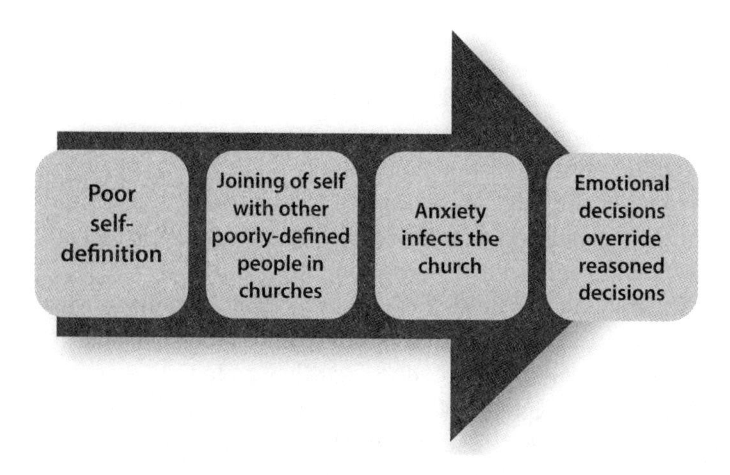

Whatever affects one member affects every other member in the system. That is, anxiety moves easily from person to person in the group. It's infectious. It is almost as if, in relationship systems, electri-

1. Peter Scazzero has written a number of books on the emotionally healthy church and the people who populate these that should prove helpful. See the further reading list at the back of this book for a sampling.

cal connections link the individuals of the system, transporting emotions and feelings from one individual to another continuously. You may have seen a herd of cows grazing in a field together. One cow accidentally touches an electric fence and startles, and then anxiety ripples through the herd as the other cows begin to experience that anxiety.

As I've said, it's the less well-defined people, those overly sensitive to the feelings of others, who are more prone to picking up anxiety as it reverberates through an organization. Churches usually set up mechanisms whereby these more fragile members can be protected from increasing levels of anxiety. Unfortunately, rather than being protected, these more fragile members are actually caught up in the organization's emotional climate. The protection paradoxically becomes an accelerator of anxiety, because the protective mechanisms often put in place create other problems within the organization.

Let's say a church is facing steep declines in membership and income and must come to grips with the possibility of cutbacks in programs and staff. This situation, of course, creates a great deal of anxiety for any organization. But it is the fragile, less well-defined members of that church and ruling board who are the first to experience the rising anxiety. And it is these same individuals who begin to act out on this anxiety (possibly missing meetings, making mistakes at work, showing up constantly at the pastor's door for reassurance, etc.). Ministers often step in to reassure the more troubled employees that all is well. And yet, these assurances merely act to increase anxiety: "Why did the pastor think he had to say that to us at this time? It's probably worse than I first thought!"

Emotional reactivity passes like a hot potato between individuals. When one anxious individual succeeds in exciting a second, the first is often relieved. In humans, this phenomenon results in nothing ever getting resolved. The problem that triggered the emotions is never addressed; emotions are merely generated and then circuited and recircuited throughout the system.[2]

---

2. The more emotionally unhealthy an organization, the more threatened these organizations by someone who is well-defined, because the presence of these people upsets the way things have always been done. The organization invariably turns on the well-defined leader. But sabotage is a sign that the leader is doing the right thing. And it's the non-anxious response to the sabotage that defines the non-anxious leader. This is the absolute standard of the leader—the one who can respond as the non-anxious presence. And

Less mature (or less well-defined) individuals, however, handle themselves emotionally quite differently. Their relationships are susceptible to a great deal of emotional stimulation. These individuals possess much more porous personal boundaries than the well-defined person (well-defined by definition requires firm personal boundaries, as discussed in chapter 3).

ANXIETY AND SCARCITY

One prominent place where anxiety constantly shows up is in the area of scarcity: Will I have enough? Arguably, the two greatest drives that each of us face as humans is the drive for security and the drive for significance, both linked to scarcity. And it is in these two realms where anxiety can work its most corrosive effects on kingdom living. Once high levels of anxiety are present, each of us has an urgency to reduce them. And, of course, the way we have learned to reduce anxiety is by intuitive measures—wealth, power, status.

Security is the need to feel safe, comfortable, stable, protected, and have predictability in our lives. Significance has to do with the need to belong, contribute, and make a difference, thus gaining respect among our peers. As I establish my security (the basic need of all humans), I am then able to look to my significance (see Maslow's hierarchy of needs for the various levels of human need). Anything I cling to for security and significance, however, is not God, it is idolatry. That's a scary thought. If this is true, then we all dance on the edges of idolatry our entire lives, which are virtual idolatry factories as Calvin once said (see his *Institutes of the Christian Religion*, I.11.8). What is the strategy for us to achieve security and significance?

SCARCITY AND SECURITY

The issue of security begins with physical security and moves on to emotional security, then relational security, and finally financial security. Anxiety associated with scarcity lurks behind each one of these.

---

this can happen in leadership at any level. This non-anxious, well-defined presence is not a static goal, but an unfolding journey, and the only way we can achieve it is to take care of ourselves.

POWER

You cannot discuss security without running headlong into the whole realm of power. Power tends to be on most people's minds, even when it's operating under the surface of our awareness. If we have power, then we'll feel more secure—physical power, emotional power, relational power, financial power. As we feel less powerful (that is, power becomes increasingly scarce), our anxiety rises and we take measures to restore our sense of security, usually by raising our sense individually or collectively by being more powerful. In the collective realm (as in the United States), we spend more on defense and the military, or locally aligning ourselves with those who have the most status (which usually devolves to those who are wealthy).[3]

But, of course, God turns this on its ear when he asks us, "Why are you trusting in horses and chariots?" Or, in our case, tanks and B-1 bombers. "They will ultimately be useless to you." Jesus puts the finishing touches on this concept as he details those who will be first in his kingdom, that those who aspire to be greatest in his kingdom must be the least and the last (see Matt. 20:25–27). At the Last Supper, Jesus demonstrated how power works in his kingdom:

> Jesus knew that the Father had put him in complete charge of everything, that he came from God and was on his way back to God. So he got up from the supper table, set aside his robe, and put on an apron. Then he poured water into a basin and began to wash the feet of the disciples, drying them with his apron. (John 13:3–5)

How's that for power mixed with vulnerability? The most vulnerable are the most powerful—which is totally counterintuitive of course.[4] The exercise of power usually equates to having regard for the powerful while disregarding the powerless ("They can't do anything for me anyway—certainly not protect me or add to my significance").

You're probably now asking: What does this look like in real time? Do we completely disarm as a nation? Do I not wear a seatbelt or

3. The very first temptation to sin in Genesis is about power, "You shall be as god." This temptation, to which the first couple succumb, should serve as a stark warning to all of us about the intuitive seduction of power.

4. See Andy Crouch, *Strong and Weak: Embracing a Life of Love, Risk and True Flourishing* (Downers Grove, IL: IVP, 2016).

take any measures to protect my identity? No, this concept doesn't preclude prudent measures in all spheres. But it does preclude an unhealthy dependence on these measures to be our ultimate protection. And it opens up avenues for discussion among kingdom citizens as to how we should live, consume, and vote.

> God's definition of power is the best place for each of us who is serious about kingdom citizenship to begin counterintuitive living, and a good place to begin that thinking is found in Philippians 2:1–9. I bring up this passage because it's so central to kingdom living. Scripture, like this passage, is saturated with this upside-down, counterintuitive way in which God demonstrates true power. Think of yourselves the way Christ Jesus thought of himself. He had equal status with God but didn't think so much of himself that he had to cling to the advantages of that status no matter what. Not at all. When the time came, he set aside the privileges of deity and took on the status of a slave, became *human*! Having become human, he stayed human. It was an incredibly humbling process. He didn't claim special privileges. Instead, he lived a selfless, obedient life and then died a selfless, obedient death—and the worst kind of death at that—a crucifixion.
>
> Because of that obedience, God lifted him high and honored him far beyond anyone or anything, ever, so that all created beings in heaven and on earth—even those long ago dead and buried—will bow in worship before this Jesus Christ, and call out in praise that he is the Master of all, to the glorious honor of God the Father. (Phil. 2:5–11)

Unfortunately, ministers, like others placed in leadership, almost invariably have difficulty with power. I've seen minister after minister misunderstand the appropriate use of power. And as a result, these ministers have usually gotten themselves and their congregations into a great deal of difficulty.

SCARCITY AND SIGNIFICANCE

My sense of my own significance begins with my identity: *Who am I? What is my "name"?* This overlaps to a degree with security: *What power do I possess? What have I achieved? With whom do I hang around?* And finally: *How am I respected?*

In each of these issues, scarcity and the anxiety associated with it play a key role. *Do I have enough power? Have I achieved enough? Do*

I have enough of the right kind of associations? Am I respected enough? If my answer to any of these questions is no, then my anxiety rises (as it did with the lack of power to keep me secure), and I initiate countermeasures to reduce the anxiety. And those countermeasures are invariably intuitive (and temporal, not kingdom-oriented), unless I can intentionally put in place counterintuitive measures.

Take a moment right now to put this book aside and consider the source where you get your greatest sense of significance. For me, the list of things (my career, books I've written, places I've taught) that create a sense of significance all tend to center on function—what I do or what I've done that has brought recognition in one form or another. Yet, I know the "right" answer when it comes to significance: My significance ultimately rests in my relationship to God, not in anything I might accomplish. Anything less than this, anything I elevate in place of God, has the danger of becoming an idol in my life. This brings us to the issue of character.

Take Action!

Tell the truth about your life and take some time to answer these questions:

- What have you been avoiding in your relationships, in your career, health, or spiritual/inner life?
- Where have you not been fully alive or showing up fully?
- What have you been avoiding telling the truth about or facing?
- What security have you been clinging that has stifled your aliveness and passion?
- What have you not started and want to start?
- What do you want to change and have not changed?
- What do you want to stop and have not stopped?
- What have you started and want to finish?
- What do you want to have and do not have?
- What do you want to do and have not done?

CHARACTER

A character trait—a virtue or vice—is a habit. As such, it's something that is intentionally, or unintentionally, developed over time through repeated actions. This makes these traits, unlike something that is inborn (e.g., personality), acquired moral qualities. As a result, we are ultimately responsible for our character.

Character germinates and grows in proportion to how well- or ill-defined I am as a person. If I am ill-defined, then emotional decisions driving actions take precedence over rational decisions and actions. Godly character requires a proper ecology in which to flourish. It grows in an environment where our decisions and actions spring from a climate where the rational position takes precedence over an emotional position. We are secure and significant within ourselves knowing our position in God's eyes.[5]

In her excellent book *Glittering Vices: A New Look at the Seven Deadly Sins and Their Remedies*, Rebecca Konyndyk DeYoung provides a useful analogy:

> Think of a winter sledding party, in which a group of people head out to smooth a path through freshly fallen snow. The first sled goes down slowly, carving out a rut. Other sleds follow, over and over, down the same path, smoothing and packing down the snow. After many trips a well-worn groove develops, a path out of which it is hard to steer. The groove enables sleds to stay aligned and on course, gliding rapidly, smoothly, and easily on their way. Character traits are like that: the first run down, which required some effort and tough going, gradually becomes a smooth track that one glides down without further intentional steering. Of course, a rider can always stick out a boot and throw the sled off course, usually damaging the track as well. So too we can act out of character, even after being "in the groove" for a long time. In general, however, habits incline us swiftly, smoothly, and reliably toward certain types of action.[6]

In contrast to this, ungodly character, where vice tends to undermine virtue, often thrives where we seek our security and significance in

---

5. I know who God made me to be (my "name") and I can rest in that. I am more dependent on Jesus and less on external promptings that elicit old story lines that raise my anxiety, making me more insecure and vulnerable to the development of vices. I depend more and more on my eternal kingdom citizenship rather than on my temporal citizenship.

6. Rebecca Konyndyk DeYoung, *Glittering Vices: A New Look at the Seven Deadly Sins and Their Remedies* (Grand Rapids: Brazos, 2009), 13–14.

the tried-and-true methods the world has devised since the Garden of Eden: methods that are intuitive and seem appropriate but often lead to idolatry. The way of Jesus, however, is *always* counterintuitive and must be followed intentionally.

In *The Road to Character*, David Brooks distinguishes between résumé virtues and eulogy virtues. Résumé virtues represent the ambitious side of our nature and, in many ways, the tried-and-true methods the world has devised for us to remain secure and find significance.[7] This side of us wants to build, create, and discover things, and along the way achieve high status and win victories. I must perform to be secure and significant. Nothing necessarily wrong with this, but it is the fast track to idolatry[8] if not constantly monitored and kept in check (a skill few of us are able to employ consistently). My kingdom significance never arises from my achievement.

The other set of strengths, which Brooks calls eulogy strengths (that which is read at our funerals), have to do with the moral character that governs our relationships with others. This side of our nature is what we usually designate as good character—the quiet but solid sense of what is right and wrong. Not just doing good, but being good.

As I become more well-defined as a person, I find that I'm able to manage my anxiety and concentrate less on performance and accumulation, and more on who I am as a godly, good person. I think that sanctification has a lot to do with this process.

Take Action!

- Striving to become ever more well-defined is an important first step in effective pastoral ministry. This is a critical forever-here-on-earth task. Taking one or more assessments mentioned—Strengthsfinders, Myers-Briggs, Enneagram, or DISC—is a useful way to begin.
- Establishing a baseline for your current behavior and attitudes is also an important step. Note the assessment below. It might be helpful if besides yourself, your spouse and/or trusted friend completed this for you as well.

---

7. David Brooks, *The Road to Character* (New York: Random House, 2016).

8. Calvin stated that the human mind "is a perpetual factory of idols."

Résumé Virtues (Accomplishments)	Eulogy Virtues (What's Read at Your Funeral)
Ambitious side of your nature	Embodies certain moral qualities
Want to build, create, and discover things	Quiet but solid sense of right and wrong
Need for high status and winning victories	Need to not just do good but also be good
Skills brought to job market	Love intimately
Contribute to external success	Sacrifice self in service to others
Conquer the world and live in a way that shows your success	Serve the world and live in obedience to some transcendent truth
Relish your accomplishments and your status in the eyes of the world	A cohesive inner soul that honors creation and your possibilities
"Success!" is your motto	"Charity, love, redemption" is your motto
You ask: How do things work?	You ask: Why do things exist, and what are we ultimately here for?
Educational system oriented around these virtues	Often renounce worldly status for the sake of some purpose
Self-help books orient here	Return to roots
Have clear strategies as to how to develop success in your career and your relationships	Exist at the core of your being = kind, honest, brave, or faithful; what kind of relationships you form
Live by straightforward utilitarian logic = effort leads to reward, input leads to output, practice makes perfect	Live by an inverse moral logic = give to receive, surrender to something outside yourself to gain strength within yourself
Pursue self-interest, maximize your utility, impress the world	Conquer your desire to get what you crave
Nurture your strengths to be successful in your work and in your relationships	To fulfill yourself, you must forget yourself; to find yourself, you have to lose yourself
Knowledge	Wisdom
Self-congratulation	Self-confrontation
Self-centered	Common-good focused
Résumé virtues lead to pride and idolatry	Eulogy virtues lead to humility and godliness
A sense of deep satisfaction is to leap ahead, which gives you the sense there must be more	Experience deep satisfaction, realizing that ultimate joys are moral joys, not fleeting happiness

BECOMING THE WELL-DEFINED LEADER ASSESSMENT

For each of the below criteria, mark 1 for strongly disagree up to a 5 for strongly agree. Note that even the résumé strengths can be set in the positive, as seen below. It's not that they are necessarily bad in and of themselves, but they can have a way of orienting us in the wrong direction.

Performance (Résumé) Strengths	
Self-discipline	1 2 3 4 5
Determination	1 2 3 4 5
Love of learning	1 2 3 4 5
Stamina in the face of sabotage	1 2 3 4 5
Decisiveness	1 2 3 4 5
Concentration	1 2 3 4 5
Resourcefulness	1 2 3 4 5
Responsibility	1 2 3 4 5
Reliability	1 2 3 4 5

Moral Character (Eulogy) Strengths	
Love and care for others	1 2 3 4 5
Sharing and/or yielding the spotlight	1 2 3 4 5
Honesty	1 2 3 4 5
Integrity	1 2 3 4 5
Humility	1 2 3 4 5
Generosity	1 2 3 4 5
Justice and fairness	1 2 3 4 5
Loyalty to others	1 2 3 4 5
Truthfulness	1 2 3 4 5

3

PROCESSES THAT SURROUND US

I want to turn now to another foundational concept that is critical to surviving in ministry. That is, to look at processes as they unfold around us. A process is a continuous action, operation, or series of changes taking place in a definite manner: for example, the process of governing a country, the process of loving our neighbors, the process of selecting the next minister of our church, and so on. Take a look at the process that is occurring here.

> "Shout! A full-throated shout!
> Hold nothing back—a trumpet-blast shout!
> Tell my people what's wrong with their lives,
> face my family Jacob with their sins!
> They're busy, busy, busy at worship,
> and love studying all about me.
> To all appearances they're a nation of right-living people—
> law-abiding, God-honoring.
> They ask me, 'What's the right thing to do?'
> and love having me on their side.
> But they also complain,
> 'Why do we fast and you don't look our way?
> Why do we humble ourselves and you don't even notice?'
> "Well, here's why:
> "The bottom line on your 'fast days' is profit.
> You drive your employees much too hard.
> You fast, but at the same time you bicker and fight.
> You fast, but you swing a mean fist.
> The kind of fasting you do
> won't get your prayers off the ground.
> Do you think this is the kind of fast day I'm after:
> a day to show off humility?

To put on a pious long face
and parade around solemnly in black?
Do you call *that* fasting,
a fast day that I, God, would like?
"This is the kind of fast day I'm after:
to break the chains of injustice,
get rid of exploitation in the workplace,
free the oppressed,
cancel debts.
What I'm interested in seeing you do is:
sharing your food with the hungry,
inviting the homeless poor into your homes,
putting clothes on the shivering ill-clad,
being available to your own families.
Do this and the lights will turn on,
and your lives will turn around at once.
Your righteousness will pave your way.
The God of glory will secure your passage.
Then when you pray, God will answer.
You'll call out for help and I'll say, 'Here I am.'"

These are the words of the Lord to the Israelites as recorded in Isaiah 58:1–9, using Eugene Peterson's contemporary paraphrase of the Bible. God is saying that although Israel was performing to the standards of the letter, they were missing the whole point in the process as it unfolded: "These people make a big show of saying the right thing," God says, "but their heart isn't in it" (Matt. 15:8).

Jesus picks up on this theme of empty traditional processes over and over in the Gospels. And in 1 Corinthians 13:1, Paul states, "If I speak with human eloquence and angelic ecstasy but don't love, I'm nothing but the creaking of a rusty gate."

More than our rote performance of some spiritual behavior or tradition, God seems to be more interested in the process. It's in the processes of our unfolding spiritual lives that the authentic or the inauthentic shines through. Let's explore this in more detail.

We are constantly involved with simultaneously occurring processes as we go about our daily life and work, which comprise the context in which we live our lives. Most of these processes are quite unconscious. We've learned to participate in them, and we go about our lives utilizing them, but never taking the time to actually stop and analyze them.

There's the process of getting up in the morning and those involved in dressing, bathing, grooming, and so on. There's the process of breakfasting and traveling to our places of work. And the processes used to accomplish work, play, recreation, and socializing. And then, of course, there are the processes of sermon preparation and delivery, building wholesome staff relations, visiting the sick, conducting funerals, and all the other processes surrounding ministry. These are largely performed automatically and unconsciously. Some of the above processes may be more conscious to you, such as preparing a sermon. But many are much more unconscious, such as time allotment for various functions (we naturally tend to allot more time to things we enjoy doing and are good at—our "sweet spot").

Remember what I said about security and significance in the second chapter. These are critical driving forces in our lives. Both security and significance have unconscious processes that develop around them, precisely because both are central to our existence. In the passage quoted at the beginning of the chapter, think about how each of these accusations against Israel's pro forma worship may in fact be processes reflective of what we've developed to attain security and significance.

People are busy going about worship and studying about God. Why? To obtain security through God's favorable consideration and thus be secure in his good graces, having him on their side.

How about significance? If I have a big church with a beautiful building and many well-connected members, I'll enjoy more significance than if I lead a small church within my denomination and the surrounding community.

LIFE UNDER THE SURFACE

So much of what happens in our unfolding lives are under the surface and not readily available to our conscious alterations without concentrated reflection accompanied by wise guidance. "We don't yet see things clearly" (1 Cor. 13:12). Since we live in the shadows, much of what we experience is a delusion. The best place to see this is in the ads on TV, which basically present a delusional world: "This car . . . this diamond ring . . . this phone . . . is what will make you contented and fulfilled!"

Because we don't tend to effectively monitor processes, they often direct our behavior in ways that at times can seem mysterious to us. Take, for instance, the issue of gaining weight. Many people in this country are overweight, and yet are basically unaware (except for the most elementary aspects of overeating and calorie counting) as to what physical, emotional, relational, and spiritual processes might be at play. As a result, simplistic solutions, such as "Just push back from the table" as a dieting strategy, are offered as solutions.[1]

And because we don't monitor processes well, the negative processes that infect our lives, the lives of those we love, and the organizations we inhabit are repeated over and over again with the same adverse results.

Lurking behind these processes are our motivations and intentions. Have you ever thought to yourself why you minister at your church every week? The logical centers in your brain will come up with the "right" answer to that: You minister at the church because you were called to do that. Yes, well, that hopefully is part of it. But there are probably other motivations at work—you like to be looked up to and feel significant and important. Your mother always said you should be a minister and you don't want to disappoint her.

The words of Captain Ahab in *Moby-Dick* as he pursues the elusive white whale are cautionary: "The path to my fixed purpose is laid with iron rails, whereon my soul is grooved to run." Those iron rails are the basic processes by which I order my life.

There are the processes that individuals perform and there are relational processes—those processes driven by the myriad relationships that surround and incorporate us. This is a somewhat arbitrary differentiation, but let's use it in our discussion.

Take Action!

Take a moment to reflect below on the processes you use to achieve security and significance. You may want someone close to you (your spouse or an accountability partner) to check your responses.

---

1. Most diets I'm aware have a common principle: Be mindful of what you're eating. Make the unconscious process conscious (e.g., count calories, keep a food diary, etc.).

Issue	Godly Process	Ungodly Process
• Achieving security	• Rest in God alone • Develop the "mind of Christ"	• Rely on political parties and processes for security
• Achieving significance	• Rest in the assumption that you are God's child	• Want a large church/staff with lots of programs in a beautiful building • A good-looking spouse

COMMUNICATION PROCESS

A good place to begin looking at processes is in the area of communication. Communication is constantly occurring, and because we all speak the same language, there's the assumption that communication is a simple process. It's not. Communication is difficult in that we communicate through different channels and we register other people's communication in different parts of our brains. Look at this drawing.

Sally has a particular intention (to get a package mailed out), but she needs to be careful in the way she communicates this intention. Although Sally's simple intention ("John, I need this box to go out") should equal how it impacts him ("Sure, Sally, I'd be happy to take care of it"), John seems a bit worried here. That's because communication has more than one channel. Her content (what's being said) also carries relational signals in the *way* she says it—body language, tone of voice, facial expressions, and so on. John looks stressed because he thinks she's bossing him around due to the signals he's receiving from her. Although her only thought is that she needs get this package mailed out, she doesn't intend to come across as demanding. Regardless, her strong signals have a major (negative) impact on how he responds to her.

When I say something to you, my words carry one message, which you hear consciously (the *what* of my message), and my body language communicates another message (the *way* of my message), which is communicated by me and registered by you unconsciously. This means that I can say one thing ("I really value women and their contribution in the workplace"), and at the same time contradict that message by my body language ("I never seek out women for their opinions and tend to value contributions only by men"). Usually, whenever there is a discrepancy between what I say verbally and how I act nonverbally (a double message), the verbal message is rejected—and any trust in me as the communicator is diminished or destroyed.

The main aspect of the trust-building process all leaders struggle with is tied up in this model of communication. Trust is built when people are authentic, or congruent—when *what* they say is backed up by the *way* they say it (which also involves the way they conduct their lives). This is, of course, easier said than done.

Beware! You may not be communicating what you hope to communicate to your hearers. The impact of your message on your hearers is what counts.

LINEAR VERSUS RECURSIVE PROCESSES

The old Newtonian way of seeing things was linear. One person acted on another: "You made me mad." "We don't have a good youth program because John didn't work hard enough." When a consultant hears a person or multiple persons explain a problem, they are almost invariably employing linear designations: "My coworker made me late to the meeting."

Linear

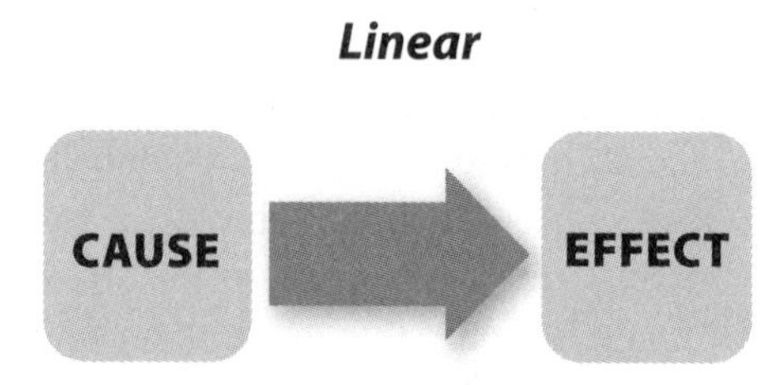

The new systems way of seeing the world has brought in a recursive sense of cause and effect. The old "You made me late" has now become "You were late because I was mad and treated you like an imbecile, which only made you later (because that was your best chance to get back at me), which only made me madder, which only made you later" and on and on.

Recursive

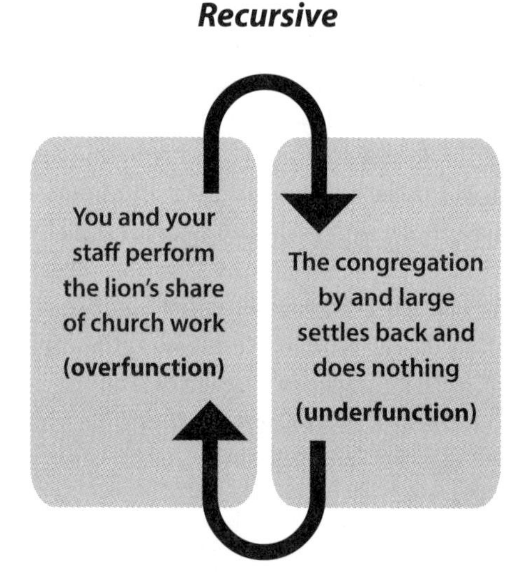

This recursive pattern makes it impossible to tease out cause and effect, because. one cause is also an effect. The pattern is self-perpetuating.

All of a sudden, we are given a new pair of glasses by which to see the world. This is a pair of glasses that looks not just at the *what* of things (the content, if you will), but also at the *way* things unfold and relate to one another—the process. Unfortunately, those of us in the Western world tend not to be very good at spotting processes.

PATTERNS RELATIONSHIPS TAKE

As anxiety and stress begin to spread through an organization, certain things start to happen within that organization. As people within the organization sense this anxiety, their tendency (especially for those who are the least well-defined individuals) is to begin to "herd"—that is, draw closer together emotionally. This drawing together then spells the further loss of each person's individuality and assumption of the group identity. Although herding together is an attempt to reduce anxiety, it actually creates its own anxiety, thus adding to the mounting difficulty in the organization.

People in the stressed organization, however, not only herd together, they also assume certain postures in an attempt to reduce that anxiety. Note a particular pattern: solutions to certain problems themselves turn into problems. In other words, as you solve the wrong problem, or solve the right problem with the wrong solution, the solution becomes the problem. You can see this throughout organizational life, and throughout history.

Let's consider an example. A minister comes to a church in the suburbs of a city. The congregation is made up of highly educated, high-ranking members who are used to thinking on their own and issuing orders. The minister is a command-control fellow who, in his former congregations out in the hinterlands, was used to shouting "Jump!" with the congregation responding, "How high?"

This minister was in trouble from the start, as a recursive pattern formed. When he gave orders to staff and congregation, they largely ignored him or pushed back. He then doubled down on his commanding style, thereby isolating himself more and more from his people. In turn, they continued to question his leadership with talk of dismissal rising. By the time he was finally dismissed, he had developed a fortress mentality and rarely left his home office to come to the church except for services.

This example can easily be reversed. Consider another minister called to a church with a dependent congregation who was used to being taken by the hand and told what to do. But this minister was more of a contemplative, mild-mannered, and not wanting to ever "upset the applecart." This congregation will have the same problem as the one mentioned above, although in a different way.

TRIANGLING

When anxiety builds in an organization, one of the automatic postures people assume together is that of the triangle. Let's say the senior pastor of a church comes to the office early the next morning following a board meeting the previous evening. He's anxious because the board was angry about the church's last quarter financial performance. The associate pastor immediately senses that the senior pastor is upset and quite possibly takes it on herself. The senior pastor transmits and the associate pastor immediately takes on his anxiety. Interestingly, as soon as she does this, the senior pastor often calms down.

Now, if one of the administrative assistants (or whoever else is part of that office staff) comes around the associate pastor, if that person is poorly defined with poor boundaries, he will also end up carrying the anxiety the senior pastor originally brought in that morning—while he senior pastor and the associate pastor feel better. So now, we have two calm church senior staff but an upset admin assistant. If this particular cycle happens often enough, with the anxiety ending up in this third party, we have a "triangle pattern." Further, if the organizational anxiety frequently tends to settle in one person (in this case, the admin assistant), then that person is likely to develop symptoms of stress (physical, mental/emotional, spiritual and/or social). This is also true of whole groups, as we will discuss below.

This onset of stressful symptoms may then add to the senior pastor and associate pastor's anxiety once again. They will begin to worry about the admin assistant (at least, if this person is important to their functioning). The more they worry about that person, the more anxious that person becomes, intensifying the symptoms, and so a vicious cycle ensues. But let's say the senior pastor and associate pastor have had a long-standing, under-the-surface conflict between them. Focusing on the admin assistant, then, takes the pressure off their conflict, and thus the triangle serves the purpose of reducing the conflict between the two principals.

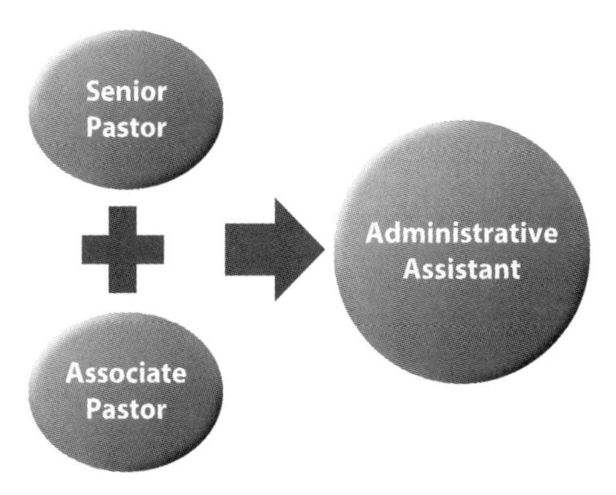

This triangling, however, may not be limited to only three individuals. It can actually encompass whole departments. As an example, let's say that the senior leadership is having tension with the children's ministry. The executive pastor jumps in to rescue that ministry, and so the children's ministry begins to experience turnover both in paid staff and volunteers. Whole departments can become symptomatic, usually by being consumed with dysfunction and underperformance. Often the solution to this is to fire the department head. But in lieu of system analysis and change, pulling one leader out and installing another will not solve the problem. Instead, the new leader merely assumes that mantle of dysfunction.

The Karpman Drama Triangle is an example of the ongoing triangling that exists between individuals and between groups of individuals, seen with regard to the stylized roles people often take toward one another.

The Drama Triangle

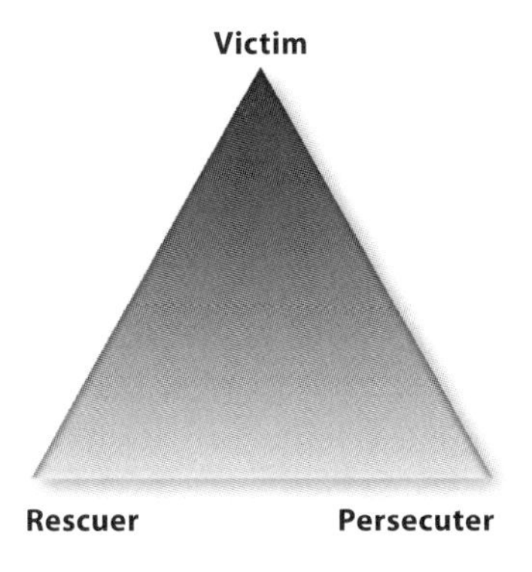

In conflicted situations, people tend to adopt three habitual roles:

1. The *person* who is treated as, or accepts the role of, a *victim* (though the victim is not really as helpless as that person feels).
2. The *person* who pressures, coerces, or *persecutes* the victim (though the persecutor doesn't really have a valid complaint).
3. The *person* who intervenes or wants to be the *rescuer* out of an ostensible wish to help the situation or the underdog.

This drama plays out when the protagonist begins in one of the three main roles: rescuer, persecutor, or victim, with the other principal player (the antagonist) in one of the other roles. Thereafter, the players move around the triangle, thus switching roles: the persecutor becomes the victim (when the rescuer starts to persecute the original persecutor for persecuting the victim), the victim becomes the rescuer, or the rescuer switches to being the persecutor.

The covert purpose for each "player" is to have their unspoken (and frequently unconscious) psychological wishes/needs met in a manner they feel justified, without having to acknowledge the broader dysfunction or harm done in the system as a whole. As such, each player acts on their own selfish "needs" rather than in a genuinely responsible or altruistic manner. The relationship between the victim and the rescuer can be one of codependency. The rescuer keeps the victim dependent on them by playing into their victimhood. The victim gets their needs met by having the rescuer take care of them.

The chief cause of burn-out is not working too much but getting sucked into other people's problems. Well-defined, non-anxious people resist being triangled, thus encouraging others to take responsibility for themselves. Non-anxious leaders are able to tolerate other people's anxiety, thereby requiring them to take personal responsibility. Anxiety is therefore diffused in the organization, allowing it to function in a healthy way.

As an example, a direct report comes into the manager's office to complain about another direct report. "Fred never gets his work done on time," Sally complains. "And that directly affects my ability to meet deadlines." Rather than storming out of his office to confront Fred (and getting triangled between the two), the manager says to the complainer, "Have you spoken to Fred about this? If not, I suggest you start there. Then if it goes nowhere, come back and speak to me about it."

GETTING ON THE BALCONY

One reason recognizing relationship processes is so difficult is because we're participating in what we're trying to observe. Ron Heifetz coined the term "Getting on the Balcony" to describe how we might best be able to spot processes that surround us. His metaphor is of a dance floor, with people swirling around with their partners to the music.

When you're dancing on a dance floor, it's hard to observe much of what's going on around you. But if you leave the dance floor and step out on a balcony overlooking it, then you'd be able to see the various patterns that develop as the people below dance with their partners as well as those swirling close by. In order not to become entangled in a hodge-podge of disconnected movements, many couples need to coordinate their dancing with those around them—a coordination process that's largely unconscious. Someone standing on a balcony observing, however, can see these processes emerge that allow many couples to enjoy the dance and maintain a sense of order, even though none of this is externally coordinated.

When we're part of a dance, we need to spend a great deal of time and practice before we become proficient at observing when we're also a part of the process we're observing. This is one benefit of independent consulting. When an organization brings in an independent consultant, they're actually asking for someone to stand on the balcony and observe the dance they themselves can't see. Getting onto that balcony is an essential leadership skill all pastors need to develop. Only then can the pastor begin to see (and diagram) the patterns of the organization.

As shown in the diagram on page 44, Fred is the senior pastor of a large in-town legacy church. He's a control freak and wants all information to flow through him. If any of his staff act independently, he becomes anxious. He therefore discourages dialogue between the other principals on his leadership team, which include Lisa (executive pastor), Bill (senior associate pastor), and Joe (church administrator).

Max, the youth director and Mary, the choir director (who is not on the senior leadership team) are in a romantic relationship. This means that Mary is privy to leadership information she wouldn't ordinarily have. Kelly, the elder board chair, is in long-standing conflict with Joe that's just under the surface and therefore highly distracting

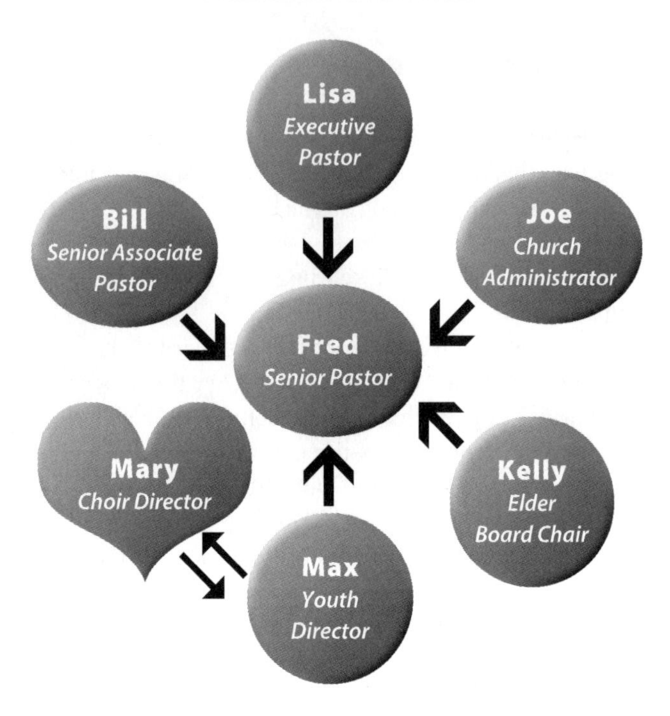

to ongoing operations. Therefore, although Fred wants all communication to flow through him, there are toxic relationship issues on his team and information that's flowing between church members outside his awareness.

This scenario is a description of a process dance that can takes place within a church staff. If we looked at their organizational chart it wouldn't help us see this informal network. To see the full picture, we would need to be on the balcony.

OVER-FUNCTIONING/UNDER-FUNCTIONING

Over-functioning/under-functioning reciprocity describes two people trying to make one self out of two. One person in a relationship (let's say one member of a small group) becomes the more dominant decision-maker, while the other (a friend who's another member of the small group) adapts to the situation by always subordinating to the other's decisions. In small group meetings, the dominant friend always initiates comments, with the recessive member always chiming in with a supportive comment.

This is one of the best examples of borrowing and trading of self in a close relationship. One may assume the dominant role with other close people who are less well-defined and thus assume an adaptive posture. The dominant one gains self at the expense of the more adaptive one, who loses self.[2]

The one who functions for long periods of time in the one-down adaptive position gradually loses the ability to make even personal decisions. At that point, it requires no more than a moderate increase in anxiety and stress to trigger this person into dysfunction. This can manifest itself in this person becoming ill physically emotionally, or socially, such as drinking, acting out, and irresponsible behavior.

The Over-Functioner

- ✓ Knows the answers
- ✓ Does well in life
- ✓ Tells the other what to do, how to think, how to feel
- ✓ Tries to help too much
- ✓ Assumes increasing responsibility for the other
- ✓ Does things for the other they could do for themselves
- ✓ Sees the other as "the problem"
- ✓ Demands agreement, bringing on "groupthink"[3]

The Under-Functioner

- ✓ Relies on the other to know what to do
- ✓ Asks unnecessarily for advice
- ✓ Takes all offered help, needed or not, and becomes passive

---

2. How one's self is established and maintained is an intriguing concept. I didn't want to expand it here, but you can explore this more fully in several of the books listed regarding family therapy.

3. "Groupthink" is when a group values harmony and coherence over accurate analysis and critical evaluation. It causes individual members of the group to unquestioningly follow the word of the leader, and it strongly discourages any disagreement with the consensus. We will look at this further in chapter 5.

✓ Asks the other to do what they could obviously do for themselves

✓ Sees self as "the problem." Is susceptible to "groupthink"

✓ Eventually becomes symptomatic

✓ Gives in on everything

By knowing about the patterns of relationships, we are able to watch for and see anxiety traveling in a system. When the anxiety is intense, the patterns are more visible. When the anxiety is low, there may be few or no apparent patterns at all.

After anxiety reaches a certain level (which is different for each person and organization), it overpowers thoughtful response. Logic is unavailable. It's as if the cerebral cortex (the thinking part of the brain) is "flooded" with anxiety. When that happens, the cerebrum is unable to function properly. Without the ability to be logical or give a thoughtful response, a relationship snag cannot be resolved. So, the anxiety continues to escalate. And as previously said, if any of the people caught in the relationship patterns were to manage their own part of the relationship differently, the pattern would disappear. But recursive patterns are self-sustaining and hard to identify and break by those caught in them.

Sufficient to say, a regressed organization or society focuses on the toxic environment they inhabit, not realizing that their own poor self-definition is a major contributor to the surrounding problems. Leaders are expected to come up with the quick-fix solution, rather than help people through suffering to take more personal responsibility. The healthier organization focuses on how people can be more well-defined and thus more mature. It's easier to focus on the external environment, since the only other option requires people to focus primarily on themselves *first.*

BOUNDARIES

One of the top five problems I've encountered with folks in ministry is the process of establishing and maintaining healthy boundaries. Healthy boundaries identify and separate the self from others and consequently are the foundation of the Blue Zone (as opposed to the Red Zone).[4] Boundaries are the fences—both physical and emotional—that mark off our world, creating zones of safety, authority, privacy, and territoriality. Boundaries are essential components because they:

- Define who we are—what we believe, think, feel, and do—where my story ends and yours begins
- Restrict access and intrusions
- Protect priorities
- Differentiate between personal (Red Zone) and professional (Blue Zone) issues

Boundary difficulties go hand-in-hand with poor self-definition. As I sink deeper into the morass of my own narrative, my personal boundaries are invariably involved, and I end up engaging others in my emotional drama in unhealthy ways. If I don't have a well-defined sense of myself, then I must borrow some of you to fill in the blanks and function more adequately.

For some people, boundaries can become too rigid. Vital information—the lifeblood of any healthy person—is greatly restricted. Stylized ways of behaving become fixed. Prejudices are constructed and maintained.

For other people, boundaries can become too porous or ambiguous. In such cases, the integrity and cohesion of the person is threatened by a lack of definition, "Who am I, other than an extension of you?"

People with boundaries that are too rigid, or too porous, are basically in the same position as to self-definition. Both are poorly defined as selves but they employ polar opposite strategies to deal with this. "I can't let anybody's opinions in, or myself will be in trouble." "I have to let everybody's opinion influence me, because my self is so poorly defined. I can't state an opinion that's wholly mine."

---

4. We enter our Red Zone when we pull up our own emotional issues and contaminate the present situation, when we should be able to evaluate it more dispassionately. The Blue Zone is when we're able to rationally assess what's occurring without any emotional contamination. We will discuss both zones in full detail in chapter 17.

We're used to the visible boundary markers of our world: fences, hedges, traffic signs, and so on. Less obvious, but equally effective, are the internal boundaries that mark off emotional territory: "These are my thoughts, my feelings, my story," or "This is my responsibility, not yours." These internal boundaries are emotional barriers that protect and enhance the integrity of individuals.

Some people can be so close-minded that no new thoughts and information ever reach them. They can also be so loose with their boundaries that they're swayed by every idea that comes along, never able to establish their own position on anything.

Here's a quick test to help you determine the strength and health of your own personal boundaries (based on ideas suggested by C. L. Whitfield in *Boundaries and Relationships*). See if you agree or disagree with the following statements:

Too Porous

✓ I have difficulty making up my mind.

✓ I have difficulty saying no to people.

✓ I feel my happiness depends on other people.

✓ I would rather attend to others than to myself.

✓ The opinions of others are more important than mine.

✓ People take and use my things without asking me.

✓ I have difficulty asking for what I want or need.

✓ I would rather go along with other people than express what I'd really like to do.

✓ It's hard for me to know what I think and believe.

✓ I have a hard time determining what I really feel.

✓ I don't get to spend much time alone.

✓ I have a hard time keeping a confidence.

✓ I am very sensitive to criticism.

✓ I tend to stay in relationships that are harmful to me.

✓ I tend to take on or feel what others are feeling.

✓ I feel responsible for other people's feelings.

✓ Now let's see if your boundaries might be too rigid.

Too Rigid

✓ My mind is always made up.

✓ It's much easier for me to say no than to say yes to people.

✓ My happiness never depends on other people.

✓ I would rather attend to myself than to others.

✓ My opinion is more important than the opinion of others.

✓ I rarely, if ever, lend my things to other people.

✓ Most issues appear black and white to me.

✓ I know exactly what I think and believe on almost every issue.

✓ I have a hard time determining what I really feel.

✓ I spend much time alone.

✓ I keep most of my thoughts to myself.

✓ I am immune to criticism.

✓ I find it difficult to make and maintain close relationships.

✓ I never feel responsible for other people's feelings.

Hopefully, the above information will give you a better sense of your own boundaries, and your own emotional responses in various situations that may cause you to compromise your boundaries. Remember, rising anxiety in particular will be a main catalyst for boundary compromises. Be aware of people and situations that create and sustain this anxiety.

MONITORING THE ENERGY

When I was in my role as a counseling psychologist, I was most interested in the energy in the room. As people's anxiety began to rise, their behavior in relationship to that energy was altered. For some people, rising energy translated into physical movement that might seem somewhat out of place. For others, it was rapid speech, or slowed speech, or particular facial expressions. Some interrupted the flow of conversation and changed the subject. Others became exceedingly quiet and withdrawn.

All of these behaviors should signal that anxiety is rising and may be approaching a threshold. Let's say you're in a church board meeting, discussing the possibility of a new program. If you're attuned to the process (and thus on the balcony), you may notice that some people in the room are becoming agitated in one way or another. They may just abruptly say to you, "Pastor, I don't like this new program." Okay, at least it now on the table for discussion. Just as likely, though, opinions may be not be clearly spoken but demonstrated by various behaviors.

One motto I've always used is "Go where the energy is." If there's no energy, then there's little anxiety present. But you should also realize that if in meeting after meeting there's little or no anxiety, this should be a signal to you that nothing of import is occurring. The rule of thumb is this: If the anxiety is too low, raise it. If it is too high, lower it.

Raising the Anxiety

This can be simply stated as: introduce issues that truly matter where there is conflict. Often the truly significant issues lie hidden as "elephants in the room." These tend to be "radioactive" with no one willing to bring them up. As a result, the issues that are discussed are noncontroversial, where everyone is basically in agreement.

Lowering the Anxiety

Let's say that one of those super-charged issues has finally been placed on the table. Predictably, people's anxiety has risen and possibly sides have been established with conflict rising. Be advised that if the anxiety is too high (when people are unable to think clearly about the issue and possible ways forward), you as leader will need to lower the anxiety. That may include saying something like, "I don't think we can productively discuss this matter at this time. Let's table it and each of us do more research."

Takeaway

You're involved in myriad dramas that are unfolding around you. Either you can be an unconscious participant, for all the good and evil that might imply, or you can become more aware of these dramas and seek to shape them in healthier, kingdom-affirming ways.

Take Action!

Sit in a meeting or a series of meetings where you don't have to be an active participant (it may be your child's school's PTA meeting). See if you can get up "on the balcony," generally ignore the content of the meeting, and note the patterns of relationships as these unfold. Who speaks to whom? How are women treated? Men? How does the leader handle that role? Who appear to be the leader's favorites?

4

BUILDING TRUST

THE FACE OF TRUST

Most pastor leaders realize that trust is foundational to their success. If the people they lead don't trust them, then how can they be expected to follow (unless it's the military, where they have to follow)? But even in the military, where there is forced compliance, leaders need to be trusted in order to exact the highest performance from those they lead.

I have said that truly effective leaders are the well-defined leaders. These well-defined leaders have a great deal of (and ever-deepening) self-awareness. As a result of this, well-defined leaders are able to first trust themselves. They have a good sense of their strengths and weaknesses. They know their talents, and they have developed these talents into strengths. They know when to employ these strengths, and when these strengths might be a detriment. They have a good sense of what it's like to be on the other side; that is, how their actions and attitudes are perceived by and make an impact on other people.

These well-defined leaders are able to most effectively build trust in their people. Being well-defined, they are internally aligned—they are able to match their words with their actions. This is directly the opposite of those person we say "speak out of both sides of their mouths." It is this congruence (actions match words) that is the key element in building trust. Let's unpack this further. Although this concept seems so simple and straightforward, it's a principle that, in coaching leader after leader, I see violated time and again.

To begin our discussion on trust, let's take a look at those elements that make for a fully functional organization, with each point building on the one preceding it:

THE FUNCTIONAL ORGANIZATION

1. Trust one another
2. Engage in unfiltered conflict around ideas
3. Commit to decisions and plans of action
4. Hold one another accountable for delivering against those plans
5. Focus on the achievement of collective results[1]

Notice that trusting one another is the foundation of a functional organization of any size. Once trust is established, the team can enter into appropriate, constructive conflict, without fear that it will turn destructive.

Trust has to do with a willingness on people's part to be vulnerable within the team and share in the team's ups and downs. It's an openness about mistakes and weaknesses. Teams that lack trust are unable to engage in unfiltered and passionate disagreement around the mission of the organization. Instead, they resort to veiled discussions and guarded comments (see chapter 17 for further discussion).

Once you have a trusting team, you can have honest disagreements that lead to decisions and plans of action *to which people are actually committed*. So much of what I see in organizations is compliance ("I'll do what you ask, but my heart's not in it"), but very little commitment. Commitment arises only after each member of a team has been able to wrestle with the initiatives presented, offer their disagreements, and grapple with all of the alternatives before arriving at a decision. Once that occurs, the team can hold one another accountable, because there is a shared sense of ownership in the decision.

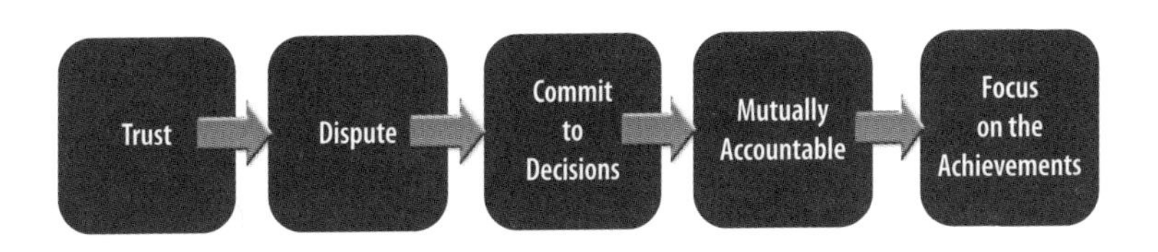

1. Adapted from Patrick Lencioni, *The Five Dysfunctions of a Team: A Leadership Fable* (San Francisco: Jossey-Bass, 2002).

In my coaching/consulting life, I've coached several people in the federal government who are responsible for over ten thousand people. That's a lot of people to direct. What I tell these leaders is that they're not actually directing ten thousand people; they're directing the eight or ten people who are their direct reports. Those are the people from whom they must win trust and lead effectively. Unfortunately, for leaders of large organizations, distractions and interruptions run high, and the ability to keep one's eye on the main thing becomes extremely difficult. It's also difficult for leaders to understand when their words no longer match their behavior, thus setting in motion the erosion of trust.

HOW IS TRUST ESTABLISHED?

Let's look at the building blocks that are critical to the growth of trust:

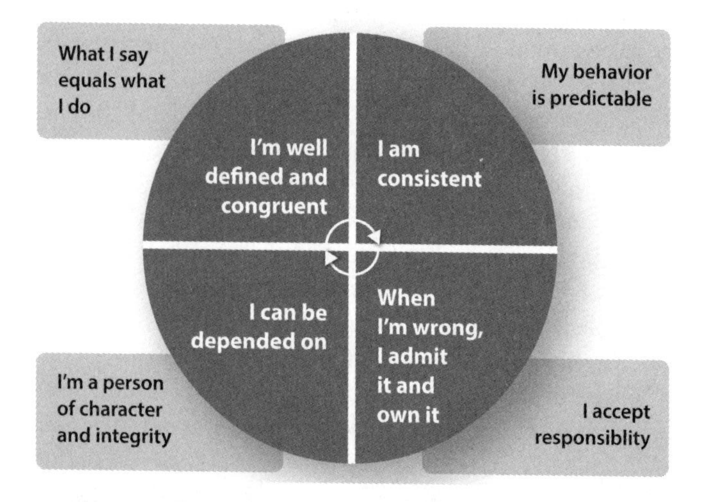

Let's begin with predictability. You're able to *predict* in advance what I will do as a leader. That's because I'm *consistent*. I do the same thing, over and over again, free from variation or contradiction. But I could be doing the same *wrong* thing, so that means I have to be *dependable*: I always get the same positive result from the person or organization. As I've said, the whole thing rests on *congruence*: I'm well-defined and internally aligned, a person of integrity. Therefore, what I say I believe and value matches how I behave.

Note now the very bottom of this graph: *When I'm wrong, I admit it and own it.* In all arenas of leadership, we've heard about the inability of leaders to own their mistakes. Blame shifting has become a leadership art form. In *Good to Great*, Jim Collins states that Level 5 leaders (or "well-defined" as I label them), when there is acclaim, look out the window, downplaying their part in the success, and sharing the spotlight with their subordinates.[2] When there's a problem, however, these leaders look in the mirror, embracing to themselves the responsibility of what went wrong.

Andy Crouch picks up this theme in his book *Strong and Weak*.[3] Truly effective and flourishing leaders are able to combine their authority with vulnerability. If my authority means I can never admit when I'm wrong, then neither I nor those I lead will flourish.

The arena in which being well-defined and congruent is on display and where it is validated is in the area of communication. Indeed, it is in communication where trust will either be won or lost. (Refer back to what I said about multi-channeled communication in chapter 3.)

BUILDING TRUST

You can either build trust with those you lead or allow cynicism to breed ("He talks out of both sides of his mouth"). Unfortunately, it's easy for pastor leaders to moan about problems in their churches and for cynicism to creep in. So, let's talk about your own, personal team.

Remember our first principle: The effective leader is one who is well-defined and self-aware. When it comes to building trust, it's critical to have a really good handle on yourself—to know where your strengths lie, where you are vulnerable (we're back to understanding yourself). Let's look at the specifics to see exactly how this works.

When leaders are well-defined and congruent, they can then go about doing the following activities that build strong trust in those they are leading. Note that each one of these often is counterintuitive as to how people normally assume leadership practices should unfold.

---

2. Jim Collins, *Good to Great: Why Some Companies Make the Leap and Others Don't* (New York: HarperCollins, 2001).

3. Andy Crouch, *Strong and Weak: Embracing a Life of Love, Risk and True Flourishing* (Downers Grove, IL: IVP, 2016).

They admit weaknesses or mistakes. The well-defined leaders who know themselves aren't threatened by admitting to weaknesses and mistakes. "I'm so sorry, I blew it" is a phrase that comes easy. Also, because they know themselves well, these leaders not only understand where their weaknesses lie, but they're able to speak of these freely so that others can have that understanding.

They ask for help. Because well-defined leaders understand and articulate weaknesses and mistakes, they are able to reach out and ask for help. For some leaders, this going into the "one-down" position is difficult. Often these people feel vulnerable in this position and refuse to assume it. But this is also a part of self-understanding: It's hard for me to ask for help, but it's also critical that I do so in order to maintain the integrity of the organization.

They accept feedback and input. Once help is solicited, well-defined leaders are able to accept the feedback and input offered. This may seem obvious, but certain people, though able to articulate weaknesses and ask for help, find themselves paralyzed when it comes to accepting the assistance offered. In fact, one critical aspect of leadership is the ability to face reality. Ron Heifetz details three realities that must be faced: First, what we say we stand for (our values) and the gaps between those values and how we actually behave. Second, the reality of the skills and talents of our company, and the gaps between those resources and what the market demands. Third, the opportunities the future holds, and the gaps between those opportunities and our ability to capitalize on them.[4]

They give others the benefit of the doubt. Well-defined leaders are able to give people the benefit of the doubt. This actually flies in the face of what is often our unconscious automatic response when we see someone doing something we disapprove: we assign immediate negative intent. "I know why you got that report to me late. You wanted me to look bad." This assigning intention, like communication itself, is a ubiquitous activity that's highly destructive to achieving and maintaining trust. It's impossible to trust someone when they assign negative

4. William C. Taylor, "The Leader of the Future: Harvard's Ronald Heifetz Offers a Short Course on the Future of Leadership," *Fast Company* (May 31, 1999), https://www.fastcompany.com/37229/leader-future.

intentions to that person's behavior. Rather than assigning intent, the far better course is to give the benefit of a doubt and inquire as to motive. "You got that report to me late. Can you tell me what happened?"

They take risks in offering feedback. Giving feedback to people can be risky, both to self and to the relationship. Often, as in the above point, feedback involves ascribing negative intent to other people's behavior. This activity of negative intent usually has more to say about the assigner than the person to whom the intent is ascribed. But honest constructive feedback can be helpful both to the person and to the organization. There are always risks, however, to offering feedback. Recipients may reject what is offered, while imputing bad motives to the feedback giver. But this possibility is diminished when the offeror is well-defined with a reputation of giving feedback that is constructive and centered on the enhancement of the person and the organization.

They focus time and energy on issues, not politics. Well-defined leaders understand those issues that will enhance the organization, and they tend to spend the majority of their time focused on these. Politics swirl around all organizations, and certainly have to be monitored. But self-aware leaders understand when they handle contentious issues appropriately, rather than sink down into political haggling that's usually more centered on personalities than on the good of the organization at large.

They share in the team's ups and downs. One glaring problem with the preponderance of leadership across the organizational spectrum is the propensity of leaders to be first in line to grab the benefits of leadership, while leaving the leftovers to those they lead.

TRUST AND THE PRINCIPLE-BASED ORGANIZATION

Human nature draws each one of us to default to self-interest and value those things most advantageous to self over other considerations (e.g., advantages to the mission of the organization). This tendency is often seen in leader after leader, especially those who have not been successful. That's why those leaders who put others above themselves stand out. These are the ones most readily followed and trusted. People know these leaders are looking out for the good of the organization.

A discussion of trust goes hand-in-hand with a discussion of values or the principles that govern our behavior. Values are like force fields that protect the organization. When leaders demonstrate a coherent set of principles consistently over time (they're congruent), these values permeate the system and influence all who come into contact with that organization. These principles are not only spoken of frequently, but they are also lived constantly. When a person comes in contact with anyone from the organization, no matter the position, that person experiences the whole organization—for good or for ill.

What's critical about trust is having a set of principles (what matters most in the organization), making sure that my life and subsequent behavior are aligned with those principles (congruent), making decisions based on these values (my operating or decision-making values, which often conflict with core values), and judging performance based on these values (we'll discuss this more in chapter 15).

When organizations are misaligned, trust is destroyed and cynicism rises. Misalignment can be compared to sails that are not properly trimmed and create a drag on the boat as it moves forward. Take a look at the core values of Enron (the company that cheated its shareholders and practically destroyed California's power grid!):

> *Communication*
>
> We have an obligation to communicate. Here, we take the time to talk with one another . . . and to listen. We believe that information is meant to move and that information moves people.
>
> *Respect*
>
> We treat others as we would like to be treated ourselves. We do not tolerate abusive or disrespectful treatment.
>
> *Integrity*
>
> We work with customers and prospects openly, honestly and sincerely. When we say we will do something, we will do it; when we say we cannot or will not do something, then we won't do it.
>
> *Excellence*
>
> We are satisfied with nothing less than the very best in everything we do. We will continue to raise the bar for everyone. The great fun here will be for all of us to discover just how good we can really be.[5]

---

5. Enron Annual Report 2000, 53, https://picker.uchicago.edu/Enron/EnronAnnualReport2000.pdf.

All these years later, the disgraced leadership of that failed company are still held in derision because of their utter disregard for these principles. That's what incongruence looks like. Obviously, the leadership of Enron posted those values, but when it came to making key decisions about the direction of the company, those values were discarded and a whole new set of values was put on the table, beginning with: *Make all the money we can, any way we can, no matter whom we hurt.*

It's therefore critical for the leaders within an organization to be aligned with the principles of the organization (which are only truly achieved when those leaders are well-defined). Now the question arises: How do we actually get people within an organization to align themselves with the values of their organization?

First, we need to remember: Stating a set of values and actually *practicing* a set of values are two different things. Our statement of values is all too often the "right" thing to value. In other words, organizations say they value people, they value honesty, they value customer service. But when they actually have to make decisions, it's as if they throw their stated values out the window and pull out a whole new set of values (operating values). Congruence has to do with alignment of values: that is, you *do* what you *say*. If you don't, then people won't trust you and cynicism will reign.

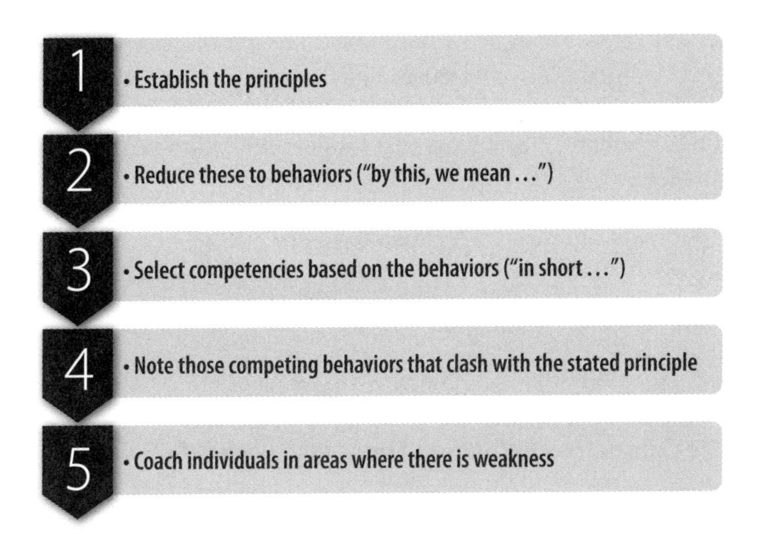

Establish the Principles

This first step of establishing the values of an institution cannot be perfunctory. What are its true core values and are they actually used as a template when decisions are made? Often, we think about values to which we aspire but don't currently employ. This can become a convenient escape hatch when it's obvious the organization isn't living out its values. An organization may declare their core value is caring for people, but then they go about trampling on their employees in a mad pursuit of profit. Their core value isn't caring for people; it's making lots of money. That value determines how they make decisions. When and if this incongruence is noted, the leadership then declares, "Well, we aspire to care for people; it's just so hard to actually do it in the real world!" Remember, when the operating and core values are aligned, there is a high level of trust in the organization. When they are not, cynicism reigns!

Reduce Values to Behaviors

In this next step, we take the values the organization espouses and begin to reduce these to specific behaviors. Okay, you care about people, so what does that look like? If I were to bring a video camera into your organization, what activities would be recorded that show how you care—something that's observable and measurable? Otherwise, you end up with subjective, airy-fairy performance evaluations that are useless to everyone. When it comes to the value of caring for people, managerial behaviors that support this value might be seen in the following:

- Takes seriously each employee's opinions
- Approaches people with an open mind and sensitivity toward each individual
- Pays attention in meetings rather than read email

Note Competing Behaviors That Clash with Principles

We'll talk more about competing values when we discuss adaptive leadership. For now, it's important to recognize that no matter what principle you establish as important to your organization, competing behaviors will emerge that will pull you away from that stated principle. Recognizing these, admitting they are there, and then navigating them are critical to successful operation. Often the competing value is financial in nature. "If we actually employ this principle, we'll lose product value, or customers, or competitive advantage."

First, let's look at the overview of our principles (usually cobbled together in a strategic planning session):

Principle	And by this, we mean behavior that readily supports this	In short . . .	Competing behaviors that clash with this principle
Empowerment	We identify gifts within the congregation, develop those gifts, and employ people to do the ministry here.	It's not the paid staff who primarily minister here; it's the congregation.	Since we're concerned that ministry is done right, we either hold tightly to ministry areas or micromanage.
Collaboration	We are stronger as a community than as individuals. The best solution is with a community rather than a single mind.	It's good to consider others but better to involve them. If we do it ourselves, then how will others grow?	We have to make a quick decision that doesn't allow the luxury of community involvement.
Integrity	We do what we say and say what we mean. We're quick to acknowledge our mistakes. We give and receive feedback.	Our actions are consistent with our beliefs.	Situations arise when we must act incongruently from what we've said.

Principle	And by this, we mean behavior that readily supports this	In short . . .	Competing behaviors that clash with this principle
Innovation	We consistently seek to improve, to discover new ways of accomplishing our mission.	We either grow or become irrelevant.	The nature of our church demands efficiency over innovation periodically.

Next, we ask questions of each principle to see how it must be operationalized. This is critical to actually driving the principles down into the organization, so that they're not just slogans on the lobby wall but actual lenses by which we monitor organizational behavior.

Principle	
Integrity	**We do what we say and say what we mean. We're quick to acknowledge our mistakes. We give and receive feedback.**
What does this look like in action?	• Being prepared • Clearly communicating expectations and asking questions when expectations are unclear • Robust dialogue, open conflict, controversy is accepted, voice of dissent is honored • Timely response • Others experience us living congruently with our values
How do we measure it?	• Feedback from internal/external communications • Demonstrated self-reflection and self-awareness regarding accountability • Quick to listen and slow to speak • Are people closing their actions and following through with deliverables?

Integrity	**We do what we say and say what we mean. We're quick to acknowledge our mistakes. We give and receive feedback.**
What happens if we fail this principle?	• Authoritative management • Trust erodes or no trust • Withdrawals versus deposits • Instability and cynicism
What's the biggest obstacle to this principle?	• Saying what others may not want to hear • Unrealistic expectations • Pace, pressure, time constraints • People's habits, personal feelings, competing values
What are the key questions?	• What additional information do you need from us? • Do customers/peers believe in us? Do we believe in each other? • Are we putting ourselves in the shoes of others? • Do I trust you? Am I treating others the way I want to be treated?

Takeaway

✓ Think of a team you were on somewhere in your life that was successful.

✓ List the characteristics that made that team successful.

Here are five questions to ask yourself concerning trust:

1. What am I doing to establish trust?
2. What am I doing to contribute to the distrust?
3. Is the lack of trust I feel a personal or a professional issue?
4. Have I done things to create feelings of distrust?
5. When I feel a lack of trust in someone, is there something I'm doing to contribute to that?

MUTUAL RESPECT

Closely tied to mutual trust, respect isn't readily given; rather, it's earned. One key difference between managers and leaders is that managers demand the respect they believe is due to them because of their title or position, whereas leaders know respect is earned through long-term consistent behavior.[6] Mutual respect is crucial in complex and large organizations, if for no other reason than one person cannot know or do it all. There should be a fundamental belief that we are in this thing together in collaboration. When addressing mutual respect issues, it's important to ask these questions:

1. What am I doing to garner the respect of those I work with?
2. What am I doing to garner the respect of those I work for?
3. What have I done in the past that would make people disrespect me?
4. What role do I think respect plays in my interactions with others?
5. How do I respect people who know more than me at lower levels of the organization?

---

6. Another way to think of this is a manager is one who does things right and a leader is one who makes sure we're doing the right things. As such, after the leader determines what needs to be done, the leader hands it over to the manager to execute whatever needs to happen to get the job done.

5

SHADOW LIVING

Investigate my life, O God,
Find out everything about me;
Cross-examine and test me,
Get a clear picture of what I'm about;
See for yourself whether I've done anything wrong
Then guide me on the road to eternal life.
(Ps. 139:23–24)

Most of us assume that our internal life is a fairly well-ordered environment, humming along with thoughts and feelings that are more or less aligned and congruent. Quite to the contrary, our internal life is a complex maze of energies, images, narratives, loyalties, and conflicting values. The likelihood of each of us becoming misaligned internally is basically 100 percent.

We are indeed misaligned, and flowing from this misalignment are particular thoughts and attitudes that lead to misaligned behaviors. The problem with these behaviors is that, in a fallen world, these are intuitive: that is, they seem to be the right thing to do. We intuitively perform the same behaviors over and over again, though more or less incorrectly from the way God intended. Conversely, as we become aligned, our behavior becomes increasingly counterintuitive, which is where the growth in faith resides. But this is not necessarily an easy task.

Take for instance the fact that we live in a consumer-driven society. Our economy is based on increasing consumption, and increasing consumption is based on dissatisfaction: I need to be dissatisfied with my home, my car, my wardrobe, my leisure time, so I'll consume more. But dissatisfaction runs directly counter to what God has called us to be: kingdom citizens who are satisfied and thankful (Phil. 4:12–13).

SHADOW LIVING

Our intuitions lead us to naturally seek out and automatically behave in ways contrary to the way God intended us to live. Even Christians embrace surrounding values without a hint of a question as to whether a certain choice is the way it should be.

Most people have difficulty distinguishing between the landscape of the mind and the landscape of actual God-created reality. What my mind assumes is so, well, intuitive! I don't even need to question my assumptions; I just know them to be correct.

Once our assumptions have solidified into our "maps" (unconscious ways of thinking and behaving that guide us in any and all situations—a liturgy, if you will), we take great pains to explain our maps. But we forget that our logical explanations emerge from a map of reality that has been constructed in our heads, not from the true map of reality. We use our map to explain our map (in a circular manner), never questioning the accuracy of our map.

Obviously, there is some overlap in my reality and God's reality. We wouldn't be able to function if this weren't true. But behaving optimally in this world (*Shalom*) would require a one-to-one correspondence between our behaviors, attitudes, beliefs, and behaviors and God's true map of reality. Although sanctification moves us in that direction, the process is never complete this side of glory.

My map of reality is a compilation of all my attitudes, opinions, assumptions, convictions, loyalties, values, influences, and experiences that have been gathered throughout my life. As I grow, my mind attempts to make sense of all it experiences—to interpret and ascribe value and meaning to it. If humankind had never sinned, then each of our maps of reality would be perfectly aligned with what is actual reality. This, however, is not the case and, as C. S. Lewis said, we consequently live in the shadows.

Because we live in the shadows, our thinking is distorted since these shadows mislead us in our perceptions as to what we're really seeing. It's hard to make out details when shadows lengthen and deepen. Because of this distortion, our authentic kingdom behavior in any given situation tends to be counterintuitive—that is, not what we would "normally" think to do. What we think should happen is probably 180 degrees in the opposite direction of the way God intended things to be. All of life is therefore twisted and distorted, and we can never have complete faith in our behaviors, much less our thoughts and intentions. What does this intuitive shadow living actually look like in real time?

- I default again and again to self-interest, pushing myself and my personal interests forward, all the while insisting I'm acting out of altruistic motives.
- I hate my enemies, while loving the lovable.
- I amass and use power in service of myself, constantly asking how I can get the most.
- I defer to the rich and powerful, realizing that they can forward my interests better than anyone else.
- I invite people over who will be able to return the favor.
- I demand my rights because I'm entitled to them.
- I allow the consumer culture to keep me perpetually dissatisfied, ever hoping to consume more and be happy.
- When people owe me or offend me, I demand satisfaction.

LIFE UNDER THE SURFACE

We live within our delusions, we walk around in a trance, never fully realizing that this isn't the way it's supposed to be. But this doesn't have to be the way things are for each of us. We can begin to think and live counterintuitively. In conclusion, consider several issues important to our existence and how we as kingdom citizens can begin to allow the Spirit to change us.

Issue	Intuitive (Not the way it's supposed to be) Shadow Living	Counterintuitive (The way it's supposed to be) True Reality
Identity	My identity springs from my function and my performance of that function.	My identity springs from my principal relationships, beginning with God.
Marriage & Family	My marriage and family ultimately are there to make me happy and meet my needs.	My marriage and family are there to make me holy and teach me to meet the needs of others.
Finances	I accumulate as much as possible, as this will add to my power and self-worth.	Everything I have is a gift from the Creator and therefore ultimately at his disposal.
Career & Occupation	I accrue to myself as much power as possible, so I grab the most powerful spots available.	We're uniquely outfitted to serve. I'm useful despite, not because of, who I am.
Church Life	I focus on meeting my spiritual needs. I am a consumer.	I focus on meeting collective needs (Phil. 2) and consider others first: that is, I'm a kingdom citizen.
Friendships & Community Life	I stick to my own kind and am wary of "the other."	I seek out those who aren't like me, "the other," and build bridges to them, especially the least and last.
Leisure & Entertainment	I distract and amuse myself in order to settle down.	I establish Sabbath in my life as a time when I can rest, replenish, and align with kingdom living.
Political Realities	I persistently protect my rights.	I persistently protect the vulnerable.

OUR MINDS ARE DISTRACTED AND DISTORTED

So why has our thinking about ourselves, about our relationships, about life in general, become so twisted? Distortions are the norm, and distorted thinking leads to distorted acting. I establish faulty priorities. I make faulty decisions. My behavior is incongruent. I say one thing but do another. Competing values twist me in knots, at least if I ever paused to reflect on what I'm saying and doing. And as anxiety rises from our incongruent living, our brains take over to reduce the anxiety by telling us all manner of nonsense to clear up these discrepancies, at least in our own minds. That's how the logical centers of our brains work: "logically." I do something against my values—let's say buy a new BMW, which I can marginally afford. My brain clears this up by stating how well these cars are engineered, how safe they will keep my kids, and how fuel efficient they are, while discounting the real reason we got it: to impress my friends how successful I am.

Christians believe that distorted living became the norm eons ago when the first humans turned against a God-directed life, defaulting to self-interest. Let's look at how distorted thinking works, especially in the lives of those who allegedly are devout.

Amadeus, a play and movie written by Peter Shaffer, is a marvelous illustration of how we delude ourselves with lies. It tells the story of Antonio Salieri, the court composer to Emperor Joseph of Austria. Salieri is ostensibly devout. He prays to God, offering his musical talents as a presentation of thanksgiving. And then Wolfgang Amadeus Mozart shows up on the scene. He's young, irreverent, brash, and libidinous—the exact opposite of Salieri's supposed piety. The only problem is that God has given Mozart the amazing gift of music. He is God's magic flute to bring the most beautiful music into the world. *How can this be*? Salieri thinks. *How can God use such a broken instrument as this? Aren't I the devout one? Doesn't God understand how much I want to use this gift to his glory*?

The climax of the play comes when Salieri tosses the crucifix into the fire, declaring that he is now going to war against God, to destroy this flawed instrument. In fact, he understands Mozart's perverted laugh as God laughing at him (Salieri) and his supposed mediocrity. *I worship God through this gift* is actually *I worship the gift, and God had better make me world-renown for my talent.* Pride and self-interest masquerade as piety. Salieri's brain has all the "right" answers. These just don't happen to square with his true motivations.

Distortions accumulate within each of us. As our thinking is compromised again and again, our distorted thinking becomes more profound. Our ability to see any sunshine out of the shadows becomes increasingly more difficult. The shadows in fact look like sunshine. We can't see the difference.

Distractions

Yes, we all experience distracted thoughts or attention. We all know what it's like not to be able to concentrate or give attention to something. The "main thing" is no longer the main thing; instead, what is minor or insignificant begin to clutter up our lives. Given the hyper-connectivity that invades our days, we are in a constant state of continuous partial attention, where people give limited attention to what they are doing—continuously. Relationships have become more superficial. Meeting attenders are also connected to social media and divert their attention in that direction.

Neurologists tell us that the human brain can attend to only one thing at a time, unlike the computer that can hum along running multiple programs simultaneously. When it seems as though we're multitasking, we aren't actually multitasking—we're diluting our efficiency and not doing anything well (studies show that if you're interrupted while working on a task, it takes fifteen minutes to get back into your project—each time). Some people can task-switch quickly. Others have a little more difficulty. In either case, they're not "multitasking," yet they still believe they're giving adequate attention to multiple tasks simultaneously. This is pure myth. This kind of distracted behavior constantly compromises our ability to focus and devote attention to what's most important to our ministries.

DEFENSES

As our thinking becomes more dissonant, defenses emerge to assist us in avoiding internal conflict and the anxiety generated by the conflict. Although I don't want to go into a psychological discussion of all the defenses that have been identified over the years, several are worth noting because they have a way of tripping up our healthy functioning and leading.

Denial

Reality isn't really reality. It's amazing to me how denial creeps into our lives, distorting how we perceive reality. There is actually total denial, when we refuse to accept in any way, shape, or form a particular truth. There is also partial denial, when we don't totally deny the particular occurrence, but we do deny the severity of the impact of the situation. "This did happen, but it's no big deal!"

Rationalization

This is an attempt logically to justify unacceptable behavior. A person might account for a bad mood or general rude behavior by explaining that heavy traffic affected the morning commute. "I didn't really want that to happen after all."

Projection

We have the tendency to project our feelings, shortcomings, or unacceptable impulses onto others. We do so because we know that recognizing this particular quality in ourselves would cause us pain and suffering. Like everyone else, there are aspects of myself I have difficulty owning and dealing with, which cause me anxiety. To reduce the anxiety, my mind keeps these aspects out of my awareness. Our minds actually censor information that could be potentially troubling. Unfortunately, I'm unable to keep my own story within myself. I project that story outward onto other people and act according to that story, not according to what that other person is currently doing.

Transference

Transference is the cousin of projection. Whereas projection involves two people—I project onto you my feelings—transference involves three people. It begins with me (the one who originates the transference), then there is you (onto whom I transfer someone else's profile), and then there is the person whose profile I "borrow" to transfer onto you. Let's say you are an authority figure (teacher, policeman, etc.). My father was my first authority figure, and he was harsh and unyielding. If I'm not careful (because fathers in particular exert a great deal of power over our thinking as we grow and separate from the family), I'll project this profile of the harsh, unyielding father onto other authority figures. Once this is done, I will no longer relate to this new authority figure according to the person they actually are. Instead, I will laminate the profile of my father onto them and act accordingly (and often inappropriately).

We usually don't approach new people as blank sheets. We transfer what we have experienced in the past into the present. Current situations are colored by attitudes we develop in the early years of family life, with the most important figures in our family continuing to emerge in present relationships.

Here's a quiz that might help you. Your answers will begin to give you insights into your own shadow aspects.

- What things really set you off and cause you to over-react?
- Do you think you read other people's minds? Whose? When do you read them? What is occurring?
- What do you fear the most? Rejection? Loss of control? Incompetence? Abandonment?
- What people or things do you hate the most?
- What characteristics do you find yourself disliking in others (especially those of the same sex)? Is there one person in your life you really can't stand? What is it about that person, what characteristics, that set you off?
- What things do you know about yourself that you try hard to keep hidden, even from those closest to you?
- What things do you *never* do, even though doing them may benefit you?
- What "strengths" do you have that, being preoccupied with them, may prevent you from being real and having fulfilling relationships (e.g., does your care of others prevent you from caring for yourself)?

- What are the themes of your dreams? Who is doing what in what context?
- What do others say about you, especially those closest to you (spouse, friends, parents)? How are you perceived in the organization to which you belong?

Groupthink

Groupthink occurs when a group values harmony and coherence over accurate analysis and critical evaluation. It causes individual members of the group to unquestioningly follow the word of the leader, and it strongly discourages any disagreement with the consensus. It happens constantly on church boards, staffs and even whole denominations, when there is almost universal agreement on issues that should require closer scrutiny.

> ***Takeaway***
>
> Groupthink often masquerades as Spirit-induced unity, and church boards are highly susceptible to this misinterpretation, so beware!

Confirmation Bias

This is the cousin of groupthink. People see what they want to see and believe what they want to believe. We like to be proven right. To change our views is to admit we're wrong. Our sense of self (our identities) is tied up in our beliefs, which are held in place by our communities (our tribes). To change our beliefs is to change our identities and risk expulsion from the tribe (see *The Big Sort* below).

As a result, we don't objectively perceive circumstances. Our tendency is to cherry-pick the data that confirms our beliefs and prejudices. We become prisoners of our assumptions. For example, those who are devoted to their political party tend to believe that their party is on the correct side of every issue. When an elected official of their party does something agreeable to them, they think, "See, my party is always right." When an elected official in their party does something contrary to their beliefs, however, they ignore or rationalize away this action.

TAKEAWAY

Much of the distorted thinking in the church is cloaked in God language. Discernment has a lot to do with being able to recognize the leading of the Spirit and discriminate it from the distorted thinking often employed.

The Big Sort

In his book, *The Big Sort: Why the Clustering of Like-Minded America Is Tearing Us Apart*, Bill Bishop demonstrates how Americans have spent decades sorting themselves into homogeneous communities that then become petri dishes for groupthink and confirmation bias—that is, where we share a common narrative that's confirmed over and over again by those with whom we surround ourselves and by the media we allow into our lives.[1]

Cognitive Dissonance

The final step in all of this distorted shadow living is cognitive dissonance. You may be asking yourself how we can actually live with our minds so bound up in contradictions and distortions. Our minds yearn for harmony, consistency, and alignment—a steady state with low anxiety. And yet, because we live in the shadows, distortions lurk within each of us, threatening to throw us into disharmony and cognitive chaos. In a sense, dissonance theory is a theory of blind spots: how people unintentionally blind themselves so that they fail to notice vital events and information that might make them question their behavior or convictions, and then congregate only with like-minded people who share their narrative.

Think about dissonance as holding two contradictory ideas or values simultaneously, one idea implies the opposite of another. For example, a belief in animal rights could be interpreted as inconsistent with eating meat or wearing fur. Or a church could affirm reaching out to the nations, while ignoring the changing ethnicity of their surrounding neighborhood. Noticing the contradiction leads to dis-

1. Bill Bishop, *The Big Sort: Why the Clustering of Like-Minded America Is Tearing Us Apart* (New York: Houghton Mifflin Harcourt, 2008).

sonance, which can be experienced as anxiety, guilt, shame, anger, embarrassment, or stress. When our thinking is dissonant, we can do two things to reduce dissonance:

1. Change our values, attitudes, beliefs, and behavior.
2. Justify or rationalize our values, attitudes, beliefs, and behaviors.

Unfortunately, changing values, attitudes, beliefs, and behaviors (in chapter 7, I call this adaptive or transformational change) is not so easy. It's far easier to rationalize away discrepancies. Our convictions about who we are carry us through the day, and we constantly interpret what happens to us through the filter of those core beliefs. When they are violated, even by a good experience, it causes anxiety that must be reduced. All of this is made much easier when we're surrounded by like-minded people, who are also attempting to cover their own dissonance and are more than willing to lend you a hand in the process.

Dissonance is most painful when an important element of our self-concept is threatened—typically when we do something inconsistent with our view of ourselves: "I'm a good person" or "I made the right decision." The anxiety that comes with the possibility of having made a bad decision can lead to rationalization, the tendency to create additional reasons or justifications to support one's choices. A person who spent too much money on a new car might decide that the new vehicle is much less likely to break down than their old car. This belief may or may not be true, but it would likely reduce dissonance and make them feel better. Dissonance can also lead to confirmation bias, the denial of disconfirming evidence, and other ego defense mechanisms. Again, the internal unconscious strategy is always to reduce anxiety.

All of us strive to make sense out of contradictory ideas and lead lives, *at least in our own minds*, that are consistent and meaningful. In order to keep our self-esteem bubbling along in high gear, our minds are forced to clear up all the discrepancies. The operation is similar to a thermostat. The thermostat in your house kicks on when the thermometer reaches a certain point. It's the same with our minds. When the dissonance reaches a certain point, rationalization kicks in to regulate the "temperature."

Cognitive dissonance also operates collectively (coupled with groupthink). Most kingdom individuals and congregations are committed to helping the poor. But there are many churches (at least in the West) that also have a blind spot: they're a wealthy congregation (at least, relatively speaking) and feel *it's their privilege* to have enjoy the benefits. After all, they did it on their own, right? They therefore rationalize that they can help the poor, as long as they stay "out there" and away from their beautiful sanctuary. Having them actually mingle with them would be unacceptable. So, they rationalize all of this by saying, *Well, we're sure they would be more comfortable congregating with their own kind.*

How Do We "Cure" Dissonance?

Self-justification! Most people, when directly confronted with proof that they're wrong, don't change their point of view or course of actions. Instead, they justify their position even more tenaciously, rationalizing their position, and employing confirmation bias to convince themselves that all evidence supports their position—beliefs being more emotionally grounded than data grounded. Self-justification is more powerful than lying (indeed, it is lying to ourselves). It allows people to convince themselves that what they did was the best they could have done.

Most human beings and institutions are going to do everything in their power to reduce dissonance in ways that are favorable *to them*, that allows them to justify their mistakes and maintain business as usual (groupthink). They probably won't be grateful for any evidence that their actions are inconsistent with their stated belief system—this would reintroduce anxiety to the system that will again need to be reduced. Note Jesus' ministry. He constantly pointed up inconsistencies, continually raised anxieties, and was ultimately killed for his troubles. Once we understand how and when we need to reduce dissonance, we can become more vigilant about the process and nip it in the bud.

On the other hand, once we begin down the path of dissonance reduction and self-justification, we will find it harder to turn back because we continue to weave a more complex web. Becoming aware that we're in a state of dissonance can help us make sharper, smarter, conscious choices instead of letting automatic, self-protective mechanisms resolve our discomfort in our favor.

The goal is to become aware of two dissonant cognitions that are causing distress and find a way to resolve them constructively, or when we can't, learn to live with them.

KINGDOM LIVING THAT IS COUNTERINTUITIVE LIVING: FLOURISHING IN *SHALOM*

In the midst of the gathering gloom of shadow living, Jesus burst on the scene, bringing a whole new way of living. Jesus' life was totally counterintuitive—the anti-hero who virtually embodied none of the expectations of those who consider leadership. Thus his day-to-day words and actions disturbed those around him, especially the religious establishment (those his life and words directly challenged). But when everyday people begin to encounter this Jesus, counterintuitive living begins to occur. There is something beautiful and joyous that emerges. Scripture terms this *shalom*, a wholeness, a completeness aligned with God's intentions, with kingdom living—flourishing.

But wait! Consider Jesus' words as to how we are to move toward that wonderful abundant life for which we all yearn. From a purely practical point of view, the vast majority of Jesus' words—and yes, the words of those who penned the New Testament—don't make a whole lot of sense to modern ears. We've conveniently censored out most of Jesus' radical counterintuitive statements, leaving behind a pie-in-the-sky spirituality that allows each of us to continue our lives basically untouched. As Dietrich Bonhoeffer stated, Jesus calls us to come and *die*! [2] Now we're beginning to see exactly why so many people, as they began to grasp what he was really saying, chose not to follow, and later aid in his destruction.

In *The Great Divorce*, C. S. Lewis picks up this same theme of hesitancy of downright refusal to follow Jesus.[3] In this book, people are given a second chance after death to enter the kingdom. But the majority find the life of *shalom* to be too solid, too real to forsake their artificial existences.

---

2. Dietrich Bonhoeffer, *The Cost of Discipleship* (repr., Nashville: Holman Reference, 2017).

3. C. S. Lewis, *The Great Divorce* (repr., New York: HarperCollins, 2001).

Who is this authentic man or woman of God? Who are those who truly live out their values, deepening their walk with Jesus? I'd argue it's the man or woman who lives counterintuitively, which is the way it was originally intended to be. Counterintuitive living is kingdom living—life that flourishes. As we move toward counterintuitive kingdom living, we inevitably advance toward *shalom*. When we begin to experience *shalom* as we come together, our communities take notice. Social processes begin to change. There's a whole new (old) way of living that is radical and enticing. Leaders are servants. Folks would rather give than receive. People put others' interests ahead of their own.

And, of course, grace is the ultimate counterintuitive action, in this case performed by God toward us, who are completely undeserving. When we become authentic Christians and experience the new birth, we are "born" into a whole new life, complete with new ways of seeing, thinking, and doing, which translate into habitual processes that cobble together into a kingdom lifestyle. This process of becoming a new person in Christ involves a radical transformation process. As Paul says, "All things become new" (2 Cor. 5:17).

This new way of living is contrary—it's counterintuitive—to anything we as changed people have ever experienced. It runs counter to everything our basic instincts tell us is the proper way of seeing, thinking, and acting. Our lives can now be reframed, allowing us to refocus and reimagine a totally different way of life.

This new way of seeing, thinking, acting, and relating is actually a reorientation to the way life was always intended to be. This reorientation, however, is also disorienting and nothing surrounding us much supports it. When we begin to move toward *shalom*, we begin to shine stronger light that drives back the shadows. But the shadows are persistent and only grudgingly yield ground over time. So particular questions begin to emerge:

- What does the true, authentic Christian life look like?
- Why do so few people seem to live that way?
- What about the corporate life of the church, business, government? Each of these seems messed up in its own way. "Wherever two are three are gathered together," things are doubly messed up!

The goal of all of life? *Shalom*. A life where peace, justice, and blessing are the rule. A life where every relationship is put right, and you enjoy it. But how is this achieved? Do we have to wait for the hereafter to see this come about? Actually, this life of *shalom* can be put into place now, as our thoughts, words, insights, and behaviors—those especially that are counterintuitive, that initially make no sense whatsoever—begin to substantially change all every relationship that surrounds us.

6

COMPETING VALUES

HOW WE CONTINUALLY MANUFACTURE *NON*-CHANGE

The final issue we must take a look at in this foundational section is the issue of competing values. Although this is a concept that has just begun to get traction in the past few years, it's critical to understand. Individuals and churches are loaded with competing values, and these competing values tend to get a lot of churches into all kinds of conflict and difficulties because they don't understand the whole process (see chapter 3). So, let's take a closer look.

I was recently coaching in two places, one right after the other. The first was at the Federal Aviation Administration (FAA) with a top executive who told me about her experience with this agency. The agency had put forth a set of values that it deemed essential to align the workforce and fulfill its mission of a safe and efficient national air space. In reality, however, she explained how one or more of these values had been violated by various leaders within the organization.

After talking with her, I then called a pastor, who essentially told me the same thing. His church had a distinct list of values that were to guide the church, values anchored in the principal set of beliefs of that organization. One of these values was respect for one another. He then detailed how the leaders of this church displayed little respect for one another, went behind each other's backs, sabotaged, blame-shifted, and in numerous other ways violated what they had stated was so important to their church (showing respect, which contrasted with their desire to gain the upper hand or to appear more competent than their fellow leaders).

What has become increasingly apparent to me is that those I work with often have little understanding of the true nature of values. They don't understand the importance of them or how these values should actually be lived out in real time. As leadership violates these core values, trust erodes and the entire organization suffers.

Values are beliefs or principles about what is important in life—a belief that a specific action or behavior is preferable to the opposite action, a statement as to what is most worthwhile. When business plans are cobbled together, or when strategic planning sessions are conducted, leaders are encouraged to identify core values, to let them emerge from what they already sense is important to them. This exercise supposedly yields the foundation stones upon which the organization will be built and maintained.

But sadly, what is often offered in these planning sessions is a list of aspirational values: principles we *should* live by or hope to live by. What so often happens is the core value list is cobbled together—a list of what we should hold dear—and then promptly filed away and forgotten. Or worse yet, these values are posted on a website or on the wall in the narthex for all to see, and then promptly forgotten. And the true list of values, the ones we actually use to make all the critical decisions within the church, is removed (unconsciously of course, which is another one of those processes, so we aren't even aware we've done this), and we go about merrily making decisions that directly contradict what we said we stand for. This is what incongruence looks like organizationally. It erodes trust and breeds cynicism.

Values are like force fields that protect the organization. When leadership of any given organization demonstrates a coherent set of beliefs consistently lived out over time (they're congruent), these values permeate the system and influence all those who come in contact with that organization. Values need to be spoken of frequently and lived out constantly. Whenever leaders violate these values, they need to be called out and held accountable.

Competing Values

Competing values exist most prominently in the realm of transformational concerns (we'll unpack this thoroughly in chapter 7). This realm resides in the deepest recesses of our being, where our values shape our attitudes, beliefs, and behaviors. But as we've already seen, we live in the shadows. These deep recesses within each of us aren't easily accessed and thus are easily distorted. Values are not neatly arranged and aligned, but in fact often compete one with another, creating cognitive dissonance. The dissonance then generates anxiety, which must be dealt with. But if not properly dealt with, these people become incongruent in their behavior, saying one thing but doing another.

There are competing values internal to each of us. And, as we saw in the above example, there are competing values that reside in every organization. Let's consider two areas that are fertile ground for developing competing values.

The gap between what we say we value and how we behave. This is the area in which we find ourselves in particular situations where we end up acting in ways that differ from what we say we value and believe about ourselves—the result of cognitive dissonance.

For example, a church that has been in the same neighborhood for the past fifty years sees the demographics of the neighborhood change to a more diverse, multicultural community. Although one of their values was always to reach out to their neighbors, they were at a loss how to do this with so many people so culturally different from them. Instead of reaching out and engaging in this new world around them, they decided instead to move to an area more in conformity to the historical profile of their members. "We'll send our teenagers back here to minister."

Competing commitments. Like individuals, organizations have numerous commitments and sometimes these commitments come into conflict. I'm committed to the youth in my church, but I'm also committed to the older folks, who provide the lion's share of the budget and demand programs that benefit them. Limited resources state that you can't have it both ways.

As an example of competing commitments, an assistant pastor was elevated to the lead pastor role during the interim when the senior pastor retired. Though this assistant had wanted to become senior pastor, leadership went a different direction. The assistant was now caught in competing loyalties. His extended family lived in the community, and he didn't want to uproot his small, growing family from grandparents and cousins. But he also knew that staying on in his position as assistant, having wanted to be the senior pastor, would undoubtedly compromise his unfolding relationship with the new senior pastor, and could create a tricky situation with the congregation if not handled carefully.

As competing values rear their heads in our ongoing community life together, people most often turn to the authorities (i.e., the ordained folks and the ruling board) to solve the problem. These authorities "rise to the bait" and assume the problem is theirs to solve, and almost invariably turn to tried-and-true tactical solutions. People are hired into ministry positions and authorized to perform particular tasks in certain prescribed ways. Leadership, however, inhabits a different sphere.

When we lead effectively, we actually help people confront these complex, knotty transformational problems that don't lend themselves neatly to tactical solutions. That's precisely because these problems involve competing values—one church constituency holding one set of values, and another group another set. By the way, this doesn't mean there is one good value and one bad value. Both are valid and good; they just compete for limited resources. That's why leadership must point up the conundrum (people usually can't see these, because they're more unconscious and buried in the processes), while assisting the stakeholders in wrestling through them. Unfortunately, because every leader is wired a particular way that bends toward a particular preference, leaders tend to move people toward one value, ignore the other, and create difficulties in the process. Here are some of these conundrums of competing values:

- Exclusion (building kingdom community) *versus* inclusion (reaching the unchurched).
- Quality (building a professional music program) *versus* quantity (allowing many congregants to participate in leading worship, thus utilizing their subpar but developing talents).
- Efficiency (the worship service needs to begin and end on time) *versus* innovation (the Spirit may take us to new places in worship, thus expanding the worship time allotted).
- Protection (congregants must feel safe at church no matter what measures are employed) *versus* challenge (we can't turn our campus into an armed camp).

- Expansion (as new people arrive, the need to alter the tried-and-true forms of worship is more apparent) *versus* preservation (we've always done it this way and must continue to do so).
- Transparency (everyone must know everything about everything) *versus* confidentiality (certain matters must be closely held because of legal and personal concerns).
- Individual considerations (what's good for and the preferences of each congregant) *versus* community considerations (what is good for the collective).
- The letter of the law (a potential board member is found to have been previously married, violating church operating rules) *versus* extending grace (a potential previously married board member has been clear about circumstances of his divorce and has embraced his own culpability in the matter).

The list can go on and on. You, the transformational leader, must first be able to spot these competing values, and then place them before your congregation (note the activities of leadership in chapter 7).

In our corporate life together in the church, one side of the competing values is often financial. "I can see the value in doing X, but we can't afford it, or we need to channel limited resources in another direction." That is how competing values look in the corporate life of your community. Let's turn our attention to our own internal competing values.

Personal Competing Values: Resisting Change

Have you ever noticed how we tend to resist the very changes we *ourselves* say we want to make? Remember, values are those things that matter most to us, the priorities that govern the decisions we make. Normally, most of us hope that our values are always aligned and consistent. Unfortunately, this is rarely the case. Life in general has a nasty habit of offering up choices based on values that aren't always aligned, values that often compete with one another.

Let's take a few examples of competing values. I worked a lot with the FAA, whose mission is to keep our air space safe and efficient. But *safety* as a value tends to compete directly with *efficiency* as a value.

In other words, as I become safer, I might find I become less efficient. Or the opposite may be true: as I become more efficient, I begin to sacrifice safety concerns.

Scripture enjoins us to reach out to the lost and bring them into the community. It also directs us to build strong community. These two values tend to compete with each other. If I want to build strong community, then it's better to close the doors and relate mostly to my own tribe and not reach out to others.

As I've said, competing values don't involve one good value competing with a bad value. That would make for easy choices. The trick is where a good value competes with another good value; they're just at cross-purposes. We usually don't realize it, but we are constantly dealing with competing values as we make our way through life. What is important is to understand how these competing values operate in our lives and how they can lead to incongruent living on our part (that is, I say one thing and do another).

Let's walk through several statements and see how competing values may in fact be blocking you from going forward in those things that are most important to you. Look first at the top row of the chart below, which is numbered 1 through 4, and note the progress.

1. You're committed to a kingdom value (which is the logical or rational value you proclaim).
2. But then, you in fact do or don't do something, which sabotages your proclaimed value.
3. That's because you have a competing value underneath (springing from the emotional centers in your brain) fueled by some big assumption you have.
4. Although this big assumption rationally makes no sense, it was laid down in your subconscious long ago and continues to exert inordinate influence on your behavior. This big assumption has to do with your unconscious blueprint for achieving and maintaining security and significance, and it triggers a great deal of anxiety when activated.

To read the four columns backward tells a powerful story. Holding to a big assumption (#4), we are understandably committed to protecting ourselves (#3). As we faithfully live out these commitments, we act in a particular fashion (#2). This in turn compromises our ability to truly realize our genuinely held commitments (#1).[1]

1 Kingdom value commitments	2 Proclaimed value sabotaged	3 Competing value underneath	4 Irrational assumption
Resting in God's acceptance of me no matter what others think.	I seek to please people, so they will accept me.	I must be acceptable to everyone, regardless.	If people don't accept me, I'll be abandoned and die (security).
At Jesus' baptism, God declares his pleasure in him, though he has *done* nothing.	I must constantly strive to achieve. The parable of the talents haunts me.	I am okay and loved, as long as I can perform and produce.	If I don't do enough (whatever that is), I'm worthless, rejected, and a failure (significance)
God reigns. There I can rest while empowering others (priesthood of believers)	I must patrol my world and try to order it, micromanaging whomever.	My control of my life drives out my sense of vulnerability, at least to a degree.	If I'm not in control, my vulnerability will leave me weak, powerless, and susceptible to *being* controlled (security)
God is completely trustworthy. I can be dependent on him.	I monitor my world, sensing danger everywhere, and activate to protect myself.	To trust is to be set up for disappointment and disaster.	If I get close and let my guard down, I'll be destroyed (security)

1. For an expansion of this theme, see *How the Way We Talk Can Change the Way We Work: Seven Languages for Transformation* by Robert Kegan and Lisa Laskow Lahey (San Francisco: Jossey-Bass, 2002).

1 Kingdom value commitments	2 Proclaimed value sabotaged	3 Competing value underneath	4 Irrational assumption
I must empower members of my congregation to exercise their God-given gifts.	I must not give people "free rein" to minister at the church without strict oversight.	I'm called to lead this church in an excellent manner. Letting others exercise their gifting might lead to sloppy, subpar performance.	If things aren't done properly, I'll be condemned for subpar performance and doomed (significance).
RESULTS			
Rational explanation: What I care about.	**Self-evaluation: My part in this mess.**	**Irrational reaction: Hidden values drive me emotionally.**	**Irrational assumption: My unfounded fears.**

As a result of all of this, we continually manufacture non-change in our lives. Oh yes, we state that we need to change, and we indeed must change. But as we set about attempting to put in place behaviors, or eliminate behaviors that need to change, we find ourselves sabotaging these changes because of competing commitments that demand to be honored. All of this is done completely out of our awareness. All the time, our minds are clearing up the discrepancies to reduce our anxiety and keep us humming right along as if our lives are paragons of virtue and consistency.

WHAT CAN YOU DO ABOUT THIS?

Here are several steps that might help:

1. Observe yourself in relation to your big assumption (BA). What do you unconsciously assume will bring you security and significance?

2. Actively look for experiences that cast doubt on your BA.
3. Explore the history of your BA.
4. Design and run a safe, modest test on the BA. After you've conducted your test, see what happens. As an example, let's say your BA is to have absolute optimal performance, and thus you rarely let others preach/teach or do any of your preferred functions. Test this BA by allowing an associate to preach who has never done this in the "big" church. See what happens. Does the congregation rise up and stone you after the service? Does giving and membership decline? Probably not.

Notice that much of what we've talked about involves delegation (aka empowerment). Delegation is extremely important for anyone in leadership, beginning with parents. Too many pastor leaders, however, get into micromanaging. There is undoubtedly a competing value at work inside of these leaders, unless they simply believe that micromanaging is the absolute best way to manage and develop their people (which flies in the face of all best management practices and doesn't lead to healthy children or congregants, who can take responsibility for their own lives as they develop their gifts).

It's important for you to begin to see how one value (i.e., delegation) gets trumped by another value (competence). Think for a moment of what competing value is inside of the micromanaging leader. There's a good chance that their need to be competent may be the competing value. What happens when you delegate? You cede quality control. You know how you would perform, but what about your children or the assistant pastor? Will they do an equally good job? The only way to know is to constantly look over their shoulder and direct their behavior in the "right way."

What This Looks Like in Real Time

Let's take a look at some concrete examples, though notice that I'm not giving concrete answers. That's because competing values don't lend themselves handily to good answers. Depending on your personality and the loyalties you experience in your congregation, you'll usually lean in one direction or another. If you're well-defined and self-aware, then you'll know where you tend to lean on various issues.

One glaring set of competing values in church settings is grace versus accountability. Of course, at its core the church is a volunteer organization, which makes things a little trickier (we'll discuss this more fully in chapter 12).

Say a small church has a janitor who is also a member of the congregation. Unfortunately, as time goes by, the performance of the janitor declines, even though the senior pastor points up his various deficiencies. The senior pastor then has to ask how much grace to extend to him. The pastor finds himself having to walk behind him and finish the jobs he's only half completed. But because he is a congregant, the pastor is in a tricky situation because the congregation considers him to be a brother in the Lord.

Another set of competing values can be seen as doing versus thinking. A church ruling board was considering relocating to a new campus. The entire board did not want to get bogged down in the details of this, so a lay team was appointed to do the "heavy lifting," with the board maintaining oversight as the process went forward. The board was anxious to get the whole process rolling, since the lease on their current property would run out in six months.

After a few months, the board realized that the relocation team was made up exclusively of doers, not thinkers—people who wanted to get on with execution. Now what? The team was moving ahead way too quickly, without thinking through ramifications of decisions made. The board realized they had the wrong people, or at least half the wrong people, on the relocation team. No one seemed to be able to grasp the complexity and understand the unintended consequences, given that relocating a church involved building issues, space utilization issues, programmatic issues, and all of the people issues a thriving congregation represents.

What to do now? They had the wrong team in place, and asking half of them to leave wouldn't work well; but just adding a bunch more people would make the group too unwieldy for optimum functioning. Note: Your mind may have already "solved" this with a technical solution. I can almost guarantee you that once your solution is put in place, that solution itself *will become the problem.*

Let's look at another scenario. A congregational ruling board received an email from one of the church member families, who was quite active in the congregation with their seven-year-old girl and five-year-old boy. A few years earlier, the parents had learned that their daughter had a severe nut allergy. Airborne allergens from tree nuts could potentially send her into anaphylactic shock, the board was told. Because of her allergy, the family asked that the church not allow nuts or nut products to be brought into the building. The church health and wellness committee, after meeting with the parents and doing some additional research, recommended that they establish a "nut-free" policy, communicate the reasons for the policy to the congregation, and ask that people refrain from using peanuts and tree nuts in baked goods and other food items that are brought to the church. Through the use of written announcements in the monthly newsletter and weekly worship bulletin, notes were sent to Sunday school families, and occasional verbal announcements were made in worship. In other words, the church followed the no nut recommendation.

In spite of the board's best efforts, however, foods containing nuts occasionally were brought into the church. When the parents (and grandparents) of the allergic daughter discovered nut items in the church, they became visibly angry and upset, sometimes in very public settings—the church narthex, the fellowship hall, and so on. As a result, a "backlash" developed against this family among some of the church members. These members believed that the parents were expecting too much from the church, that the parents were not taking enough responsibility themselves. The parents, on the other hand, believed the congregation was not taking the issue seriously enough. The church board then created "nut-free" signs that were posted in various locations within the building.

Even these actions, however, resulted in some tension. The parents wanted to display signs that were larger and more prominent than the ones used. The poor pastor in this true story fully understood and supported the desire of the parents to make the church a nut-free environment. He, along with the board chair, communicated to people the reasons for the nut-free policy, both publicly and in one-on-one conversations. On the other hand, he also tried to convey to the girl's family that they could never guarantee that no nut products would ever be brought into the building, and that their angry outbursts were counterproductive.

The question then became: How does a congregation best accommodate the special needs of individual members (individuality), while attending to the needs of the congregation (collective)? And what is the role of the pastor in helping people to see things from the perspective of the other "side"?

Values, though constantly yet often unconsciously directing our activities, tend to rear their heads most prominently when we are considering change. Let's first consider the nature of change, especially the three profiles that change assumes.[2] Over and over, ministers miss this point and pay a high price as a result.

TAKEAWAY

✓ Problems within the church usually fall into three distinct categories: tactical, strategic, and transformational. The biggest error pastor leaders face is applying tactical solutions to transformational issues.

✓ If you're not careful, your unaddressed internal competing values will lead to misalignment on your part, eroding trust among those who follow you.

---

2. For a much more thorough discussion of the leadership triangle, see *The Leadership Triangle: The Three Options That Will Make You a Strong Leader*, by Kevin Ford and Ken Tucker (New York: Morgan James, 2014).

PART TWO

What Do You Do as a Leader?

In part one, we laid the foundation of discovering who you are as a church leader. As we saw, to be an effective leader, you must have a growing awareness of yourself and of the processes that surround you. You understand that your thinking can be compromised and distorted, especially by competing values. Now we will look at what you actually do as a pastor, and how to be most effective at these various responsibilities and tasks.

7

YOU, THE LEADER

The job of pastoring has been compared to that of a homemaker: many different tasks to perform, none of which corresponds with any other in any appreciable way, and no one standing over you to make sure each task is done properly. As a result, homemakers and pastors both tend to experience a great deal of anxiety as each confronts the beginning of their day or week deciding what tasks to tackle, in which order, and with what amount of intensity. Added to this are the leadership challenges every pastor faces. Let's begin there.

THREE LEADERSHIP CHALLENGES

My business partner and friend, Kevin Ford, has discussed thoroughly what he calls the Leadership Triangle.[1] These concepts denote that there are actually three leadership challenges that present the pastor with three options to confront them.

At the core of leadership is our belief that different kinds of leadership challenges call for different types of leadership options, choices, and postures the leader must assume. The most pressing leadership question of the moment is not just about church attendance or giving patterns or resource allotment. It is asking what it means to lead in such a way that your church can adapt and thrive. This is the case whether you're leading a family, a business, a department, a volunteer board, an army, or any other organization.

Let's now look at the three primary types of leadership challenges: the technical (or tactical) challenge, the strategic challenge, and the transformational (or adaptive) challenge.

---

1. See Ford and Tucker, *The Leadership Triangle*.

Three Primary Leadership Challenges			
	Technical (or Tactical)	Strategic	Transfor-mational (or Adaptive)
Role:	Expert	Synthesizer	Facilitator
Tone:	Confident	Vision casting	Creative
Key questions:	What's wrong?	What's the focus?	What's the question?
Problems are to be:	Solved	Planned	Reframed
Interaction:	Train	Inspire	Free-flowing and robust
Tense:	Present	Future	Past, present, future

In my work with hundreds of organizations, I've observed that successful leaders use these three primary modes of leadership.

Technical (Tactical) Problems

When the problem is technical (tactical), leaders take on the role of an expert or an expert-finder. Their tone is confident: "We can apply our current base of knowledge to solve this." They ask, "What's wrong here?" and then work on solving the evident problems. As they interact with their people, they function as a trainer, an authority figure if you will, bringing knowledge to bear. And they function in the present tense, asking "How can we solve this problem right away so that our today can be better?"

Tactical problems are solved by experts. If the roof leaks, hire a roofer. If your computer network is down, call the Geek Squad. If you break your leg, find an orthopedist. If a congregation is unclear on a theological issue, instruct them. Most ministers function in this mode most of the time. Leaders rise to the top of their organizations precisely because they expertly handle the various situations that have confronted their companies. So, with their "subject matter expert" (SME) hat firmly in place, they go about directing the organization forward.

Ministers bring their own expertise to the table: theological, financial, technological, managerial, and so forth. If the church is considering a new building project or capital campaign, it's appropriate for others to bring their expertise to the table. To solve a tactical problem, simply find someone who has the expertise and authorize that person to solve the problem. Tactical leaders exercise their will through their expertise. But be very careful. Something that appears on the surface to be technical often has a great deal of transformational material lurking under the surface.

Strategic Challenges

When the problem is strategic, ministers take on the role of a synthesizer, bringing together knowledge of the internal organization, the external constituency, and the broader climate. Their tone is that of casting vision, introducing an inspiring picture of the future that takes advantage of and confronts the changing landscape. Their key question is "What should be our focus?" and they realize that the main way to tackle problems is through innovation and integration. Their interaction with their congregation is best described as inspirational, and they focus on the future tense: the imagined and aspired-to results of careful adherence to a clearly articulated strategy.

Strategic challenges relate to external changes and are future oriented. They are about major transitions. Such challenges require more than a tactical fix. Strategic challenges require strategic leadership, the art of leveraging strengths in order to minimize weaknesses and capitalize on opportunities. But strategic leadership often involves dealing with opposition, as congregants may resist the needed change. Strategic leaders are on a quest to understand their external environment, and they must ask big-picture questions.

Transformational (Adaptive) Challenges

When the problem is adaptive (transformational), ministers take on the role of a facilitator, inviting dialogue and discovery, particularly in the areas of values and beliefs. In church life, we see transformational challenges emerge constantly. New programs are introduced and old ones are discontinued. Worship takes on new forms, and music along with instrumentation evolves. These challenges require churches to clarify values, develop new strategies, and learn new ways of operating.

In these situations, pastors can no longer be seen as an expert. They must develop a whole new way of leading. The tone they strike needs to be one of creativity, whether in problem-solving or in conflict! They know the key question now is itself: "What's the question?" They know that problems aren't so much to be solved or planned for as much as navigated and reframed—considered in an entirely new way. They know that group interaction at this level of leadership needs to be free-flowing and robust—everything on the table—and that their focus is not only on the present but also on the past and the future.

Transformational challenges are the very stuff of leadership and require a leader operating at full creative capacity. It is in this arena that most ministers, and leaders generally, have the most difficulty. And the first problem they have is in actually seeing that there is a transformational issue lurking, the temptation being to default to the tactical expert.

An issue requiring transformational change is much more complex and is sometimes hidden within the systems and structures and hence the culture of the organization. We are seldom aware of transformational issues. They mostly revolve around competing values. This is why strategic direction often surfaces transformational issues. The new direction challenges the status quo (we'll discuss this more when we get into culture in chapter 11).

Transformational (adaptive) issues are often hard to identify clearly, require changing hearts and minds, and often are championed by someone who cares but may not have the authority to effect change. When adaptive issues are involved, people have to learn new ways and must choose among what appear to be contradictory values. Technical or tactical issues can be *managed*. Adaptive issues require leadership to help the stakeholders navigate them—hence the name transformational or adaptive leadership.

Adaptive leadership is difficult work. It's difficult because it involves helping individuals make hard value choices, and because it challenges what people hold dear, thereby generating resistance from many of those affected. When people resist adaptive work, their first goal is to preserve what they have, and that means shutting down those advocating the change.

Transformational issues always bring competing values to the fore. They aren't easy decisions. Transformational issues require different skills than tactical problems, especially the ability to manage and occasionally even orchestrate conflict. Very few people in positions of leadership have developed these skills.

Let's look at an example. Historically, First Church was a pastor-driven, pastor-controlled church. It generally worked well for many years, when they had extraordinary senior pastors who could get it done. The last pastor was a gifted teacher and a warm and friendly caregiver who was also was autocratic (historically what the church was used to). The congregation was aging, and the senior pastor had a vision to reach out to younger families. Thinking tactically, he changed their traditional worship into blended worship (that is, more contemporary than traditional). Although this caused great conflict, as long as the senior pastor was present, he was able to have the power and authority to keep things going. Over the years, the elder board had been a "Yes Board" in the fullest use of that phrase.

The underlying conflict and unhappiness of the older members (the vast majority of the membership) continued. The elder board finally couldn't take it anymore and let the pastor go (another tactical solution that usually solves nothing, or merely drives the conflict underground). Everyone personally liked the fired pastor (even most who were unhappy), and his being let go didn't sit well with the membership. The elder board then decided to change the culture of the church from a pastor-centered/pastor-led church to an elder-led church (another tactical solution with major transformational implications). The elder board studied Scripture, studied board governance models, and prayed. About six months of hard work went into a total rewrite of the constitution. The one thing they didn't do was engage the stakeholders (i.e., the congregation) as they carved out this new document.

The new constitution gave the senior pastor (now called the teaching pastor) no power over vision or strategy, and none of the staff reported to him. This, in the board's mind, freed up the pastor to teach and preach. At the same time the elders made this change, they told the worship team to return to more traditional hymns and less contemporary music. Made up almost exclusively of baby boomers and older, who didn't like all the loud drums and guitars, the elder board wanted to go back to the church of the 1950s: "the way it should be." As of this writing, the church has yet to fill the position of teaching pastor.[2]

The elder board simply couldn't understand why the people were so upset. They really did their homework, or so they thought. They had many meetings to explain the new governance model to the congregation (of course, they never really asked for feedback). This was not a quick change in their eyes. Nor was it a grab for power. In fact, since the elder board had all of these new responsibilities, they were working harder than ever, already becoming burned out from the workload, not to mention the arrows the staff and members were firing at them for being "control freaks." Welcome to the land of transformational challenges!

WHAT LEADERS DO FROM DAY TO DAY

Let's turn to the specific behaviors that each leader must employ in order to be successful. Consider this list (which undoubtedly is partial) of potential responsibilities:

1. Prepare to preach and/or teach
2. Preach
3. Teach
4. Visit (sick, shut ins, new members, etc.)
5. Counsel
6. Team build
7. Hire staff
8. Lead the church board
9. Train and develop staff
10. Disciple
11. Manage the budget
12. Fundraise
13. Develop various programs: e.g., outreach (evangelism)

Let's graph these thirteen responsibilities (see below). Notice that each responsibility is given equal weight. Everyone knows that each

2. Well, duh!

of these responsibilities is not coequal to all the rest, but which responsibilities are more important than the others? Is preaching more important than counseling or budgetary monitoring?

Look at these responsibilities and try to ascertain which ones you are good at and are thereby energized by when you perform them. Then note those you're okay at but would rather someone else perform. Lastly, note those responsibilities you are frankly poor at and need to off load as quickly as possible.

For pastors in a small church situation, they will find themselves responsible for most if not all of the above list. For those who minister in larger churches with multiple staffs, the ability to parcel out some of these tasks is much greater. But even pastors in much larger churches often get caught trying to fulfill the majority of this responsibilities list.

The Central Problem

There are at least three difficulties as pastors consider this list of responsibilities:

1. This list is a recipe for burnout. Attempting to perform all of these tasks adequately, just from a time point of view, requires a 24/7 schedule that's impossible to maintain.
2. No one person, no matter how wired, can successfully perform more than four or five of the above. As an example, people who are good with other people (visiting, teaching, counseling) usually make poor administrators (hiring, developing staff, managing the budget, etc.).
3. We invariably default to our areas of strength, where we are energized and receive our highest accolades. Therefore, the four or so areas of our strength will receive the lion's share of our time, while the other areas (especially those four or five we do extremely poorly) will languish. If I'm good with people, I tend to ignore the administrative part of my job (unless our church is big enough that I can offload these tasks to a more competent subordinate). If I like to preach, teach, and do research and study, then I tend to ignore visitation and possibly administration.

We have already looked at the concept of the sweet spot: the cumulative elements of our talents, our experiences, and our learning that together sets us apart and makes us unique. It is that zone in which we perform optimally, while feeling energized rather than drained.

When we're functioning in our sweet spot, we're extremely focused, lost in the moment. Sufficient to say, effective leaders spend a preponderance of their time functioning in their sweet spot. This place represents that convergence of our talents-turned-into-strengths where all of our faculties are combined in a harmonious order. We perform at our peak, getting lost in the process, and losing a sense of the passage of time. We can work for hours and are actually energized rather than depleted by the experience. At these times, we are authentically centered in the true sense of ourselves—we are well-defined. We pursue our sweet spot for its own sake, not worrying about the residuals that might flow from its successful prosecution. We pursue this special place for its own sake, not worrying about the residuals that might flow from its successful prosecution.[3]

---

3. This seems to be the thrust of Proverbs 22:6: "Point your kids in the right direction—when they're old they won't be lost." I would agree that

Remember what was previously said: those who can combine their career with their sweet spot will be those who function in those careers at the highest levels, at the same time maintaining a sense of accomplishment and fulfillment that unfortunately few of us realize. Those who are rarely if ever in their sweet spot will usually find themselves depleted. These folks may also turn to artificial stimulants to produce the synthetic high that working in our sweet spot naturally produces (although these artificial means often lead to addictions and a host of associated problems).

THE MATH

What I find in my coaching of ministers is often a group of people who are over-worked and burning out, attempting to do tasks and functions for which they are poorly 'wired.' Yes, they may go off to various workshops in an attempt to bring up their very poor performance to at best marginal levels of performance. But is that the answer? Attempting to raise poor performance to marginal performance? Or is it better strategy to, as best we can, given our circumstances, choose more of our weekly tasks among those that fall within our sweet spot, leaving the rest to others who are better suited to perform them?

Your Sweet Spot and Responsibilities

I want you now to consider the specific responsibilities you have to perform in your role of minister. Using the example below, write in your own specific responsibilities in the blank spaces. Below that, break down each responsibility into specific behaviors needed to successfully complete this task. Then, in the second column, rank this responsibility as to its priority to fulfill the church mission. In the third column, score yourself from 1 to 5 (1 being poor, 5 being excellent) as to how you rank yourself actually performing that behavior. If you want, you can also give this chart to a trusted person or two who know your performance to see how they'd rank you.

"they won't be lost" is their id. That's why they don't have midlife crises and abandon their chosen careers.

Pastor's Responsibilities	Priority A, B, C	Score 1 to 5
Staff functions		
Builds trust among team members as leader and for one another		
Engages in healthy conflict		
Commits to decisions and actions		
Builds team where everyone holds each other accountable		
Focuses on collective results		
Be with People		
Visiting hospitals		
Visiting shut-ins		
Counseling		
Preaching and Teaching		
Administration		
Leading the Church Board		

Those responsibilities above where you scored 5 probably fall within your sweet spot. Those are tasks that only you can do. Those where you scored 4 and 3 probably fall within those tasks that others can be trained to do. Anything below 3 falls within those tasks anyone can do. It is best to leave these lowest scored tasks to others to perform.

YOUR TEAM

I would argue that it's critical to *always work within a team*, even if you're church planting. My friend Todd Hahn, who has planted a couple of successful churches, told me that he always begins with a team, realizing that he doesn't possess all of the gifts necessary to be successful. Team members don't have to be paid members. In fact, this may not even be possible depending on your situation. But well-chosen volunteers can function just as well performing certain critical functions that you as the pastor do not possess.

Selecting the Team

Team selection is usually problematic throughout the organizational spectrum. When leaders select teams, they usually make two glaring mistakes:

1. They don't have a clear idea as to the talents that will be critical for the team to successfully complete its mission.
2. They go about selecting people who are: (a) just like themselves (therefore duplicating talents rather than expanding talents), or (b) people they would like to hang out with and have as buddies, not people with complementary talents.

Working with and through the Team

One primary responsibility you the pastor have is to actually pastor your team. In turn, the team are the primary ministers to the congregation in the various functions they perform. From Jesus sending out his disciples two by two, to Paul taking along a ministry team, Scripture illustrates over and over that we are not called to "Lone Ranger" ministries. We can't be. The metaphor in 1 Corinthians 14 is that of a body, with each part essential to the proper functioning of the whole.

Much has been said and written about team functioning., In "The Five Keys to a Successful Google Team," Julia Rozovsky describes what Google considers key ingredients to successful teams, which I have found helpful:

1. *Psychological safety.* Can we take risks on this team without feeling insecure or embarrassed? This is the critical foundational issue for teams, and revolves around the whole notion of trust. Teams with high trust are able to admit mistakes, are able to enter into mission-focused conflict, are generally able to be vulnerable. As a result, these teams are able to "think out of the box" and make significant strides that other teams can only dream about.
2. *Dependability.* Can we count on each other to do high-quality work on time? This kind of dependability requires mutual peer accountability.
3. *Structure and clarity.* Are goals, roles, and execution plans on our team clear?
4. *Meaning of work.* Are we working on something that is personally important for each of us?
5. *Impact of work.* Do we fundamentally believe that the work we're doing matters?[4]

Takeaway

- ✓ Knowing your own id (your unconscious instinctual needs and drives) and working as best you can within that sphere, is critical to your own emotional well-being.
- ✓ It's critical to surround yourself with a team that can shore up those areas where you don't perform optimally.
- ✓ And maintaining that team as a high-functioning entity is critical to the well-being of your church.

Take Action!

In the chart above (p. 104), I had you mark down your specific responsibilities, the priorities of each, and how you see yourself performing in each of these areas. At this point, it would be good to get feedback from others in your life as to how they see you doing. Below is a survey you can take for yourself. In addition, give a copy to your

4. Julia Rozovsky, "The Five Keys to a Successful Google Team," *Google People Operations*, November 17, 2015.

spouse, the chair of your ruling board, key staff people, and one or two other leaders in your church. Their answers will give you a better handle on how you're perceived by those you lead.

Directions: Go through the following competencies and mark each according to the key below. Having spouse, several friends, and key church leaders take this will also be helpful.

Key:

1 = Rarely or Never
2 = Sometimes
3 = Often
4 = Most of the Time

Survey of Performance				
Spiritual Leadership				
Provides spiritual direction to the church	1	2	3	4
Demonstrates personal spiritual maturity	1	2	3	4
Leads others toward spiritual maturity	1	2	3	4
Is personally committed to spiritual disciplines such as prayer and Bible study	1	2	3	4
Comments:				
Preserves the Core Values and Purpose of the Church				
Communicates the values and mission of the church (what the church is all about)	1	2	3	4
Lives out the values and mission of the church	1	2	3	4
Makes decisions based on the values and mission of the church	1	2	3	4
Protects what is most important to the church	1	2	3	4
Comments:				

Survey of Performance				
Mentors People				
Invests intentional time to develop leaders	1	2	3	4
Shares responsibility with others	1	2	3	4
Gives permission to allow others to take initiative	1	2	3	4
Provides constructive feedback in helpful ways	1	2	3	4
Comments:				
Empowerment				
Provides knowledge and resources to enable others to solve problems	1	2	3	4
Provides encouragement and feedback	1	2	3	4
Encourages risk-taking	1	2	3	4
Provides strategic direction, without micromanaging	1	2	3	4
Comments:				
Basic Management				
Demonstrates competence in financial/budget issues	1	2	3	4
Demonstrates effective time management skills	1	2	3	4
Demonstrates effectiveness in basic technologies for communication	1	2	3	4
Leads meetings effectively	1	2	3	4
Comments:				

Survey of Performance				
Team Building				
Pulls together the right people for projects or ministries	1	2	3	4
Builds consensus decision-making at the team level	1	2	3	4
Keeps the team focused on the strategic direction	1	2	3	4
Encourages brain-storming and idea generation	1	2	3	4
Comments:				
Conflict Management				
Encourages healthy debate around ideas and issues	1	2	3	4
Keeps conflict from becoming personalized	1	2	3	4
Addresses conflict when it emerges	1	2	3	4
Effectively resolves conflict	1	2	3	4
Comments:				
Pastoral Essentials				
Is an effective teacher/preacher	1	2	3	4
Shows care for people	1	2	3	4
Creates a safe environment to discuss difficult issues	1	2	3	4
Demonstrates integrity	1	2	3	4
Comments:				

Survey of Performance				
Leadership				
Initiates action, motivates others, and inspires people to follow	1	2	3	4
Maintains own opinions while considering others' opinions (knows when to appropriately maintain own opinion when not in the minority)	1	2	3	4
Coaches, encourages, and assists others, and inspires people to follow.	1	2	3	4
Understands impact her/his personality and behavior has on other people	1	2	3	4
Comments:				

8

CRITICAL INTERPERSONAL SKILLS

Certain people are extremely effective in interpersonal relationships, whether in circulating at a party, group facilitation with the staff, bedside manner during hospital visitation, or whatever the social situation demands. Others seem to have varying degrees of difficulty in relationships, often pushing people away or shutting them down rather than drawing them closer. Certain pastor leaders are extremely adroit at building trust and directing people. Others tend to have difficulty building confidence and marshalling consensus to move people and churches forward.

But the vast majority of people, whether effective or ineffective in relationships, have a foggy understanding of the particular skills that either assist them or work against them.

Social investigators have attempted to understand these interpersonal processes to see if particular skills could be taught so that individuals could become more successful in their interpersonal relationships. I think the answer is, yes, these skills can be taught. Some people seem to grasp them more naturally than others. But whether you come by these more naturally because of your internal hard-wiring and upbringing, or you need to work harder to develop one or more of these skills, I believe they will make you much more effective in your ministry.

Let's look at the basic skills I think are crucial for ministers in attempting to move people forward. When I mention the first, you'll probably roll your eyes, but I want you to pay attention. And let me say that each of these skills assumes you are in the Blue Zone (rational rather than emotional) and focused on the mission. Once you get into the Red Zone (emotional rather than rational), all bets are off. This where you default to your own story and become unable to employ any of these with effect.

PASTOR LEADERS AND OBSERVATION

To be truly effective, pastor leaders must simply pay attention. In his book *The Attentive Life*, my friend Leighton Ford argues that this is exactly what God wants—an attentive servant—which is the path to becoming like Christ.[1] Many things in modern life crop up to distract us. Not the least of which is busyness. The pastors I know and have worked with over the years are incredibly busy people. Distractions of all kinds crowd into their lives, pulling them from paying attention.

Probably the single most notorious distraction creator is the need on minsters' part to meet the expectations of those they serve. Every congregant has at least one and usually multiple expectations of you. There are the usual expectations of good preaching and teaching, but then there are the subtle expectations of availability: "Pastor, I expect you to be available to me and my family whenever the need arises. And, by the way, don't send an associate, much less a volunteer. Only you will suffice." If you wrote down all the expectations of your congregation, ruling board, community, and so on, I think you'll find there aren't enough hours in the day or even week to meet even a fraction of them.

And yet, I've met pastor after pastor running all over the church community trying as best as they can to meet this myriad of expectations, frankly wearing themselves out, all the while losing their own spiritual vitality.

Mark this down: Your task is not to *meet* expectations. Your task is to *recalibrate* expectations. Did you get that? This is a critical issue you simply must understand or you will fail in your ministry.

Many people who go into ministry are people pleasers. As such, they are fair game for the competing demands and expectations of the congregation. And for those of you who are parents, you know that to be effective in your parenting role, you can't go around meeting every demand and expectation of your kids. If you did that, you'd manage to raise narcissistic, entitled kids. And Lord knows we don't need any more of them!

Dr. Rick Hanson, a neurologist who wrote *Buddha's Brain: The Practical Neuroscience of Happiness, Love and Wisdom*, states that "at-

1. Leighton Ford, *The Attentive Life: Discerning God's Presence in All Things* (Downers Grove, IL: IVP, 2014).

tention shapes the brain."[2] In other words, what we pay attention to is literally what we build in our brain tissue. Our neurons become wired in response to whatever we focus on.

A fascinating article in *Psychology Today* focuses on paying attention.[3] The author states that we often confuse paying attention (a neutral function) with judgment (a critical function). Judgment assumes we must evaluate, categorize, and then take action on the thing observed. We rush to get beyond what we observe, deciding whether to fix it or just let it alone. But this is not true paying attention. Paying attention can actually promote healing and transformation as we give our world attention and thus rewire our brains

We can talk about paying attention to God's creation, which helps restore and refresh us, but others have written on this more elegantly than I on this. Regarding ministers, I think the best place for their concentration is in the area of relationships. When you give someone your undivided attention, you send a message to them that they are worthy. You convey to them that you notice, concentrate, and focus on what they are saying and feeling—both verbally and nonverbally. By listening, you step into their shoes, trying to understand their frame of reference, different though it may be from your own.

Undoubtedly, all of us have had conversations with someone who wasn't giving us their full attention. I find that disconcerting and often maddening. This conveys to me that what I have to say isn't as important as whatever else is on their mind.

A lot of ministers I know pride themselves on their "multitasking" abilities. But remember what I said about so-called multitaskers out there: There's no such thing as multitasking! This therefore brings us to the obvious conclusion:

Great leaders are great listeners!

---

2. Rick Hanson with Richard Mendius, *Buddha's Brain: The Practical Neuroscieance of Happiness, Love, and Wisdom* (Oakland, CA: New Harbinger, 2009).

3. Alison Bonds Shapiro, "Paying Attention," *Psychology Today* (July 11, 2010).

PASTOR LEADERS AND LISTENING

Most folks in positions of leadership—pastors, CEOs, educators, physicians, or what have you—die with their mouths open. Instead of listening, they're either chattering away or thinking of their own next comment as they wait their turn to talk. Leaders, however, must know how to listen. They need to want to listen—they must value listening, and they must see listening as a difficult art that must be learned. Of course, the subtext here is the belief that people around you are valuable, that their opinions and disagreements matter. If you don't believe this, then you probably think your opinion is the only one with merit and the rest of this discussion will be useless to you.

Good listening is fueled by curiosity and empathy: It's hard to be a great listener if you're not interested in other people. Again, this ties us back to the basics of leadership: leading is about people, taking an interest in them, developing them, and motivating them.

Some of the great leaders in the airline business are good examples of listening: Jan Carlzon of SAS (Scandinavian Airlines System) in the early 1980s, Colin Marshall of British Airways in the early 1990s, and Herb Kelleher at Southwest Airlines. These are leaders who flew their own company's planes, talked with customers, listened, and encouraged ticket agents and baggage handlers. This can be called a "dynamic listening" mode—asking questions all the time. Furthermore, great listeners don't always provide answers. A good leader is one who acts more as listener and facilitator, precisely because the stakeholders themselves must wrestle with the competing values.

A warning here: When asked a question, many subordinates remain silent. This is because other situations have conditioned them to believe that their opinion is not really sought after. The manager is merely asking a rhetorical question, which the manager will answer. So, you'll need to be patient at first, and remind your protégés and those who report to you that what they have to say is truly valued.

Great Listeners Listen Musically

Great listeners listen musically as well as analytically. Jimmy Carter is an example of a president who was "tone deaf." He relied on "rational discourse" to weigh the pros and cons of various initiatives. People prepared papers that he would sift through in private. This enabled him to listen to their arguments analytically, but not musically. Jimmy Carter did not enjoy being in meetings where there was posturing, arguing, and haggling. You could say he was conflict-averse. But as I said about great teams, they are loaded with conflict.

We don't have conflict for conflict's sake. All of that arguing and disagreement give us clues. What do people really see is at stake here? What are their values or the subtext that includes the history of the situation and the personal stakes they bring to an argument?

Listening musically attends to the tone of voice and the intensity of the argument, which in turn point to the subtext. Listening musically enables leaders to get underneath and behind the surface to ask, "What's the real argument we're having?" And that's a critical question to answer, because in the absence of an answer to that question, you get superficial buy-in. People go along in a pseudo-consensus, or in a deferential way, but without commitment.

If Curiosity Is a Prerequisite for Listening, Then What's the Problem?

Another thing to remember. Grandiosity is the problem! Pastor leaders need to check their sense of self-importance. This goes hand-in-hand with the sense that your perspective is the one true perspective. This can grow into the myth of certainty—that you know exactly what's best in all situations. This doesn't arise from bad intentions. It usually grows out of the normal human need to feel significant (discussed in chapter 1). I don't know any human being who doesn't want to feel important, who doesn't want to matter to other people.

Those of us who have a strong need to be needed—I happen to have that need, so I know a lot about it—spend our lives solving other people's problems because it makes us feel needed: "Surely, you have a problem I can solve." But that orientation creates its own kind of problem. The more we demonstrate our capacity to take problems off other people's shoulders, the more authority we gain in their eyes—until, finally, we become a senior pastor or a CEO. By then, the tracks lie so deeply inside our brain that it becomes hard for us to stand back, listen, or learn from others. Our normal need to feel important—"Let me help you"—transforms into grandiosity: "I have all the answers." This, as I've already said, is the opposite of the adaptive leader.

Consider the following points about active listening. Although you've probably seen these before, they're worth repeating. Here's what you need to do to be an active listener:

1. Face the speaker
2. Maintain eye contact to the degree you both remain comfortable
3. Minimize external extractions
4. Respond appropriately to show you understand
5. Focus solely on what the speaker is saying
6. Minimize internal distractions
7. Keep an open mind
8. Even if the speaker launches a complaint against you, wait until they finish to defend yourself
9. Ask questions for clarification to make sure you didn't misunderstand. But once again, wait until the speaker has finished. Start with, "So you're saying . . ."

PASTOR LEADERS AND QUESTIONS

Let's begin with a point that's probably counterintuitive to the way you think about leading:

Great leaders ask lots of questions and offer few answers except as needed.

Unfortunately, in so many organizations, people are elevated to places of authority because of their expertise, and they're often the smartest people in the room. Because of this, most leaders think they have to be the answer person whenever their subordinates have a question.

Consider what you're authorized as a leader to do. Doling out answers—especially when people themselves should be wrestling through the issues, the competing values, or whatever—is not only *not* helpful, but it also builds dependency on you. Leadership is not about building dependency. It's about having people wrestle through key issues because they are the key stakeholders (remember the leadership triangle).

True, these concepts are hard to grasp quickly, so think about this: Leaders think their power comes from being smart, from having answers, but power is actually somewhat paradoxical. It comes from having a non-anxious presence that understands unfolding processes and allows those you lead to find their way while managing their anxiety.

Just remember, your job as leader is not to dole out answers but to frame good questions that allow your direct reports to delve into the issues more intentionally. When these folks show up at your door, here are some questions you could ask:

- What steps have you already taken to solve this problem?
- Where are you having the most difficulty solving this particular problem?
- When you see that your tried-and-true solution to most of these problems didn't work in this case, what alternatives come to mind?

Powerful questions . . .

✓ come from a place of genuine curiosity

✓ are direct, simple, and usually open-ended

✓ generate creative thinking and surface underlying information

✓ encourage self-reflection

Here are some examples of powerful questions you can ask:

- How would you like to use your gifts here at the church?
- How have the talents and gifts of other people helped you in your ministry?
- What do you want out of life?
- What's holding you back from achieving this?
- What is it costing you to continue holding back?
- Do you see yourself changing your mind on that topic?

- What new habits will you put in place to fortify your new mindset?
- What is the most meaningful action you could take now?
- What new skills or support systems will ensure your success?
- What would happen if . . . ?
- With hindsight, what can you see?
- If you were an expert in this field, what would you do?
- If you had a magic wand, what would you do?
- What dreams did you or do you have for your life?
- In what area could you make a contribution?
- In your view, what is stopping you from realizing your dreams or getting to your goals?
- What are you afraid of?
- What do you believe must happen before you can realize your dreams and visions?
- What are the actions you haven't taken to make your dreams come true?

PASTOR LEADERS AND PACING

Let's look next at an old word with a new meaning: *pacing*. I'm using the word *pace* here not as in relation to movement but rather to follow along with another person's whole demeanor—what they say and do—which gives them a sense that I understand their reality.

Pacing and listening are probably the two most powerful tools you can use to gain rapport with folks. And why would you want to gain rapport? To gain *trust*. And why do we need to gain trust? So that people will follow us!

Remember what I said earlier: trust is the first big hurdle you must get over with anyone. If people don't trust you, they won't follow you or do whatever it is you want them to do. In the past, leadership has been seen as a simple two-step process:

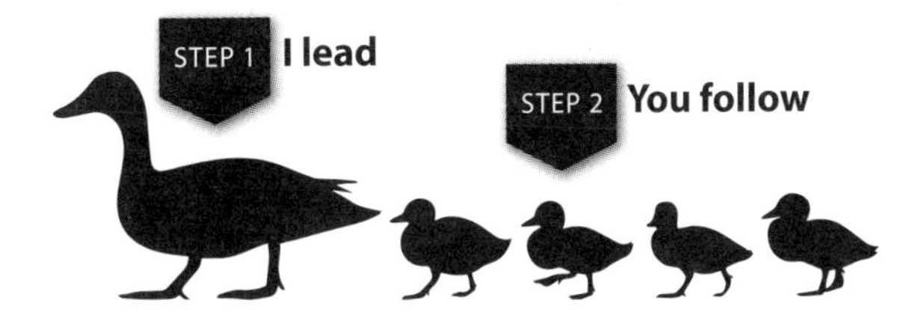

Actually, however, it's a three-step process:

Remember the trust element: You've got to gain trust to lead. And to gain trust, you've got to build rapport. Brain scientists tell us that the more primitive parts of our brain are constantly asking the same question when a relationship is first forming: "Can I trust this person? Will I survive this encounter?" It makes sense. If those questions aren't answered in the affirmative, then all bets are off.

Pacing means stepping into another person's world for a moment, meeting the person there to let them know that you're truly "with" them. Then, you lead them in the direction of change. People won't follow someone unless they're certain this leader can be trusted.

And they won't give their trust until they sense that they're being understood.

Being understood, however, is one thing and agreeing is quite another. At this point, you don't need to give them the impression that you agree with them. It would be ludicrous and downright manipulative to give the impression of agreement if in fact you don't. What is critical at this stage is to hear the other person and give them the impression that you understand them.

THOSE INTERESTING BRAINS WE HAVE

Humans have massive brains with which we're able to internalize our behavior through the complex processes of abstract thought such as language, philosophy, mathematics, and allegory. Even though much of our action with others tends to be internal (as just mentioned), there are still many simple actions we all perform. These actions are inborn and genetic (e.g., sucking as an infant) and may be discovered by ourselves, or we absorb them from society or learn them formally. In fact, far from being free-flowing, human behavior is divided into a long series of separate acts that follow each other unconsciously and spontaneously. Let's consider several categories of those actions that can enhance our understanding of relationships.

Gestures

The first class that can enhance our understanding entails gestures. A gesture is any action that sends a visual signal to an onlooker. We are obviously so accustomed to gestures taking place constantly around us that generally we tend not to take particular notice of them. They are there merely as a punctuation to our existence. Desmond Morris, a student of human behavior, divides gestures into two types: incidental and primary.

Incidental gestures are mechanical movements that involve personal actions such as cleaning, rubbing, wiping, coughing, yawning, and stretching. These gestures carry secondary messages to the observer. We can learn about people by the way they do these mechanical actions. If you're near someone right now, set this book aside for a moment and observe them—but do so in a way that they're not aware of being observed. Notice some incidental gestures. See if you can guess the person's mood. Then try to make some assumptions about the person's personality. Are they outgoing? Tentative? Shy? Sincere? Flighty? Whether or not you're right is irrelevant. The point is that you can make these assumptions about a person merely by noting incidental gestures. Unfortunately, we make many unconscious judgments about people with this limited information.

By contrast, primary gestures involve deliberate signaling. The face and hands are the most important parts of the body that give these gestures. First, think of the face. The more highly developed the species, the more elaborate the facial muscles. Humans have faces capable of myriad poses; in fact, the human face transmits the bulk of nonverbal signaling. The subtle changes our faces make as we talk with someone constantly sends information to that other person. For example, just the eyebrow position alone can convey moods of dismay, anger, or joy.

We also use our hands to convey small mood changes. We tend not to consciously notice when hands punctuate verbal communication, unless they move in pronounced ways. Try muting your television and then watch the characters gesture to one another. Notice their faces and hands. Watch how varied and subtle their movements and changes can be.

Posture

Another class of actions involves postural changes. Let's focus on the ways people who are in agreement assume particular postures in relation to one another. It's interesting to note how friends, who are conversing, unconsciously act in unison. First, they adopt a similar posture. If they're particularly friendly and share an attitude on the subject being discussed, their actions will become almost identical to each other. This is a natural, unconscious display of companionship and rapport.

Slow-motion filming of this phenomenon has shown that there is a "micro-synchrony" of small movements that is so sensitive it's hard to see with the naked eye. These movements include tiny, momentary dips and nods of the head, tensing of fingers, stretching of lips, and jerks of the body that become matched for the two people with strong rapport. Evidently, the right side of the brain unconsciously registers the movements of the other, matches these through similar movements, and then registers the feeling of warmth to the other person. One reason why mental patients *are* mental patients is that they literally are not in "sync" with the rest of the world.

Most people are surprised by how much we actually communicate at any given time. James Lynch is a doctor who has spent years researching changes in heart rate and related factors as people talk to one another. He states that for too long we, like Descartes, have viewed the body as a machine that's isolated in its functioning. Lynch cites study after study that demonstrates how the organs of the body respond and change dramatically with something as seemingly innocuous as human dialogue. He also states that many people tend not to realize their internal conflicts—conflicts that become manifest in physical problems like hypertension and migraines.[4]

Keep in mind what I said about people who agree and get into "sync" with each other. These are people who trust each other. As a result, they begin to mirror each other's posture, rate of delivery, tone of voice, and so forth. And this is exactly what pacing entails. Pacing involves matching the verbal and nonverbal behaviors of the other person so that they unconsciously sense that we're in "sync" with them, that we've entered their world and truly understand.

Here's my reality and your reality (remember what I said about our reality and God's reality). There is some overlap obviously in the way the two of us perceive reality. Pacing gives us the sense that there's much more of a correlation between my reality and your reality than is actually the case.

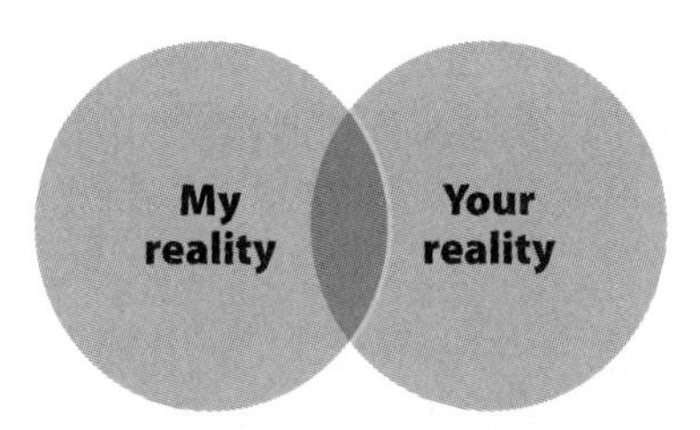

4. Note these helpful books by James J. Lynch: *The Broken Heart: The Medical Consequences of Loneliness* (New York: Basic Books, 1970), and *The Language of the Heart: The Bodies Response to Human Dialogue* (New York: Basic Books1985).

Now let's turn our attention to words, and how our conversations can reinforce or mitigate pacing another person.

VERBAL PACING

Verbal pacing involves several things. Look at these three questions I want you to ask when you're pacing someone.

1. What Did the Other Person Say?

Look at this first question: *What was just said*? Sound simple? It's not. Think back to what I said about listening. Most people are just plain terrible at listening, waiting their turn to talk.

The first, and possibly most important, part of verbal pacing is hearing what the person just said and then *acknowledging it*! It also involves knowing what the person didn't say, but what you note in their demeanor. Here are some examples of what I mean:

> "John, you look as though you've lost your best friend."
>
> "Mary, if looks could kill, I wouldn't want to be the recipient of your frown."
>
> "Mark, you look perplexed."

Remember, people constantly send us nonverbal clues as to their interior emotional status. If you can verbally note it, then that person will feel you understand.

2. What's This Person's World?

Words match a person's world—where they live, work, play, worship, shop, and so on. Look at the chart below. For the first profession, pilot, I provided words to describe this person's world. Look at the other professions and write down the words you might use to pace their world. Since everyone listed below has a different function, you pace them accordingly. Remember, we're trying to build rapport, which leads to trust and allows us to lead effectively.

Profession	Language used to pace
Pilot	Soar, glide, take off, land
Nurse	
Construction worker	
Computer programmer	
CPA	

3. What's the Representational System?

Lastly, we live in a world dominated by words. We therefore tend to believe that our thinking is mainly accomplished through words. But thinking is basically the manipulation of memory images, and the greatest source of these is our senses. This means we literally think in sensory images—making mental images of tastes, sights, sounds, and feelings.

One group of scientists, neurolinguistic programmers, interested in human behavior has taken this idea and considered how sensory thinking can be used. These researchers found that when we experience data consciously, we choose one sensory mode to gather the information, organize it, and express it. The sensory modes we use are the visual (seeing), the auditory (hearing), and the kinesthetic (touching). Of course, we use all three modes, but we each tend to have one in which we're more sensitive and will use to make the finest distinctions.

As an example, if someone asked you to remember the last concert you attended, you would go back into your memory and bring up that experience to consider. If you tend toward being a visual person, then you would primarily (not totally of course) remember how the orchestra looked, how the hall was arranged, where you sat, and so on. If you tend toward the auditory, you'd remember the music played and how it sounded. The kinesthetic would first note the feelings evoked from the experience (the temperature of the room, the upholstery on the chair).

The highly visual person translates information into a visual image to represent its meaning. This person then relies on visual images at the expense of hearing and feeling. The hearing-sensitive person obviously would emphasize sounds more, and the kinesthetic would use the feeling mode.

It would be ideal for a person to be able to use all three modes as appropriate to various contexts. A symphony is best enjoyed if the auditory channel is primary. Driving a car requires the visual mode to take charge. Appreciating a back rub needs kinesthetic awareness. You use all of these modes depending on experience, but undoubtedly, you also limit your experience when you force all experiences through your primary mode.

- Auditory people use words such as *hear, told, listen, tell myself,* and *sounds like.*
- Kinesthetics would use words such as *grasp, feel, handle, in touch with,* and *contact.*
- Those who are visual actually see pictures in their head, and describe what they see with words such as *see, look,* and *observe.*

NONVERBAL PACING

Let's now consider nonverbal pacing. Here are some questions to ask:

- What's the eye contact?
- What's the posture and incidental body movements?
- What's the tone of voice, rate and amount of speech?

Here, various aspects of a person's body language are noted and mirrored, including eye contact, breathing, voice tone and rate, body posture, and other movements. When you're pacing nonverbally, only one or two of these behaviors need to be copied. In fact, one effective way to do this is to pace one movement with another movement—that is, you're pacing the rate of movement. For instance, the person you're pacing is tapping his foot. To pace with him, trying tap your finger on every second or fourth beat.

Remember what I said earlier about people talking with one another who are in agreement. They get into an unconscious symmetry, matching breathing, tone of voice, rate, and amount of speech. We're now using that information to build rapport. This does need to be unconscious. If you're so blatant about it, mirroring a person's every move, so that it becomes obvious to that person, they'll become uncomfortable and there will be no rapport.

It's only effective when done inconspicuously. The best place to practice pacing is in social situations or at home with your family. By the way, those who are chronically isolated and alone in our society never really learn how to pace. They're perpetually out of sync with the rest of the world. They can be the most brilliant person, but nobody quite trusts them.

PASTOR LEADERS AND REFRAMING

Reframing is one of the most profound and powerful ways to help people shift perspective and widen their map of the world. A good definition of reframing is to put a new or different frame around an image, a thought, or an experience. This has the effect of transforming the meaning of your experience. The reframe creates a different perspective or context.

Let's start with the idea of perspective. Basically, everyone has a perspective on virtually everything, and your perspective of any given situation colors your feelings and informs your actions. Take for example an experience where you're home alone at night and you hear footsteps in the house. If your perspective is that it's an intruder, you feel frightened and your action is to run or grab a weapon. If your perspective is that it's your spouse or one of your kids coming in, then your feelings are warm and you prepare for a hug.

The perspective we each bring to our experiences is a function of our development. We all lived a particular story as we grew up. And in that story, we incorporated an infinite number of perspectives that make up our map of reality. I use the metaphor of a map, as we discussed in chapter 1. Although a road map is not the actual terrain, it does represent the terrain.

My map of reality is a compilation of all my opinions, assumptions, convictions, values, influences, and experiences. As I grow, my mind attempts to make sense of all it experiences—to interpret any given experience and ascribe meaning and hence value to it. Remember these two circles?

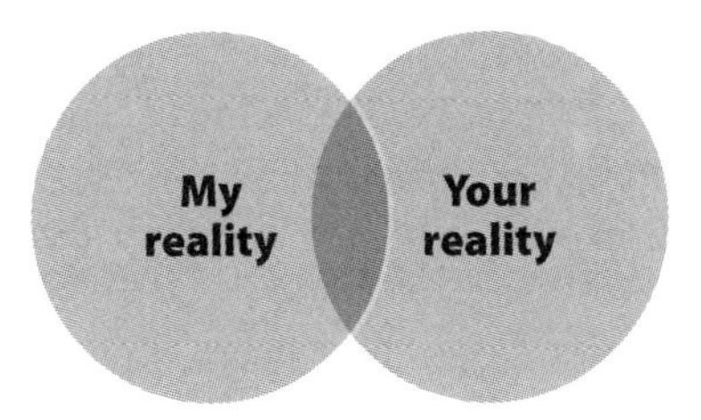

There's my perspective on reality and yours. Note that there's some overlap. If there wasn't, then I suppose we wouldn't get anything done. Most people, however, think there's a total correspondence between their reality and yours. They're frankly dismayed when you didn't like the movie that they thought was sensational.

People operate out of their internal maps. As they encounter new experiences, they take out their map to give themselves the perspective (or frame) of those experiences, and then they project their frame of this experience onto the experience unfolding in front of them.

We direct ourselves through all of life using our maps to guide us. The map works much the same as the embedded commands that are part of a word-processing program: embedded commands tell the computer how to react to certain sections of the text.

Unfortunately, we rarely take out our map and analyze it. We don't see the map, we see *with* the map, all the while believing that the way we perceive the world and our unique experience of it is what is truly real.

Interestingly, researchers find that the left side of our brains (the logic side) is committed to interpreting all of our overt behavior and emotional responses. Evidently this is done so that the brain can have a consistent story of what's happening at any given time. Sometimes the left side will go to bizarre lengths to correlate events into a coherent story, even constructing explanations that contradict the tenets of our map. Competing values and double messages are the result.

Therefore, our perspective or frame helps us interpret the meaning of our experiences. But note that our perspective and its usefulness is context bound. In other words, a particular frame that suits us just fine in one context, may in fact be detrimental in another.

Your job as a leader is to listen carefully (again, there's that word *listen*) to hear how people are framing the situations in which they're involved. Note to yourself whether these frames are helpful in moving forward the project, the relationship, or the organization. If the frame isn't helpful, and in fact is miring things down, your job will be to reframe the situation so that people can see a different perspective on what's occurring.

You have to first listen carefully in order to pace and gain rapport. Then you must get a sense of the person's perspective (frame) on the issue. Then you need to think of a reframe.

Successful reframing . . .

- ✓ Understands there is always more than one perspective underlying every problem. Even problematic behavior usually has a positive intention.
- ✓ Provides a legitimate alternative view.
- ✓ Is valid.
- ✓ Provides a positive option.
- ✓ Allows someone to take action.

Exercise		
Take a look at the experiences in the first column, then the frame in the second column, and finally the reframe in the third column. I've done the first row for you. See if you can come up with your own frame and then a reframe for the next ones.		
Experience	**Frame**	**Reframe**
• Jack concerns himself with every detail. • Mary spoke to me with a harsh voice. • John challenges me on the theological accuracy of my sermons. • Kelly said nothing to me when I came into the church. • The church lay board isn't permitting my initiative to set up a homeless shelter.	• Jack is a micromanager.	• Jack is concerned with excellence.

PART THREE

Getting Started

At this point, I've covered the foundational issues relating to self and the processes that are critical to understand, and we have also looked at crucial pastoral responsibilities and skills. Now we turn to those areas that need attention when you consider a new call, and then how to get started in that new call to build a congregation that increasingly reflects kingdom citizenship.

We'll first look at critical questions that are helpful as you evaluate a new call. Then we'll consider your first ninety days in that new call. After that, we'll consider how you can build trust and then a healthy culture.

9

QUESTIONS TO ASK WHEN CONSIDERING A CALL

One of the most important decisions pastors make throughout their career is the decision to move to a new ministry. It all starts when a search or pulpit committee from a church conducts a thorough investigation into a minister's credentials and general suitability for the position. The minister under consideration, however, tends to have no idea how to investigate that church. These ministers need to know whether or not this new position will be a good fit for them, and the underlying processes and conflicts that might be boiling under the surface.

To help these deciding pastors, we developed a set of considerations and attendant questions they should find useful in considering a new ministry. First, it would be beneficial to read Kevin Ford's *Transforming Church*.[1] His discussion in that book will give a basis for the categories and questions listed below.

In the following, I provide categories in which you can mold particular questions and provide specific questions to help you probe areas that are critical for you to gain a full understanding of this new church situation.

COMMUNITY

A healthy church community is one where people find a combination of several factors. Here members experience social connections, caring relationships, and feelings of personal connection to the church's overarching purpose.

---

1. Kevin Ford, *Transforming Church: Bringing out the Good to Get to Great* (Colorado Springs: David C. Cook, 2008).

- *Are people at this church "consumers" or "partners in ministry"?*
- *What is the level of relational commitment to the church, and how much relational community do they experience?*

Equipping the Members

A healthy church is composed of healthy, positive members who know how to relate to one another in healthy ways. Subsequently, they are equipped to authentically minister to one another and to those outside the church.

- *In what ways do members here come together, besides during formal worship and other programs?*
- *In what specific ways does the church assist members to be more effective in their everyday lives?*

Conflict

A healthy church contains conflict, which centers on the mission of the church. It is not primarily personal. Personal conflict by definition tends never to be resolved—it goes underground and can last for years, being passed down through generations.

- *Tell me about conflicts that have been ongoing here, that don't seem to reach resolution.*
- *In what areas have conflicts tended to reside? Choir? Children's Ministry? Pastoral Staff?*

Church as Community

A healthy church is a network of inter-related, interacting associations. Churches are also spiritual communities. Members manifest certain gifts, bear the burdens of one another, and generally become intentionally involved in one another's lives to the betterment of the individual and the building up of the community (a.k.a. body life).

- *How specifically does the church help members identify their unique gifts and talents?*

- *How are the gifts of individual members developed?*
- *Tell me about this church as a caring community. In what practical ways do folks here feel responsible for one another, to care for one another and be intentionally involved in one another's lives?*

Healthy Communication

For a church to be healthy, it needs to be alive with open and free-flowing communication.

- *Do people generally feel as though they are informed as to what is happening here?*
- *What specific channels of communication have been put in place to inform members about the church?*
- *Do you experience the church as open, or are there things that have gone on here that remain somewhat nebulous and mysterious?*

Belonging

The degree to which church members feel valued and loved in the church will demonstrate how solidly committed members are to the community.

- *What strategies have been put in place to assimilate new people coming to the church?*
- *Are there certain groups of people (e.g., singles) who feel less assimilated than others?*

CODE

A church's code is its identity, or personality—its DNA. Do people here have a deep personal connection to what the church is all about? What is the general sense of excitement and enthusiasm about the church? Is personal spiritual growth occurring through the church? Does the church have a unique sense of focus?

Church Code

A healthy church knows who it is, what it does, where it's going, and how it is going to get there.

- *Tell me, as you understand it, what the primary mission of this church is.*
- *What is the primary population(s) that the church is attempting to reach?*
- *Where does the church see itself in five years?*
- *What practical steps are being taken to realize your desired future?*
- *What do people here feel is the heart of this church?*

Connection to the Church's Purpose

A healthy church is one in which members understand and align with the church's goals and direction (vision of the future).

- *How well do members here understand who the church is attempting to reach and serve?*
- *How committed are you (church members) to where the church is headed in the next few years?*

Trust in Church's Direction

A healthy church is built on trust.

- *Have the last few pastors here generally been trusted?*
- *Have any of them done anything that caused the congregation to distrust them? If so, how was that handled?*

Personal Spiritual Growth

Is the church doing an effective job in emphasizing personal spiritual growth?

- *What specific programs/strategies have been put in place to help people here grow spiritually?*
- *How specifically does the church help members identify their unique gifts and talents?*

LEADERSHIP

In many circles, leadership is often too narrowly defined. In my research, I found that leadership that mobilizes people for ministry is a combination of several factors: effective leaders raise important and difficult issues with the people, engaging them in dialogue and discussion; various points of view are respected, and people are free to speak their minds; members need to trust that leaders have the best interest of the church in mind; they need to know that the church's financial resources are being effectively managed; and they need a sense that the church has clear objectives that are well communicated and executed.

Leadership and Assimilation

A healthy church is built on strong, wise, inspiring leadership at all levels of the organization.

- *How has the leadership here (both lay and ordained) engaged the congregation around the tough issues that have faced the congregation?*
- *Tell me how members within the congregation see their own personal responsibility for the ongoing work of this church.*

Former Pastors

Congregations have a way of perceiving new pastors in the same way they perceived their former pastors. Their expectations tend to be similar (and the unspoken expectations are the most important).

- *Tell me generally how the last pastor was perceived.*
- *Was this person a beloved parent? An overbearing tyrant? A detached administrator? A good teacher, poor leader?*

Staff Relations

You may be considering a church with a paid staff. You need to know that relationships among staff members, and between the staff and the pastor, are critical to the overall functioning of the church.

- *Have there been staff who have engendered some controversy?*
- *What have been the successes and weaknesses of staff development?*

Board Relations

Ruling boards of churches play an integral part in the life and leadership of the church.

- *How does the board understand what it's authorized to do?*
- *How effectively are new board members assimilated onto the board?*
- *Have there been particular issues in the board that have been difficult? If so, what were they and how were they resolved?*
- *In what areas does the board spend the majority of its time? Fiduciary matters and technical issues? Strategy? Adaptive (transformative) issues facing the church community?*

Boundaries

A healthy church is composed of individuals, divisions, and/or teams that maintain healthy boundaries.

- *Were the expectations (contractual) of the former pastor clear to the leadership and congregation in general? If not, where were there problems?*
- *Did your former pastor(s) take their allocated days off?*
- *What were the general feelings when your former pastor(s) was on vacation or study leave?*

Member Satisfaction

A healthy church is made of members with high levels of satisfaction.

- *Are you happy to be a member here?*
- *Would you be willing to have friends attend with you here?*

Financial and Management Communication

Finances are an area where poor communication can lead quickly to misgivings and distrust.

- *Do most people here feel that the church effectively manages its financial resources? If not, in what areas are there questions?*
- *Are financial matters discussed openly with the congregation?*

OUTREACH

An outward focus is evident when a church meets a variety of needs. It includes meeting the needs of various demographic segments (children, seniors, singles, etc.). It also includes making a contribution to the local community.

Mission, Outreach, and Evangelism

A healthy church should exist for those outside the church.

- *What is the overall orientation of the church toward outreach?*
- *How is this orientation specifically implemented?*

Programming for Various Age Groups

In order for members of a church to minister effectively with one another, and to those outside the walls of the church, specific programs to equip the membership must be effectively administered.

- *How do the programs of the church specifically prepare members to minister to others inside the church?*
- *What about reaching out to your community or neighborhood?*

Making a Difference in Community

To fulfill its commission effectively, the church must reach beyond itself and make a difference in the lives of people in the community.

- *How does the surrounding community perceive this church? Is it positive? Negative? Indifferent?*
- *If the church disappeared tomorrow, would anyone in your surrounding community care?*

CHANGE

A healthy church must be able to reinvent itself. Change is inevitable, and how a church handles change is critical. Care must be taken to examine the communication surrounding change, whether or not the church's members embrace change, and how innovative or creative the church is in its approach.

Managing Change

A healthy church navigates transitions and responds effectively to changing conditions.

- *When changes in worship, programming, staffing, or buildings were instituted, how were these generally received by the congregation?*
- *What change, instituted in the last five years, received the most resistance? How was this handled?*

The Right Direction

Members perceive that the church is moving in the right direction, and they embrace the changes that are necessary.

- *Does the average member have a sense of where the church is going in the next five years?*
- *Is there general agreement about the direction of the church?*
- *What strategies/initiatives have been put in place to move in this direction?*

Innovation and Creativity

If the church is innovative, then it probably relies on staying ahead of the curve in new products, services, and programs as a means to accomplishing its goals. This novel approach works well when efficiency is not hugely important.

- *What programs/initiatives/strategies have been implemented in the past five years that you would term "innovative"? How were these initiatives generally received by the congregation?*
- *Are there currently initiatives on the "drawing board" awaiting implementation? Who is responsible for these initiatives?*

A SENSE OF THE CHURCH

To get a sense of the overall mood of the church, how it perceives itself, and how it carries on its business, it's best to ask members for stories that are reflective of the church. Below are some areas you may wish to explore with behavioral questions (e.g., *Tell me a time when you were involved in a creative initiative the church was conducting*).

✓ *Creative vs. unimaginative*

✓ *Warm vs. cold*

✓ *Formal vs. informal*

✓ *Innovative vs. unoriginal*

✓ *Contemporary/cutting edge vs. traditional*

✓ *Family-oriented vs. individual-oriented*

✓ *Loving vs. uncaring*

- ✓ *Upbeat vs. pessimistic*
- ✓ *Fellowship vs. animosity*
- ✓ *Outreach vs. inward focus*
- ✓ Worship

Worship is the one time when members gather collectively, relating to one another and expressing devotion to God.

- ✓ *Do members enthusiastically recommend the worship service to friends outside this church? Have the sermons proved helpful and challenging in people's everyday life?*
- ✓ *How does the music enhance the worship experience?*

Christian Education

- ✓ *Do the programs of the church effectively teach the faith to children?*
- ✓ *Teens?*
- ✓ *Young singles?*
- ✓ *Young families?*
- ✓ *Older people?*

Building and Facilities

Buildings and other facilities not only provide space for the ongoing work of the church, but they are also visual representations of the church and its mission in the community. Below are some issues to ask yourself as you peruse the facilities.

- ✓ *Are the church buildings and property visually appealing from the outside and highly visible to people in the local community?*
- ✓ *Because of the location, can newcomers easily find the church?*
- ✓ *Do the buildings feel welcoming?*
- ✓ *Are the buildings and facilities effective in supporting the various ministries (children, teen, young adult, adult, senior, etc.)?*

- ✓ *Are there any current plans to expand facilities? If so, what are the plans and in what stage of development are they?*
- ✓ *Have any plans to expand facilities been scrapped recently? If so, why?*
- ✓ *Are there any off-campus facilities (owned or rented) that are currently being used by the church? If so, what programs reside there?*

Obviously, these are a lot of questions, and your opportunity to sit down with leadership within the potential new church situation will be limited. At the very least, this list should help you gain a sense of the areas that are critical to healthy church functioning. Therefore, if you have these questions in the back of your mind, especially the various and important areas, then they should prove to be an essential prerequisite to due diligence as you consider your call.

10

THE FIRST NINETY DAYS IN YOUR NEW MINISTRY

Congratulations! If you're reading this, then you must be starting your role as pastor in a new church. You've cast aside the security blanket of your previous assignment (or seminary). You've survived the emotional fits and starts of the search/call process (which is often convoluted and confusing). Now, brimming with confidence, you arrive for the first day of work, secure in the knowledge that of all the candidates, you were the one the church identified as having the right combination of skills and attitude for this important ministry position.

Possibly lingering in the back of your mind, however, are those inevitable questions about whether you truly heard God's call and made the right move, whether your contribution will be valued, and whether the reality of this new position will live up to its expectations. How you channel those hopes, dreams, and doubts in the first ninety days will set the tone and tenor of your work with your new church. You have a limited window of opportunity to create a sustainable advantage for "brand you."

Although there is no magic formula that will assure a smooth honeymoon, or a genetic code governing interorganizational relationships, the following steps can help you make the most of your new opportunity.

HOW DO YOU SEE YOURSELF DIFFERENT FROM YOUR PREDECESSOR?

Take some time to figure out exactly how your predecessor was "wired," how they actually carried on the functions prescribed, and how they were perceived by the various factions within the church. Then think about your own profile. How are you "wired"? How will this affect the organization you now lead?

If you are following a founding pastor and/or a pastor who served at the church for many years, then your task is particularly challenging. There will be many ideas and expectations (many unspoken and some unconscious and therefore unknown to the holder) that will transfer to you. Often those who follow long-standing ministers are assassinated in the first few years of ministry, and much of the pent-up conflict and hostility is unloaded on the new person.

You must realize that your new church has two ways of considering you: there's your true self (which very few if any congregants know and will ever know), and then there's your role as pastor (which receives all of the projections from the congregation, beginning with you as the "good parent" or "bad parent," depending on each congregant's upbringing). When congregants come against you, casting all manner of aspersions upon you, realize they're casting these accusations at your *role*, not at you. They don't know you well enough to authentically criticize you. But if they manage to target an area where you yourself struggle (e.g., your competency as a preacher), then there's a good chance the criticisms will land hard on you and you'll react poorly as a result. When you have a chance, read *Thriving through Ministry Conflict* by Jim Osterhaus, Joseph Jurkowski, and Todd Hahn.[1]

TAKEAWAY

- ✓ Be especially careful with those in your congregation who adore you, the ones who always want to compliment you on everything from sermons to appearance to family life, who want to be around you and your spouse as much as possible.
- ✓ Although this is probably what you want to hear (as opposed to criticism), these people are usually the least well-defined and are looking for and projecting onto you the "good parent" material from their childhoods.
- ✓ The reason they're so dangerous is because they'll be the first to turn on you when you disappoint them (which you are bound to do, because their expectations are way too high).

Let's now turn to the critical questions you must ask as you begin this new season of your journey.

1. James P. Osterhaus, Joseph M. Jurkowski, and Todd A. Hahn, *Thriving through Ministry Conflict: A Parable on How Resistance Can Be Your Ally* (Grand Rapids: Zondervan, 2010).

WHAT LEGACY DO YOU WANT TO LEAVE BEHIND?

It's never too early to begin to think about your legacy. This will take you to the "end game," what you hope to leave in place to make this church a better organization than you found it.

If you don't already make a practice of keeping a journal, this might be a good time to start. Write down your hopes and dreams for the future of your new ministry. Be specific, but also realize this will change and morph as time goes on and circumstances change.

WHAT ARE THE CHALLENGES YOU NOW FACE?

What are the *internal* challenges? Each new position we assume carries with it a particular set of challenges that must be understood, met, and properly handled. Many of these challenges revolve around the political landscape of the church, and we'll discuss each much more fully in chapter 13.

What are the *external* challenges? What are the demographics of the surrounding community? How have the surrounding constituencies regarded your new church? What are the particular legal covenants and laws unique to this area that must be acknowledged?

WHAT'S THE CULTURE OF YOUR ORGANIZATION?

One critical aspect of church life you must begin to grasp is the unique culture of your church. Although we'll discuss this more fully in chapter 11, it's sufficient to say here that rarely is culture overtly discussed or understood within churches. But to disregard culture is to pay a high price. Culture eats strategy for breakfast, as Peter Drucker once said.

Do Your Homework

Much of your success during the first ninety days comes before you report for work on the first day. Take the time to learn all you can about your new church. Ask for materials about the church—such as any founding documents, services, and strategic plans—anything that will allow you to gain a little extra knowledge. Jot down key questions you want to get answered.

It's critical for you to be aware of past conflicts that have gone unresolved and underground. Often congregations are haunted by these conflicts and the residual damage caused by them. These conflicts may have centered on sexual indiscretions on the part of leadership, power struggles as to who ultimately was in charge (pastor versus lay board), policy and program disagreements, and so on. Congregations tend to be allergic to conflicts, and they handle them poorly with devastating results.

One good way to know that a conflict was never resolved is in the response from congregants when you mention it. If the congregant quickly dismisses it with, "Oh, that was a long time ago, and everything's been fine since that pastor left," know that the issue was never truly resolved. A dismissive answer usually signals that denial is taking place and that the incident in question has generated a great deal of anxiety the congregant now wants to avoid.

Unresolved conflict has a nasty way of rearing its head in the present. As an example, let's say that the former pastor (or three pastors ago) spent discretionary funds for personal vacations and was dismissed when discovered. What could remain from this incident is a prevailing distrust on the part of the congregation and lay leadership on you now. This might show up in the form of a harsh policy as to how you need to account for your use of discretionary funds. You need to understand that this mistrust is not about your misconduct but is residual from someone else's misconduct.

Another common mistake is the failure to recognize the full set of stakeholders whose expectations will influence your mandate. It's important for you to develop a working understanding of the broader political, cultural, and regulatory environment within which you operate so that you're better able (1) to comprehend and predict the areas that are likely to be priority concerns in your leadership position, and (2) to tailor your own action plans so they conform and support those priorities. Understanding the big picture will not only keep you on track with your church's expectations, but it will also greatly facilitate your ability to anticipate and adjust to shifts in those expectations. Ask yourself the following important questions:

- Who are the key stakeholders?
- What are their priorities?
- What are their main concerns?

Start with a Clean Sheet

Just as you research the church, conduct an in-depth personal inventory of your own skills, behaviors, and attitudes. Think about previous positions and experiences: what worked for you, what didn't, and why (see chapter 7). You now have an ideal opportunity to build the new and improved professional you. Write down those personal characteristics you'd like to improve. Then develop a strategy to maximize your strengths and minimize your weaknesses. For instance, if you were never prepared for meetings, then write down ways to improve your performance. If you were always late on assignments, then develop a routine that will keep you on time. Develop a reputation for honesty and integrity, which is something you must earn over time. And then live up to that reputation at all times—at work and everywhere else.

Orient Yourself

As part of your orientation, your church should have done a number of things to bring you up to speed and get you plugged in as fast as possible. But you can't bank on the organization taking the initiative. Sadly, few churches recognize the value of making orientation a priority. Don't worry. Remember the old phrase, "If it's to be, it's up to me." Design and implement your own orientation program. Set up meetings with the key people with whom you will interact. Visit all small groups. Remember names. Find out who in particular you will need to work with. Look for resources you need or that you can draw on.

Send the Right Message

Dress conservatively (along the lines of how members of your congregation usually dress). Don't let your clothes attract more attention than your ideas. Hold in check any behavior that could be deemed offensive to others, including drinking alcoholic beverages over the lunch hour or at professional or social events where congregants are present. Be careful in using profanity.

Stay Grounded

Churches exist to reach and serve congregants and the surrounding community. Find out all you can about your new church's demographic base—income, vocations, and so on—as well as the demographics of the surrounding communities. What attracts your congregants to your church? Continually ask, "Why did you first come to First Church? Why have you stayed? Why have some people left?" This also will alert you to conflict that has been resident for many years (again, often underground).

Get Cultured

As already mentioned, Peter Drucker once said, "Culture eats strategy for breakfast." It's therefore vital that you have a grasp on the culture you've now joined. That culture now surrounds you and infuses everything and every way that your church operates. One of the most important ingredients of success in any new position is not the skills you bring to the table. Those are already well recognized. You need to know how those skills will mesh with the church culture. Look for clues about how the church operates by finding answers to these questions:

- How does your leadership like information: an impromptu face-to-face meeting? Memo? Email?
- Is it an open-door environment, or are formal meetings preferred? How are they conducted? Who needs to be involved?
- Who needs to be in the loop and when?
- Is the church formal and business-like, or is it more laidback and personable?
- Is the church innovative and ready to adapt new procedures and programs (looking forward), or is it very much about legacy and conserving past achievements?

Although there's little you can do to fight the church culture, the more you know and understand about the unwritten rules, the more effective you will be. One rule of thumb: Regardless of the church culture, always be early to appointments and meetings. It shows respect. Keep in mind that your selection as pastor had much to do with the search committee's sense as to how you aligned with their culture. If they celebrate that culture, then they will have seen you as aligning very nicely. If they have major issues with the culture, then they will have seen you as a major change agent (although that doesn't necessarily mean they'll go along with your change initiatives).

Listen Up

Your short- and long-term success depends on other people. The team you're joining was in place before you arrived and will be in place after you leave. Look for ways to fit in, to build a sense of camaraderie and become a part of the team. Don't go it alone. You have to work in concert with those around you. That means understanding the personalities and capabilities of those above you, those below you, and those beside you. More important initially is not what you do but rather how you do it. You should focus on five conversations:

1. ***The Situation Conversation.*** Your goal with the "situation conversation" is to gain an understanding of how church leadership sees the state of your new church organization. Is it a turnaround, a start-up, a realignment, or a sustaining-success situation?

2. ***The Expectations Conversation.*** Your agenda with the "expectations conversation" will be to clarify and negotiate what you are expected to accomplish. What is expected of you in the short term and the medium term? Be advised that these expectations will undoubtedly be totally unrealistic, and you will need to begin early to recalibrate these expectations to something that makes more sense. Otherwise, you'll burn yourself out in the first ninety days.
3. ***The Style Conversation.*** The "style conversation" is about how you and your staff (if you have one) and how you and church lay leadership can best interact on an ongoing basis. What

is the preferred form of communication—face-to-face, email, voice mail, memos? How often are status reports expected? What sorts of decisions do they want to be consulted on? Yes, there is church polity that lays out the structure, but within all of these structures is a myriad of individual processes shaped by the particular culture in which you find yourself.

4. ***The Resources Conversation***. The "resources conversation" is actually a negotiation for critical resources. What do you need to be successful? These resources are not limited to people and funds. Negotiate for resources. As you seek commitments for resources, keep these principles of effective negotiation in mind:

   ✓ *Focus on underlying interests*. Probe as deeply as possible to understand the agendas of your church board and any others to whom you will need to apply for resources. What's in it for them?

   ✓ *Look for mutually beneficial exchanges*. Seek resources that both support your leadership's agenda and advance your own.

   ✓ *Link resources to results*. Highlight the performance benefits that will result if more resources are dedicated to your interests. Create a "menu," laying out what you can achieve (or not achieve) with current resources and what different-sized increments would allow you to do.

5. ***The Personal Development Conversation***. The "personal development conversation" is a discussion of how your tenure and performance in this job can contribute to your own growth. This will involve study leave and sabbaticals. Make sure you have already thought carefully about what your needs will be. Get the particulars spelled out in writing so there's no misunderstanding with current and future leadership.

Confirmation Bias

The church represents a complex situation, beginning with the idea of competing values (and thus priorities). Each of us can see any particular situation only from our own point of view. Instinct in making decisions is reliable in situations where we have about a decade of experience in the situation, having confronted multiple competing values along the way. If you're a pastor taking over a position in a church you know well and an environment you know well, then you should definitely trust your instincts. If you're taking over a new position, a new group, or a new functional responsibility, then you might want to hold back for a while and consider different options and alternatives. Confirmation bias happens when information that's consistent with your initial hypothesis—that supports what you initially believe—is more readily available and attractive to you. Take the time to look for reasons you might be wrong as well as reasons you might be right.

Keep Perspective

The allure of a new position can be intoxicating. It's easy to be infatuated with the people, processes, and purpose of your new church. You will be tempted to overlook the blemishes and ignore the warning signs, because you want this position to be better than your former one. But is it really better—or just new? The newness will fade, so you need to keep your cultural antennae raised. While these imperfections may be insignificant, they may provide evidence of deeper personal or corporate issues you will need to deal with down the road.

Earn Your Stripes

You've come to your new assignment with a list of questions and ideas from your previous position that you want to import. You want to hit the ground running. Establish a reputation for yourself. Prove the church made the right decision when they brought you on. Unfortunately, that's a fine line. Come out too aggressively, and you could be perceived as a threat to the status quo and an assault on the church culture. Remember, the organization hired you to lead. They didn't hire you to shake up the place. They want you in their boat pulling in the same direction, not off in your own speedboat making waves. Bide your time, be patient, and the opportunities to make changes will come. Keep in mind that this is a long-distance race. Before you start a full-out sprint, you need to walk a mile (at least) in their shoes and pace yourself so you don't flame out too early. An excellent book to read on this is *The Leadership Triangle* by Kevin Ford and Ken Tucker, as well as Ford's *Transforming Church.*

Start Small

Coming from the outside, you'll see lots of things you'll question and be tempted to change. Remember, though, that you can't possibly change everything at once. Focus on one or two initiatives you see as critical to success, and then gather a coalition around those initiatives and move forward. In other words: be still, listen to what's going on, and set your sights on small, achievable victories. Here are several actions that could prove helpful:

- Express thanks to everyone who had something to do with your being there.
- Be especially grateful to God for calling you here.
- Introduce your family.
- Ask the congregation to regularly pray for you and your family.
- Write a letter to the whole congregation expressing many of these same points.
- From the moment you arrive until you finally conclude your ministry at the church, say *nothing* negative about your predecessors.
- Visit all homebound congregants your first month there (but don't announce you're doing this).
- Think of your newness as a bank account. Think carefully as to how you will spend this account. You get only one chance to spend it.
- Be especially wary of those congregants who adore you (who, of course, are the most appealing because of the adoration). This adulation should tell you that these people have poor personal boundaries and extremely high expectations of you (which you will not be able to meet). When you don't meet their expectations, they will be the first to turn on you.

- If the former minister happens to continue in your congregation, say this (and mean it):
    - "Pastor so-and-so has a well-earned place in your hearts, a place I will never be able to replace. Hopefully, as time goes by you will be able to find another place for me."
    - "If you want Pastor so-and-so at your weddings and funerals, I'd be happy to have him/her assist, as long as the invitation comes through my office."

Share Credit

One of the quickest ways to gain acceptance for you and your contributions is to include other people—both staff and congregants. Involve them from the get-go and they will help you steer through political minefields, polish your ideas, and make for a better contribution. When something works, give them the credit. If it bombs, shoulder the responsibility. When you make mistakes, take responsibility for them immediately. Failure to do so will only intensify ill will. And don't make the same mistake again. Replace "I" and "me" in your lexicon with "we" and "us." You will quickly engender a flood of support and good will. The object is to create trust and engender loyalty and commitment.

Be Tactful

Don't rush to judgment. That strategy you're knocking may well be somebody's pet project. Let go of your own preconceived notions and try to understand why it was developed and how it has been implemented. You may learn something. Even if you don't, by showing your understanding and support, you may be able to make thoughtful contribution.

Set the Right Precedents

In your gung-ho rush to please, you may be prone to tackle more of the workload, work long hours, or involve yourself in areas beyond your sphere of influence. Beware of the fact that precedents can be hard to overturn. When you scale back or slow down, it could be perceived as a waning of commitment or enthusiasm. Over and over again, I see ministers trying to *meet* everyone's expectations. Your goal is not to *meet* everyone's expectations, it's to *recalibrate* expectations: "I know I've said this before, but I can't say it enough!" This will involve disappointing people: "No, I'm sorry. I can't be there at that meeting." But in the process of disappointing, you'll also be teaching them about the limits of your abilities and the priesthood of all believers (that we are *all* tasked with ministry, because no one person enjoys all of the promised gifts).

Keep Balance

In a similar vein, don't forget the other priorities in your life—your family, your health, your hobbies, your friends. If all facets of your life are not in alignment, then there's no way you can find fulfillment in the position. Remember, you work to live—you don't live to work.

Takeaway

- ✓ What are the expectations being placed on you? By whom? Are they aligned?
- ✓ What expectations do you have of your people? How are you communicating these?
- ✓ What is your understanding of the culture of the organization? What has been your experience of the culture of the management of this organization?
- ✓ What are the most significant obstacles you now face?
- ✓ What is the church doing right? What are its best practices?
- ✓ What is the church doing that adds no value that it should stop doing?
- ✓ What should you and the others start doing? Prioritize!

11

CULTURE-CHANGE ROAD MAP

WE HAVE A CULTURE AT OUR CHURCH, SO WHAT?

Most ministers I talk to haven't given much thought to culture—especially not the culture of the church where they minister. But whether or not you attend to it, your church has a culture. Remember once again Peter Drucker's quote: "Culture eats strategy for breakfast." In other words, you can plan all you want about where you want your church to go, but the culture of that church will work against you if not carefully noted and respected.

Although the strategies you craft for your church may announce the path of your voyage, culture is the gyroscope that holds the ship steady in all kinds of seas. It prevents "roll" and gives position, orientation, and momentum. Without that gyroscope of a clear and healthy culture, leadership has to continually monitor and apply external pressure to counterbalance internal habits and inclinations.

Culture is the carrier of meaning. It provides the story of not just the "what" of your church's narrative but also the "why." It points to what is truly important, what should be valued, and who should be valued. It focuses attention on various symbols, why they are important, and thus why you should pay attention to them.

Sufficient to say, your church will thrive and grow, or plateau and diminish, based on your understanding of your church's culture and what you're planning to do about it. Be advised that culture tends to hide much more than it exposes, especially to those who participate in that culture. You also need to be aware of the political landscape of your church, which we will discuss in chapter 13. Politics and culture go hand-in-hand, and these two issues will make your life truly miserable if you don't pay attention to them.

So where is this hidden culture? It's buried deep within the church's basic assumptions, attitudes, rituals, and buildings. My friend Rex Miller has written about culture being most clearly seen in spaces we inhabit—in our case, in our church buildings, grounds, and other facilities. In *Change Your Space, Change Your Culture*, Rex discusses that culture is not about behavior, it's about a person's sense of identity.[1] As such, people choose environments with which they can identify. People will visit your church, but they'll stay only if they align with its culture. As I mentioned earlier, there are three churches I know well in my area that are in the same denomination. I go to one of them. Two of these churches are on the opposite end of the spectrum—one "high end" and formal, which the other is freewheeling with an air that "anything can happen." My church is somewhere in the middle.

Culture in any organization flows from the top down, so the leaders of the organization must embody what they want the organization to become. And every leader must understand the culture in which they exist in order to successfully grow their organization and move it forward. Every organization also has a distinct culture. Sometimes that culture is highly cultivated. Usually, however, an organization has a default culture owing to the fact that leadership never took the time to consider how their culture operates.

Culture not only shapes your people, but it also determines how successfully you will achieve the purpose for which your church exists. As we talk about culture, keep in mind that people have three needs:

1. They need to feel as though they belong.
2. Not only do people need to have a sense of belonging, but they also need to know that they contribute to that culture.
3. And not only do they need to belong and contribute, but they also need to sense that their contributions make a difference—they know they're helping to forward the mission of that organization.

---

1. Rex Miller, Mabel Casey, and Mark Konchar, *Change Your Space, Change Your Culture: How Engaging Workspaces Lead to Transformation and Growth* (Hoboken, NJ: John Wiley and Sons, 2014).

Some people think that the mission, vision, and values of the church are in fact the culture and all that needs to be said about culture. But time and again, I've seen mission, vision, and values statements crafted by church leadership that has little or no impact on how the church functions—certainly not on the shadow culture that lurks beneath the surface. That's because culture actually exists in a much broader dimension as it shapes behavior within the church. Therefore, in considering a strategy on how to help a church achieve its desired future, I start with culture, not mission, vision, and values (since all are already included within the culture).

Whether the culture is evident or not, it is vital to the life of every organization. Culture establishes the environmental conditions that enables the execution of function and tasks, shapes leaders, directs the alignment of the organization, and determines productivity. The leaders within any given organization shape the organizational climate, set the tone for leadership effectiveness, and focus on how to engage their workforce in meaningful contribution to the organization's mission. These are the necessary conditions and ingredients to optimize productivity and performance.[2]

But over and over again, I've seen that church cultures tend to be far from life-giving kingdom expressions. This is because most of them aren't intentional about crafting their culture. Then as time passes, these churches, which were undoubtedly vibrant at some point in their past, become irrelevant and even toxic. Strategy is important and necessary, but it requires a cultural environment that will support the strategic direction or else the best-laid strategic plans are dead on arrival.

If we are going to address successfully opportunities around worship, programming, outreach, employee engagement, leadership development, succession planning, and a whole host of other church activities, then it is essential to design and build a thriving culture.

Being intentional about crafting the right culture for your church is the primary work of leadership.

---

2. Some large organizations, Southwest Airlines being one of them, have special departments set up within the organization whose sole task is to monitor the organization's culture and make needed adjustments.

THREE CULTURES

One way to look at culture is in three aspects: legacy culture, shadow culture, and crafted culture. Let's look at each one.

Legacy Culture

This is the culture in your church that was created in the past; and if your church has been there for any length of time, the folks responsible for its creation are probably no longer around. This culture undoubtedly has been meaningful to many and frustrating to others (many of whom have probably moved on to more favorable climes).

Shadow Culture

This culture was never intentionally or unintentionally created; it just exists. It lies buried inside assumptions, attitudes, and rituals. We usually become aware of it only when there is an attempt to change it.[3] This shadow culture can be frustrating in that, because it is largely invisible, its elements cannot be readily seen and acted on. But it exerts a great deal of influence on the overall trajectory of the church. And it is never good. That's precisely why it exists within the shadows of the organization. Evidence of such a culture lies in conversations like the following:

"So, why do we do things this way at the church?"
"I don't know. It's just the way we've always done it."

Shadow cultures are regulated through personnel, programs, and behaviors. These are found in deeply held beliefs, assumptions, values, attitudes, practices, and traditions—all of which shape every important (and even the most unimportant) decision. Always there, you only begin to see it when you get involved in the church's activities. You may observe it by sudden whispers, closed-subject conversations,

---

3. This is where pastors coming to a new congregation often run into a great deal of trouble. They immediately see that certain things need to change. But then, as they attempt to make those changes, the shadow culture rears up and resists.

topics discussed only behind closed doors, and discussions that end with, "We just don't do things like that around here."

I worked with a church that had George Washington on its ruling board two hundred and fifty years ago. In the shadows of its culture was an elitist, tradition-bound mentality that tended to color all decisions. It was hard to tease this shadow culture into the light, mostly because the people within the organization didn't understand themselves in these categories, which created cognitive dissonance and the attendant anxiety.

It's important to realize that culture hides much more than it reveals and that, strangely enough, it hides these things most effectively from its own participants. But understand: to allow your church's culture to remain hidden is to invite difficulty and hardship as you attempt to move toward your desired future.

Crafted Culture

This is the culture that is intentionally forged. It's this culture that establishes the environmental conditions enabling the execution of function and tasks aligned with the mission, and it shapes leaders and directs the alignment of the organization. Pastor leaders, who take their culture-crafting responsibilities seriously within their individual churches, are the ones who shape the organizational climate, set the tone for leadership effectiveness, and focus on how to engage their staffs and congregations in meaningful contribution to the organization's mission. It is those pastors who are consciously aware of their influence on culture, and who set about leveraging that influence to bring about a desired culture, who experience the most successful ministries.

Many of the seeker-friendly churches of the past thirty or so years have carefully crafted cultures, detailing who they were targeting and what elements (buildings, programing, and staffing) would be the most appealing to that target audience. Over and over, we found pastors in these congregations who were intentional about the type of culture they wanted to create.

Let's take a closer look at this process to create a healthy culture. When people feel they belong, they're more likely to contribute significantly, and with significant contribution comes the ability to make a difference.

FIVE ESSENTIALS TO A HEALTHY CULTURE

Here are five characteristics in organizations my former colleagues worked with that set these organizations apart and created vibrant, healthy cultures.[4]

Congruence

Congruence is about resonance. It is alignment around core nonnegotiable principles that literally rings true with those who hold similar value propositions. To ensure this alignment, it's critical for churches to point every component and person in the same direction, moving in a certain cadence, and honoring the essence of the organization, team, and individuals. When shared principles are honored, the energy that's produced propels the team and organization forward with greater ease and fluidity.

When individuals are at odds with the principles embraced by their church, the activities and outcomes necessary for organizational success will always be compromised. The same is true of teams within an organization. The leader's role is marked by constantly noting the principles in question that underlie every initiative, navigating competing principles that are inevitably present, and discerning the difference and impact between operating on default principles (those we actually use for decision-making) versus core stated principles (those sets of principles or values we hang on the wall, declaring to everyone that what we *say* we believe).

Organizations, teams, and individuals must also have congruence between their stated mission, vision, and objectives. Misalignment can result from incongruence in principles, in mission, in direction, or in execution. Knowing the plan, the direction, the approach, and what fuels the "why" will provide the right platform in which to set up optimal organizational focus and success.

Connection

All of life is about relationships. People rely on others to create a meaningful existence and connect in their work. It's in this

---

4. Trevor Bron, Shane Roberson, Rich Hurst, and a team from my former consulting firm (TAG) cobbled together these points.

connection that people better understand themselves, others, and how to integrate meaning and purpose into their vocation.

Most organizations are structured into basic relational units or teams. The power of the team solidifies when the contributions and value of each person is understood and everyone leverages the best of what's brought into an atmosphere of mutual respect and trust. Connection refers both to the relationship people have with one another as well as the relationship the individual, team, and department have with the overall mission and direction of the organization.

Designing and building the right culture for a church requires forging connections that lead to a deeply held trust between people and teams. To forge trust, people must begin with awareness of self and others—recognizing what everyone brings to the table, the strengths, weaknesses, blind spots, passions, idiosyncrasies, and experiences (see chapter 4 on building trust).

The great jazz musician Charlie Parker said, "If it isn't in you, it can't come out of your horn." Recognizing and tapping into what is "in you" creates awareness of self. Simultaneously, doing likewise with others, recognizing what they bring to the work relationship, shapes perspective and deepens the bond of connection. It's helpful to think of trust as the steel that re-enforces the concrete. Without it, the concrete may look strong, feel solid, and hold up for a while. Eventually, however, it will crumble and fail.

A growing awareness of self and others leads to a mutually held respect for what each person brings to the team and organization. Even when people experience conflict, they can respect the value and contribution of the other. Cultivating connections requires honoring the contributions of each person, recognizing that they have something to give and add that is of value. "Respect for" leads to a "trust in." If awareness is created and respect is developed, then the right conditions exist for trust to be forged. And where there is trust, there is greater capacity for synchronization of mission and purpose.

Additionally, connection also refers to the relationship between self and team within the mission of the organization. If people follow us for our "why," then it's paramount that there's a clear connection between the individual, the team, and the organization's reason for existence. For the mission to matter, individuals must feel deeply and be able to express the value they bring, providing a sense of ownership and buy-in for the mission.

When organizations honor the insight and experience of their members and stakeholders, they honor this sort of connection as well and craft a culture that honors the individual.

Commitment

Author, speaker, and futurist Simon Sinek says, "People don't buy what you do. People buy why you do it. People follow you for why you do what you do, not what you do."[5] They follow you for what you believe, what pulsates forth from what you fundamentally believe to be true. By "why," we mean: Why does your organization exist? What's your cause? What's your belief? Why do you get out of bed in the morning? Why should anyone else care? There is something that should set your church apart. It's your "why" not your "what." Commitment focuses us on the culture that distinguishes us and sets us apart.

Commitment reinforces the "why" question. It involves individuals, teams, and organizations seeking clarity and commitment around their "why," their purpose, and belief about why they do what they do. An essential yet often missing ingredient for teams and organizations is to know not only where they're going, but also a compelling reason for others to want to follow them. Healthy churches define their why, possess a clear sense of mission and purpose, and provide opportunities for their people to contribute to that "why."

Gaining commitment is not a static destination—something that's achieved and then checked off the list. Rather, it's a dynamic journey that requires constant attention and cultivation, due to the external and internal factors that tend to distract organizational focus. Never assume that the message is clear or understood or that the purpose is consistently honored. One of the roles of leaders is to assist people in navigating the roadblocks that attempt to distract and deter away from the why. Leaders need to become vigilant about constantly clarifying the why.

Commitment is about alignment and focus, the North Star, the pull of the compass for the organization. Every business unit, department, task, function, product, and strategic initiative center needs to have clarity around the organization's "why." Organizations that are

---

5. Simon Sinek, *Start with Why: How Great Leaders Inspire Everyone to Take Action: How Great Leaders Inspire Everyone to Take Action* (New York: Portfolio / Penguin, 2009).

intentional about their "why" find themselves in a position of optimal performance, profitability, and productivity. The work it takes to craft thriving culture, however, is not for the faint of heart. Although it's a never-ending process, we believe it's the one factor that will set your church apart from all others.

Creativity

The essence of creativity explores a better method, a different way, or a unique perspective. It's about being able to look at a situation, challenge, or problem with a different set of lenses than the rest of the world uses.

As Albert Einstein once said, "We cannot solve our problems with the same thinking that created them." Regardless of the organization, the more challenges faced, the more this statement rings true. One of the most vital parts of the human spirit is the ability to create, to think outside of normal routines and rhythms, to disrupt static nature with a dynamic force of innovation. Creativity is not just something we do when we have spare time. It's a fundamental piece of who we are as people and thus as people who contribute to making up organizations.

Creativity is life-giving both for people and the organization itself. Giving life to an idea, expression, thought, movement, or a construct is vital to organizational health and directly impacts the mission. Thriving organizational cultures that value and prominently prioritize creativity shape an environment where individuals offer more to the team, leverage their skills, talents, and resources, and propel the organization forward as an industry shaper.

Innovation shouldn't be delegated to the solitary work of one or two staff or congregants. Every church has within its ranks the creative answers to the most challenging questions that church faces. Everyone in the organization has something to offer. In fact, some of the best ideas come from those given the space and permission to wrestle with the challenges their organization faces.

As I'm writing this, COVID-19 has been plaguing our country and the rest of the world, causing every organization to radically rethink priorities and implementation. This is markedly true of every church. We have always met inside our sanctuary sitting in fixed pews, but that doesn't work during the present crisis. What do we do when we can't conduct business as usual?

Many churches, without even being aware, inhibit creativity. Not intentionally, but churches don't always provide the cultural context to offer new solutions and best new practices. The answer to every challenge can be found in the room where people who "do" the work exist. Some recognized inhibitors of creativity include: the thought that new ideas can be seen as a threat to the establishment, a general fear of failure or a limiting philosophy about failure, a structure that doesn't allow for out-of-the-box kind of thinking, micromanaging, not enough time or the permission to utilize one's "work" time to be creative, the physical environment and the way in which the workspace is designed, lack of support for idea-generating venues; and authority and power structures that limit the generation of new expressions and ideas to only certain senior leaders or appointed positions.

Clarity

Clarity is all about communication that's clear enough so everyone can be on the same page and align. Under "Commitment" above, I talked about people joining an organization or movement because of the why—why the organization exists. Clarity has to do with communicating that why. This is not a one-time communication. The why must be perpetually communicated in many settings (sermons, church board meetings, etc.) so that people are clear on why an organization exists and how whatever we are currently doing aligns with why we exist.

INTENTIONALLY CRAFTING CULTURE

Now we turn to the crafting of culture. Remember, as you begin to think of crafting a new culture in your church, you should first consider what needs to change and what needs to be preserved. Once you establish these two factors, however, expect to receive a certain amount of resistance to your new direction. Indeed, there could be a great deal of resistance. All of this falls under the category of "transformational change," which needs to be handled in a specific way (revisit chapter 7).

I have coached a number of young pastors who took over churches with strong legacy and shadow cultures. Almost without fail, each pastor jumped right in and start changing things immediately, only to face stiff resistance from their leadership boards and congregations.

Culture is constantly shaping people's behavior. And people become committed to these behaviors. Thus when you begin to change your culture, this will immediately have an impact on people's behavior. This will create anxiety, and anxiety will generate resistance and push-back (and then we're into the world of transformational leadership as I discussed in chapter 7).

At this point, think of what we have discussed: the well-defined leader, the place of anxiety in our lives, the processes that surround us, and the competing values that inhabit us. Each of these concepts will be critical to keep in mind as you approach your church with a view toward changing the culture. You will need to be the non-anxious presence who is able to spot the processes as change unfolds and exert leadership in the three arenas I've detailed (tactical, strategic, and transformative), for all three of these arenas will be brought to bear as you initiate change.

Say you've decided that the church you lead needs to change, and that its culture is simply not adequate to support the way forward toward your desired future. You even have some sense as to the direction your church needs to go in. Let's say you're in a neighborhood where the traditional demographic is rapidly changing. You know that the culture of your church mirrors this other long-standing demographic, but you also know that trying to maintain the church's old culture (especially its worship service) in order to appeal to this older—and rapidly decreasing—demographic is no longer be viable. So, what can you do? Let's look at the following steps.

Establish a Sense of Urgency

The majority of churches I've experienced were never able to create enough urgency to prompt action. Without motivation, people won't help and the effort goes nowhere. Pastors underestimate how hard it can be to drive people out of their comfort zones. In the more successful cases, the leadership group facilitated a frank discussion of potentially unpleasant facts: the changing neighborhood dynamics, the new megachurch in town, flat giving, decreasing attendance, or other relevant indicators. It's helpful to use outsiders (consultants, the unchurched, people from other denominations, or regional or national staff people) who can share the "big picture" from a different perspective and help broaden the awareness of your members. When is the urgency level high enough? When 75 percent of your leadership is honestly convinced that business as usual is no longer an acceptable plan.

Form a Guiding Team

Change efforts often start with just one or two people, and should grow continually to include more and more who believe change is necessary. The need in this phase is to gather a large enough initial core of believers. This initial group should be pretty powerful in terms of the roles they hold in the church, their reputations, their skills, and their relationships. Regardless of size of your organization, the "guiding coalition" for change needs to have three to five people leading the effort. In turn, this group helps bring others on board with the new ideas. The building of this coalition—their sense of urgency, of what's happening and what's needed—is crucial. Involving respected leaders from key areas of your church in this coalition will pay great dividends later.

Have Lots of Informal Conversations

Everyone knows that informal conversations take place constantly in the parking lot. Most ministers fear these and are reactive to them, so why not get proactive instead? Let people know there are informal conversations, and warn against coalitions, confirmation, and group think. Then ask for feedback as to what is actually transpiring in these informal forums. It's hard to describe the impact of "obeying" this command.

Leaders who manage change are, by definition, busy men and women. The good ones know they must listen to their people so they can understand, filter accurate information from people who say "what the boss wants to hear," and communicate personal care and concern for the team. There are a wide variety of recommendations offered for formal structures to accomplish these goals: emails sent directly to the leader, town hall meetings, focus groups where the boss reads the transcripts, open-door policies during set office hours, and so on. Although there's nothing wrong with any of these, none pack the power punch of tons of informal, off-the-clock, in-the-moment unplanned conversations. Some of the very best leaders I've worked with schedule unscheduled time. Yep, you read that right.

They build into their calendars time for no formal meetings, phone calls, or strategic planning. They simply get out into the office, the field, or the congregation and talk to people.

We think of the pastor of a large church who routinely showed up at Sunday morning "huddles" where church volunteers met to plan and pray for that morning's activities. On any given Sunday morning, the pastor simply materialized at the gathering of children's workers or parking lot volunteers or greeters. This allowed him to have quick, unscripted conversations, take a moment or two to communicate vision, and thank the people giving their discretionary time and energy. Especially during an effort to change the culture, such small yet impactful moments are a key ingredient in the "secret sauce." The leader is a visible, incarnational presence—not someone a long way away randomly hurling change initiatives like thunderbolts from on high.

During all of this, it's important to keep your eye out for any adaptive (transformational) issues as they arise, which they undoubtedly will. These will involve anxiety generated by the impending losses various people will anticipate and experience (loss of status, of familiar forms of worship, etc.; review chapter 7). When adaptive issues emerge, you must create a safe place where the competing values, loyalties, and losses can be openly discussed.

Create a Safe Place → Create Safe Forums

Many churches are rife with division and, worse, they often mirror secular workplaces that are full of petty politics and backstabbing. Leaders leading change must ensure that their people feel safe, safe to express their opinions, even when those opinions challenge the status quo. Safe to be themselves, to bring their gifts and talents to the table. Safe to face conflict and not just avoid it or survive it, but to thrive through it. In our experience, leaders often overestimate how safe their followers feel. The consequence is that these same leaders are often shocked when people bail for another opportunity or actively work to undermine them when the opportunity presents itself. Ask yourself, Leader, is your place a safe place?

Manage Anxiety Levels

As I said in chapter 2, anxiety is the unseen, internal fuel that drives us. If you're leading cultural change, there will be loss for some people; and when people feel the threat of loss, their anxiety goes through the roof. It's imperative that you be able to manage your own anxiety as a leader—and, rest assured, you will feel it if you're engaged in the work of change leadership. People you lead will undoubtedly feel anxiety as the culture they have known changes. Therefore, create a safe place for them to share this anxiety so they won't be overwhelmed by it.

Not only must you recognize the anxiety within your church system, but you must also regulate it. If the anxiety regarding what you're doing rises above a certain threshold (where the anxiety is too high to move forward), you'll need to reduce that anxiety. I have seen pastor after pastor get on the bandwagon about a change initiative, push harder and harder to implement it, only to see the whole thing come crashing down because they moved too fast for the congregation to catch up and feel okay about what was happening.

Allow Failure and Experimentation

Because anxiety is high during a time of culture change and formation, tolerance for risk is low. This goes both ways. Leaders are anxious, knowing their jobs could be on the line, so their tendency is to make incremental, technical changes only. Followers become caught up in the tension and anxiety of uncertainty when too much changes around them, so they're inclined to keep their heads low and plod forward. Wise leaders know that part of the "secret sauce" in culture change is the ingredient that says, "You can risk and experiment. We won't tolerate such; we will encourage it. We will reward you for trying new things and taking risks." Nothing lessens anxiety more than the sense that someone can think, "I can try and fail and still have a place here." By the way, that goes for life and human relationships as well as work.

Gain Input—Not for the Sake of Consensus but for Making Good Decisions

I once heard a management consultant say, "Don't move ahead until you have gained the approval and agreement of everyone on the team." This is bad advice. It's critical that a change leader builds a guiding coalition of influential team members who can influence others. At the end of the day, it's better to have more people brought in than not.

We've learned through hard experience, however, that when you're in the process of forging a healthy culture, not everyone will buy in. Some can't deal with the anxiety of change. Others have a vested interest or key alliances rooted in the old culture. Others just won't get it. Others are simply oppositional by nature. Not everyone will buy in—at least, not everyone will buy in right away. This is where the leader has a most challenging yet invigorating balancing act. It's vital to engage people in the process of change. But once a leader has made a directional decision, input is not about approval. It's about helping the leader make good decisions with as much information as possible. Here, it's all about framing and expectations. Although there are both formal and informal structures for gaining input, it has to be clear what the input is for. It's not a vote. Respectful requests for wisdom earned from experience will help the leader be the best steward possible as the cultural change is implemented.

Give It Time to Percolate

Remember, time is on your side. Recognizing that a change in culture is necessary is much of the battle. But remember that your culture didn't get to where it is overnight. And it won't change overnight. Remember that as a leader, you see further ahead than followers because your job is to see the big picture.

Raise Competing Values and Conflict—and Raise the Temperature

I don't know if there's a more important leadership lesson than this one. The work of a leader is not to squelch but rather to spotlight competing values, especially around matters of belief and behavior. Transformational leadership is where the real work of leadership is done. Real change cannot happen unless people are allowed to see where their values compete, where they differ, and where this is done in an environment of acceptance. Once these competing values are surfaced, the work to define, clarify, and hone the values can begin.

In *The Practice of Adaptive Leadership*, Ron Heifetz talks about "creating urgency," and this is what he means. Wise leaders look for critical points where they can say, "Look, we're not in alignment here. We have to look at why, even if it's uncomfortable and hurts." Competing values often try to hide in dark corners. Bringing them out into the open casts light in and allows for everyone to see the same thing.

Give People Opportunities to Continually Belong, Contribute, and Make a Difference

Remember that these three things are at the heart of what it means to be human. And because this is true, these three things are at the heart of what it means to have a great culture of an organization of which humans are a part. I suggest that you make these three things—belong, contribute, and make a difference—part of your scorecard, one of the metrics by which you judge the success of your organization. I recommend being overt in telling your people, "I want these three things for you, and I will leverage my influence to make sure you have opportunities to fulfill them." Think about the power of that: you're speaking to the deepest, truest, most universal aspirations of the human heart—something innate to everyone—and saying, "What's valuable to you is valuable to me, and as a leader I want to create space for those things to happen for you in the course of your work life, your life as a volunteer." This is what creates employee and volunteer engagement.

Allow People Space to Grieve as the Old Becomes the New

Grief emerges as people lose something important to them. Change, even for the better, generates a sense of loss. We lose what is familiar and expected. We lose that sense of how to navigate the world.

CULTURE INVENTORY

Culture work is serious business. It is also critical business. If you don't take the time to intentionally craft a culture, a culture will develop in the shadows that may ultimately be detrimental to your church. Be advised that you have to move slowly when you're in the business of crafting culture, but your efforts will ultimately pay off with a culture that is healthy and aligns with the why of your church.

Here are some questions to help you consider the culture within your church:[6]

- What stories are legends, and what values do they convey?
- Who are legendary people presently and in the church's past? What are the prime characteristics of these people?
- What behaviors at your church and among your staff are rewarded? Denigrated?
- Where and how is your church actually spending its resources—time, programs, staffing, buildings?
- What rules and expectations here at the church are followed? Enforced? Ignored?
- Do people at the church feel safe and supported talking about how they feel about the church and what they need?
- What are the sacred cows (that is, ideas that are unreasonably immune from criticism or opposition)? Who is most likely to knock them over? Stand them back up?
- How is vulnerability—uncertainty, risk and, emotional exposure—perceived? How prevalent are shame and blame? How are they showing up (e.g., in your sermons)?
- What is the collective tolerance for discomfort? Is it the discomfort for learning, trying new things, and giving and receiving feedback? Is a high premium put onto comfort? How does that look?

---

6. These were crafted by my friend Rich Hurst.

PART FOUR

Negotiating Choppy Ministry Waters

Now that you've selected a new ministry opportunity, negotiated the first ninety days in that ministry, and considered the culture of your new ministry, it's time to consider the issues you'll invariably face as your ministry unfolds.

12

UNDERSTANDING YOUR CHURCH'S ORGANIZATIONAL MODEL

John, senior pastor of a large Midwestern church, was facing a possible $150,000 shortfall in the church budget due to an economic downturn in the area. He knew that some hard decisions would have to be made. Some of these decisions would be driven by the shortfall coupled with ministry philosophy shifts. Other decisions would be driven by the hard realities of personnel, whose skill sets no longer fit with the retooled positions.

By the time the smoke cleared at the church, two full-time and two part-time people had been let go. After two contentious town hall meetings, John realized that this congregational storm would take time to weather, with people second-guessing decisions. Paradoxically, this storm hit just as ministry numbers and a general response to ministry began to trend upward.

Downsizing church staff is only one instance that introduces challenges that almost any other organization doesn't understand. The particular trauma of letting staff go within a church setting occurs because the church involves an organizational model that hardly, if any, other organization faces.

I have consulted in basically all of the organizational models that exist, from government to private nonprofit, to multinational corporation. Among these, I have never encountered the complexity the church world presents organizationally. To make matters worse, few church leaders have been trained to understand this complexity, much less how to navigate it effectively.

ORGANIZATIONAL MODELS OF THE CHURCH

Let's now take a look at this complex organizational model we call the church by considering the three arenas of business, family, and faith community that all work within the church. What generally makes church life and functioning so confusing is the fact that, like no other organization in society, church encompasses expectations of business, family, and the faith community.

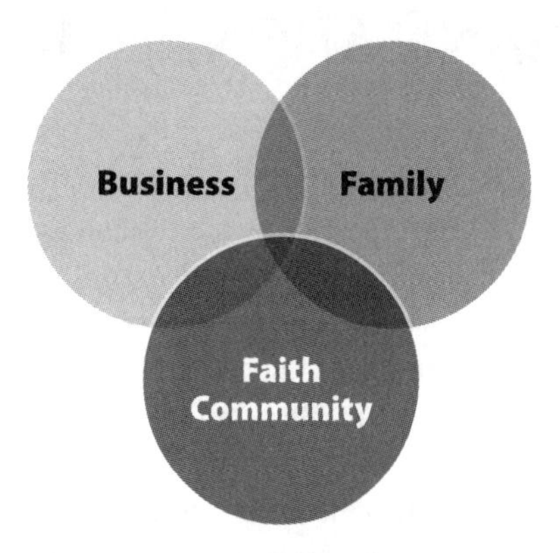

Each of these elements must be held in tension, and each must be understood clearly, or else confusion will ensue. Because churches operate much like families, and those who work on staff are often church members, emotional-impact decisions (such as being downsized) have the same repercussions of someone saying, "My family just threw me out," and the congregation chorusing, "You can't let go of Suzie! She's family!"

THE BUSINESS ARENA

Churches, especially those with multiple staffs, have management considerations that require the best principles of business: people are hired to do particular types of work according to their individual skill sets, performance standards are established and maintained, salaries are set, and work is accomplished and evaluated. When work falls below par, accountability kicks in and people may be fired for poor performance. When there is a budget shortfall, considerations as to staffing needs cannot be avoided.

As the church grows and staff is added, senior pastors often find themselves attending more and more to management concerns. For those pastors (which is most of them) who are neither adept nor interested in management, this can become a problem. Staffs that are ignored tend to become misaligned with everyone (beginning with the senior pastor), defaulting to self-interest.

Church staffs that grow to a certain size need to be managed effectively. Historically, churches have turned to hiring executive pastors (ordained) or executive directors (lay). These people function as chief operating officers attending to the daily operations of the church. Ideally, this should free senior pastors to function within their skill set unencumbered by management concerns.

In some sense, you need to see yourself as a businessperson wearing a business hat. I realize this is contrary to why you chose ministry as your vocation. But if you can't see yourself in this hat, then leading the church will be problematic.

One critical aspect of your ministry-as-business obligation is alignment. Alignment has to do with configuring all the resources of the church (staff, programs, buildings, budget) so that the mission of the church is carried out. In recent years, churches have turned to some form of strategic planning in order to align rationally.

Strategic planning helps churches understand the current state of the church, helps determine what the church is called to be, and provides tangible and immediate action steps for the next part of the journey. It provides focus, structure, and alignment. Strategic planning helps determine the realities of the church, shape or sharpen core values, mission, and strategy, and point to next steps to move the church from being good to being great.

Every church should start with a clear sense of its True North—its core values, mission, vision, and strategy. Once that's clear, the other elements should then align to that True North. The problem most churches face is that one of the other elements tends to become more important than its True North. We've all seen churches where their brand (often the senior pastor) is what the church is known for. In other churches, the support structures take over (buildings, finances, professional staff) and replace the church's mission. I have worked with several churches where the building was True North. One church was in a decaying steel town, its gleaming white building stood amid crumbling buildings around it. The ruling board therefore saw their main mission as preserving their pretty building.

Alignment will be accomplished and maintained when you are able to constantly "sing" the following four "theme songs":

- ♫ "This is our mission"
  (Why our church exists and for whom)
- ♫ "These are our values"
  (What's most important to us)
- ♫ "This is our vision"
  (Where we're going and our desired future)
- ♫ "This is our strategy"
  (How we intend to get there)

Unfortunately, many if not most churches are sloppy when it comes to these four themes. Oh yes, they may come up with a mission statement and something about values and maybe even vision. But once posted on the website, all is forgotten.

But let me be clear: these four themes should be like a pair of glasses that helps you focus clearly on everything you do, every building you build, every staff person you hire, and every program you initiate. In church after church with which I've been associated, they don't have such glasses to help them see what's most important and what should be jettisoned. Consistently, church programs and personnel grow without any particular direction in mind. It's imperative that you focus clearly on these issues clear and then use them in church board meetings, church town hall meetings, and in staff meetings to align everyone around the why that your church exists, where it's going, how it's going to get there, and what's most important.

Not only do you have to "sing," but you also have to coach; and as a coach, you need to get good at the following (and this goes for staff and volunteer):

- *Selecting your players* (determine what skills each position requires and who has them)
- *Setting expectations for your players* (determine clear performance criteria for each position and conduct regular, specific performance evaluations for each staff member)

- *Motivating your players* (understand each player's motivational needs)
- *Developing your players* (help your players grow and flourish in their positions)

Consider these points and questions when in the business arena:

- There's hierarchy here: What's the organizational chart? Who answers to whom?
- Who's above you? Who's below you? Who's beside you?
- How does authority (power) really work here? Who are the persons and/or families making (usually but not always the biggest donors) that exert the most influence on decision-making?
- The system is perfectly designed to give you the results you're getting. So how is this system actually designed? (This could look different from your organizational chart). Who's allied with whom? Against whom?
- When is the hierarchy honored? Violated? By whom? In what situations?
- What are the ongoing conflicts (now probably under the surface) that have never been resolved?

THE FAMILY ARENA

When we look at the church as a family, clergy are perceived as parents and congregants operate as siblings.[1] Church members feel as though they're coming home and therefore have particular idealistic expectations as to what they'll find and how they'll be treated. When paid staff members are also church members (i.e., "family"), the expectations rise beyond the average business employee.

1. Sibling rivalry is created by treating one sibling as special. As ministers elevate one or more parishioners to places of prominence (they're special), or even friendship, often hurt and angry feelings and general dissatisfaction is generated among those less favored.

An apocryphal story might prove the point. Pastor John calls the church custodian, Bill, into his office. Bill is also a church member. "Bill," says the pastor, "we need to have a talk. For the past six months, I've watched your performance deteriorate. You haven't been cleaning properly. Your set ups and take downs haven't been effective. All in all, your performance has been awful, though I've pointed this up to you over and over. Bill, I'm afraid I'm going to have to let you go. And now, Bill, I have to change my 'hat' from being your employer to being your pastor. Bill, I just heard you lost your job. What can I do to help?"

All of this adds up to the fact that getting rid of employees who are church members is difficult. Everyone who works for a church has a constituency around them—a constituency that holds them in high regard and who is willing to come to their defense when termination looms. And this constituency rarely if ever is aware of any performance issues that may lead to termination.[2]

I have worked with several churches that had to let go key personnel who were underperforming (in the business circle) but were greatly loved by church members (in the family circle). One such person had worked at the church for over twenty years. This person had begun a ministry for which a number of congregants volunteered. The problem? This person refused to take direction from the senior or executive pastor, had rarely attended staff meetings, and had basically never participated in church functions other than this person's own ministry. In other words, this person was a bad employee and bad team player. But the people who volunteered in the ministry didn't know any of this. And when this person was finally terminated, many in the congregation were up in arms at the senior pastor. Plus, this terminated person's story was the only story being told. For the senior pastor to state why exactly this person had been terminated was to invite a defamation lawsuit.

Transference versus Projection

Let's revisit two concepts I noted in chapter 5: transference and projection. Pastors need to get a sense of these two concepts in order

---

2. Clergy are usually unable to be candid about performance issues with the congregation at large. To be clear about why a person was fired or disciplined is to invite a law suit. Usually there is only one story broadcast as to why a person is let go, the story of the person who was let go.

to understand many of the issues that swirl around them. Let's first take a look at transference.

Transference. Transference is actually a three-person dance: you the pastor, a staff member or parishioner who is present, and someone from that parishioner or staff person's past (who is not present or even alive physically, but who is very much part of the relationship the pastor has with them). Transference takes place when the other person transfers that absent person's qualities, feelings, behaviors, and so on onto you and then reacts to you as if you were the other person. Let's say your parishioner had a father who always yelled at her whenever she asked a question, calling her stupid and ill-informed. That parishioner then transfers those feelings about her father onto you. You're the pastor, and in certain traditions you're even called Father or Mother. As a result, the parishioner acts toward you the way she did toward her father (who may be long dead, but that doesn't matter).

In a sense, transference is like looking at a person but seeing someone else. And once I see that past person in the present person, I begin to act accordingly. People who are less self-aware or emotionally healthy are the ones who will be ensnared by this transference the most. They are the ones who often divide the world, or at least the leaders who affect them, into two categories: the good parents and the bad parents. The good parents are those leaders who will (as they unconsciously wish) heal all of their childhood wounds. Consequently, when a new pastor appears at the church, these are the people who are most joyous and celebratory. As I've already mentioned, be cautious of those who initially adore you. These are the ones who will turn on you in a second when their expectations go unmet. And, of course, they will go unmet because they are totally unrealistic. There is no way you will heal all of their childhood wounds, nor should you even try. You now shift in that person's mind from the good parent to the bad parent in a heartbeat—the person who once adored you now is leading the cabal to remove you.

Projection. Projection is a less complex concept. While transference takes three people, projection needs only two. It happens when someone projects their own qualities, feelings, behaviors, and so on onto another person. You might be wondering why anyone would do this. Those qualities they project are in fact qualities they find difficult to own for themselves—those horrible qualities, behaviors, attitudes, and so on they must guard against in themselves to keep their self-esteem humming along. When they look at that other person, they don't see that person: they actually see *themselves.*

When projection is directed at you, what you are hearing from that other person is autobiographical: "Pastor, I want to give you some constructive criticism about your [preaching, your personality, whatever—fill in the blank]." The next words you hear will undoubtedly be a self-description of the person speaking to you. Now understand, if you act on what they say (the criticism actually strikes a chord in you: *I actually haven't been putting enough time into my sermons recently*), then you'll own the criticism, and it's now about *you.*

Discerning When It Happens

To manage someone effectively, you need a basic understanding as to how you will effectively manage. With a basic understanding of transference and projection, you first need to take note of when you're experiencing these things within yourself and learn how to see people for who they are. But also remember that as a minister you're absolutely a transference and projection screen. So many of the criticisms and compliments that come at you are borne along by these two forces, which are actually at work constantly within each of us. This is why I said in the first chapter that it's essential to maintain a growing self-awareness.

Consider these points and questions when in the family arena:

- Hierarchy is still a factor: there are parents and there are siblings.
- Clergy are seen as parents (good until expectations aren't met, and then bad by those who are more emotionally precarious as unrealistic expectations go unmet).
- Depending on childhood wounding and subsequent healing → "You as good parent are to heal all of my childhood wounds"—until you fail in your healing powers, and then all bets are off.

- What is often said to you is not actually about you (unless you embrace it). You are a screen for projections and transference. Those who adore you and those who undermine you are to an extent living out their own unresolved childhood stories.
- As a family the church community is a cauldron of swirling emotional issues and needs that are constantly bubbling up and contaminating the best efforts to move the church in any particular direction. You need a great deal of discernment and wisdom to effectively navigate all of the competing needs and loyalties, any one of which can derail even the best-intended clergy and/or church board strategy.

THE FAITH COMMUNITY ARENA

Churches are also spiritual communities. Members manifest certain gifts, bear the burdens of one another, and generally become intentionally involved in one another's lives to the betterment of the individual and the building up of the community (a.k.a., body life). Unlike the above two arenas of business and family, community members have no assumed hierarchy ("neither male nor female, slave nor free"). There is mutual accountability, with no one being "more privileged" than another.

Often ministers and their spouses join small groups within the church community for fellowship, learning, and mutual accountability. But care must be taken as to how the minister is perceived (what "hat" they are wearing) in these small groups. You may think you're on an equal plain with all the other members of the small group. But your parent "hat" may loom large to certain group members, who will then defer to you as parent, thus destroying the mutuality the group hopes to maintain.

Many ministers decide that their principal friendships and accountabilities must be maintained outside of their church. To draw congregants into their personal lives invites misunderstandings; but if they do so, then they must exercise with great care.

Consider these points and questions when in the faith community arena:

- No hierarchy. We're all on the same plain.
- We're all brothers and sisters in Christ.
- There's mutual accountability. You're accountable to me as much as I am to you.
- We bear one another's burdens.
- If I choose to draw close to one or more of my congregants, are these people mature enough to handle the relationship appropriately?

Unfortunately, as often happens, these three separate functions become confused. When business considerations are handled with family patterns, problems arise. Likewise, if community and family aspects are treated as a business consideration, then misunderstanding arises. These three models must always be appreciated and negotiated.

Volunteers

And now the wild card: volunteers! In every church, volunteers surround these three interlocking organizational models. This one aspect of church organizational life can add a great deal of angst to the work of the pastor. Let me illustrate with just one question: How do you fire a volunteer? Good luck, especially in a church setting where being a family is one of the three premium organizational models in play.

There are a number of good articles and books on effectively managing volunteers, so I won't say much here. But attending to several key issues when dealing with volunteers will cut down on headaches considerably.

1. *Communicate clear expectations.* This should include clear job descriptions and an orientation to the church organization as a whole.
2. *Provide tools and training to perform job tasks.* Volunteers who have a positive experience will enjoy their assigned job and will be excited about helping.

3. *Recognize volunteer contributions.* People like to be recognized for a job well done, so incorporate this recognition into your collective church life.
4. *Celebrate successes.* Celebrating a successful event is a great way to acknowledge all of the hard work that went into it.

Dual Relationships

Keep in mind that all I've said above about the complicated church organizational model is absolutely fertile ground for dual relationships to develop. Dual relationships occur when a person has multiple roles with another person. That doesn't sound so bad, and it's not some of the time. But it can also be tricky and problematic at other times. Let me give you an example. I was coaching a minister who mentioned during our first meeting that he had been playing golf with several church board members. I commented to him, "Well, I assume no church business was discussed." The minister looked sheepish and asked, "Is that wrong?" I responded, "No, it's not wrong if the entire board was part of your foursome, and Roberts Rules were clearly in play."

In the above example, the friendship "hat" of the minister got confused with his leadership "hat." He thought, "I can be out with a few board members, have a nice round of golf, and discuss church business." Wrong! And yet, this happens all the time when people get confused and fuzzy about what relational "hat" they're wearing at any given time.

I have several minister friends who refuse to have any close relationships with those in their congregations. One minister told me he had been burned too many times when dual relationship matters surfaced. You as a minister may think you're just having a social interaction with friends, but hidden agendas may lurk that could potentially confuse the relationship.

WHAT CAN YOU DO ABOUT THIS?

When you're in leadership, you must take into consideration what "hat" you're wearing as you prepare to act. On only particular occasions will you need to ask yourself if you're the parent of a family, the CEO of a business, or a fellow Christian). You always need to be clear to your staff and congregants. Otherwise, your differing "hats" will confuse you and them if you aren't clear in going forward. Then, the following considerations are important.

In the Business Arena

- What are the best business practices you need to be aware of so you can manage this church effectively?
- Where in this operation are people, programs, or facilities misaligned? What steps need to be taken to bring about alignment?
- Are you "singing" the mission-values-vision-strategy song clearly and often enough?
- Are you doing due diligence appropriately when it comes to hiring and developing staff and volunteers?

In the Family Arena

- Do you understand how projection and transference color relationships within the congregation? Do you monitor these tendencies so your ministry isn't adversely affected?
- Are you able to keep on top of swirling emotional issues that can contaminate the unfolding ministry? If you have trouble in this area, do you have people you can rely on to help you see clearly what themes might be unfolding that need attention?

In the Faith Community Arena

- Trust is the critical foundational element to the healthy functioning of a faith community. What are you doing to enhance trust, beginning with your staff?
- Do you provide instruction in authentic community building, and do you yourself participate in an authentic community where you're known, understood, and held accountable?

13

POLITICAL RELATIONS WITHIN YOUR CHURCH

Most pastors I know fail to appreciate the political landscape that surrounds them. Although political considerations seem to exist in a world far from the church, more than any other issue, politics is what gets most pastors into trouble. Not knowing and understanding these political dynamics can be deadly.

I worked with a pastor friend of mine who took over a legacy church that was foundering. He had big plans for its future health and thriving culture within its surrounding community. He had initially laid out his plans to the search committee that had called him; and during his "honeymoon" period, the church leadership supported him.

They he began to get vibes of discontent coming from various quarters of the congregation. As he dug more into this, he found that these negative vibes were emanating from one prominent family. Although they had no positional power within the church, they had been there for generations and had exerted a great deal of influence over the direction of the church throughout the years.

At first, my friend barely knew of their existence. They hadn't been involved at all in either his call or his initial strategy sessions with leadership. But over time, their influence and wishes slowly began to emerge. Not that this family was totally against all my friend wanted to accomplish. But they were dead set against a number of the most important proposals he hoped to implement in order to achieve his overall goal of influencing the surrounding community in positive ways for the kingdom. The main focus of this family and the contingency of older families, however, was on the church building itself. That building was the most striking feature in an otherwise deteriorating downtown, and these older families wanted it to stay that way.

Reaching out to the surrounding community would divert funds from maintaining a beautiful building. As time went on, opposition to my friend's plans solidified into outright disapproval of all he wished to accomplish in the coming years, and he finally resigned in frustration.

Politics has to do with people living together in groups, the way people live in groups, and how decisions are made and by whom. When we talk about making decisions, we enter the realm of power. Decision-makers have power within groups to determine the direction of those groups. Often these powerful decision-makers have positional power. But often as not, these powerful people, as in the above example, don't have formal positions but still exert an inordinate influence over decisions and direction of the church.

Remember what I said about power in chapter 2: Power tends to be on most people's minds, even when it's operating under the surface of our awareness. If we have power, then we sense we'll be secure—exerting our physical power, emotional power, relational power, and financial power in ways that influence decisions. When we feel less powerful, our anxiety rises and we take measures to restore our sense of security—usually by raising our sense individually or collectively of being more powerful. In the collective realm, we align ourselves with those who have the most status—usually those most powerful in an organization.

Understanding the political relationships in your church is key to seeing how your church works as a system. This activity, what is called "thinking politically," can help you design more effective strategies for leading adaptive change. The key assumption behind thinking politically is *that people in a church seek to meet the expectations of their various constituencies* (even when that constituency is yourself). When you understand the nature of those expectations, you can mobilize people more effectively.

To think politically, you have to look at your church as a web of stakeholders. For each stakeholder, you need to identify the following:

- *Their stake in the challenges the church faces.* How will they be affected by resolution of the challenge?
- *Desired outcomes.* What would they like to see come out of a resolution of any particular issue you're facing?
- *Level of engagement.* How much do they care about the issue and the church?

- *Degree of power and influence.* What resources do they control, and who wants those resources?

Equally important, you must identify the following factors for each stakeholder:

- *Values.* What are their commitments and beliefs that guide their behaviors and decision-making processes?
- *Loyalties.* What obligations do they have to people outside their immediate group (such as those on the ruling board)?
- *Losses at risk.* What do they fear losing (status, resources, a positive self-image) if things should change?
- *Hidden alliances.* What shared interests do they have with people from other major stakeholder groups (such as peers in another department) that could lead them to form an alliance that could build influence?

PEOPLE WITH POWER IN THE CONGREGATION

Let's begin with those in your church who have power. In his book *Strong and Weak* (which I highly recommend), Andy Crouch talks about how the concept of power is elusive—and when it comes to following Jesus, it's counterintuitive. But for the purposes of what you will undoubtedly face as a pastor, certain people within your congregation have more power as decision-makers than others.

Taking time to determine the people of power will undoubtedly prove invaluable in understanding the political landscape of your church. It will also help you understand why there is pressure and pushback coming from individuals and collectives of people. Take a few moments to think about your church and then fill out this chart below.

People with positional authority who are powerful	People without positional authority who are powerful

Allies

Allies are those who share many of your values, or at least your strategy. You can't assume they'll always be loyal to you; they have other ties and loyalties to honor. In fact, a key aspect of what makes allies extremely helpful is precisely because they have other loyalties. This means they can help you understand competing stakes, conflicting views, and missing elements in your grasp of a situation. They can pull you by the collar and say, "Pay attention to these other people over here. You're not learning anything from your enemies." It's with allies that you can form coalitions to move forward your key initiatives. You can never go it alone, especially in the face of significant opposition (see chapter 11 on changing the culture).

I worked with a pastor who didn't take the time to form a solid coalition of allies with staff and ruling board around an initiative that was dear to his heart. Therefore, when it came time to implement the preliminary steps in his initiative, he faced opposition. Although he had a number of congregants in favor of what he wanted to do, they didn't have the power to bring about the initiative. This pastor had spent all of his time with the people in the congregation who adored him and cheered him on. But these people didn't possess significant power to create movement.

Sometimes pastors make the mistake of treating an ally like a confidant. Confidants have few, if any, conflicting loyalties. They usually operate outside your church, although occasionally someone close in, whose interests are perfectly aligned with yours, can also play that role.

Confidants can do something that allies can't do: they can provide you with a place where you can say everything that's in your heart and on your mind, without having to be tactful. You can spill out your feelings without fear of judgment or retribution. Then, once the whole mess is on the table, you can begin to pull the pieces back in and separate what's worthwhile from what's simply ventilation

Confidants can put you back together again at the end of the day when you're all broken to pieces, and they can remind you why it's worth getting out there and taking risks in the first place. When you ask them to listen, they're free to care about you more than they do about your issues.

- Who might be your allies?
- Why might they be allies?
- What's their main objective? To support you, the initiative itself, or the church?
- How can these allies best help you successfully implement your program/initiative?

Confidants

Confidants, as I said above, are those usually outside the system who can give you honest feedback about yourself as a leader in the system. They are those who can help you stay aware of your own "Red Zone" (see chapter 17) and attend to your self-care. Most pastors I know find these confidants outside of their church, and many pastors I've worked with have experienced betrayal from those they assumed were confidants, only to have confidences revealed with destructive consequences.[1]

- Who are your confidants?
- What perspective do they offer?
- What do they need to fully support you?

Opponents

Potential opponents are stakeholders who have markedly different perspectives from yours and who stand to risk losing the most if you and your initiatives go forward. Once you've identified the opposition, stay close to them, spend time with them, ask for their input on your initiative, listen closely to their reality (especially where it differs from yours), and take their temperature to assess how much heat you're putting on them and how desperate they're becoming. Regularly get together for coffee, include them in meetings, and let them know you value their perspective and insights. Of course, it's not a lot of fun to spend time with "the enemy." Your intuitive tendency will be to keep your opponents as far away as possible, never seeking

---

1. One critical thing to remember is: Beware those who adore you. They may appear as confidants, but they have undoubtedly transferred onto you the "Good Parent" and have little perspective on who you are as a person. When you disappoint them, they usually turn on you in unpleasant ways.

their advice, but you'll regret holding these people at arms' length. I have seen this happen again and again with the seniors within the congregation (see below).[2]

- Who might be your opponents?
- Why might they be opponents?
- What do they stand to lose if your initiative succeeds?
- How might you neutralize their opposition or get them on your side?

Casualties

Resisters to your initiative are people who feel most threatened by it. They may believe that they won't be able to make the changes you recommend, that they might lose their job, or that they'll be worse off in some way if the initiative is carried out. You may agree or disagree with their perception, but it's their perception that counts for your purposes. Resist any temptation to try "straightening" them out. My experience suggests this would be a fool's errand and could actually set you back by stiffening their resistance. Nobody likes being told that they "shouldn't feel that way." Instead, accept that what you're trying to do isn't in their interest. Compassion and empathy have their own reward in heaven, but they're also critical tools for comprehending the potential losses at stake for your opposition.[3]

- Who will be casualties of your program/initiative?
- What will they lose?
- What new skills would help them survive the change and thrive in the new church?

---

2. A key question you need to ask yourself is if you have the capacity to hang in there when opposition to your plans is at its highest. If you've developed the emotional stamina (translated into a non-anxious presence) to stay true to your principles when nasty reactions and sabotage are most evident, then the process will often reverse itself and the followers will begin to adapt to you, the leader.

3. Remember to stay calm, stay connected, and stay the course. Keep these relationships, but don't become the anxiety sink for the system.

- How might you help them acquire those skills?
- Which casualties will need to leave the church?
- How could you help them succeed elsewhere?

Dissenters

The group that's probably the most vocal, the most annoying—and at the same time, the most useful—are the dissenters. These are the folks who have the frustrating habit of voicing the most radical ideas or mentioning the "elephant in the room" at the most inauspicious occasions, or who genuinely seem to delight in being all things disagreeable. This is the group you'd like to throttle and/or send down the street to your competing church. Oddly enough, these are the people you need around you and must protect.

While they may not have the social skills and awareness that would make them more effective in voicing their ideas and concerns, what they have to say is often valuable and needs to be protected and heard. Also, these people usually aren't alone. They're giving voice to a constituency. Ignoring them or giving a flippant answer to their concerns will only exacerbate the problem. So, I want you to catalogue who these people are and begin to see them for the value they bring to the table.

- Who are the dissenters in your church—those who typically voice radical ideas or mention the unmentionable?
- What ideas are they bringing forth that might be valuable for your program/initiative?
- How might you enable their ideas to have a hearing?
- How can you protect them from being marginalized or silenced?

What to Do with Those Pesky Seniors

I would argue that this senior demographic is an excellent place to begin to think about a discrete political constituency (by the way, I'm one of them!). They are probably the most untapped resource in any congregation. They can also represent the most troubling political entity. Unfortunately, a common theme often emerges from the pastor: "I have a number of senior citizens in my congregation. Virtually, all of them complain that I don't spend enough time with them, that they feel neglected and resentful."

It is this contingent that often contributes the lion's share of the budget. And when it comes to church life, people tend to vote their approval or disapproval with their wallets and their feet (by going elsewhere).

- Who are the senior authorities most important to your program/initiative's success?
- Why are they important?
- What signals are they giving about how the church perceives your program/initiative?
- What might you say or do to secure their support as your initiative is being implemented?

Listen and Acknowledge Them

Unfortunately, as you interface with your senior congregants, a pattern emerges. I call this a recursive pattern (see chapter 3): the very thing you do elicits exactly the behavior you don't want from others, and then their response is the very thing that elicits from you your original behavior. When you ask someone in this pattern who's to blame between them and another person, they'll invariably point to the other person. You may think to yourself that the reason you stay away from these people is because they only assault you with complaints. But if you do that, then you'll never help them understand or appreciate how their own behavior keeps the pattern going.

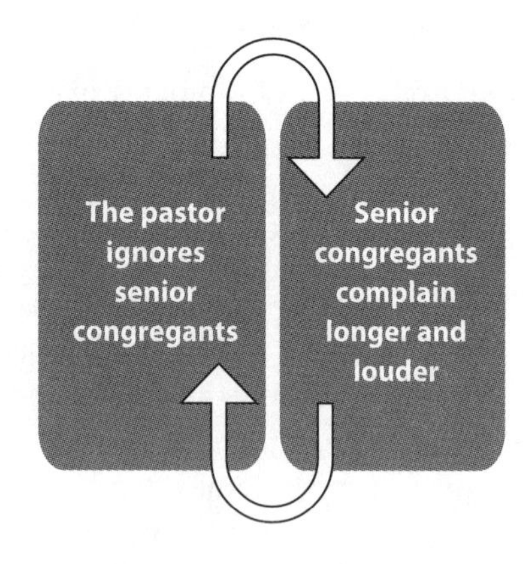

The more seniors complain, the more the pastor ignores them. And the more he ignores them, the more they complain and possibly organize to disrupt church functioning. If you ask either group what the problem is, the seniors will say that the pastor ignores them and the pastor will say that the seniors do nothing but complain.

Since neither contingent understands their own role in this conundrum, the first step—though it may be painful, depending on how long you haven't listened to them—is to sit down and hear them out. Try not to be defensive and answer them point by point, however, as this defensiveness will merely say to them that they just don't understand.

If you can really sit and listen to them (and I'm not talking about agreeing with them, merely hearing them), then you will be able to get an opportunity likewise to really be heard by them about what you wish to suggest.

Present Them with a Legitimate Need That Will Make a Difference

Your goal is to turn complaining consumers (the seniors) into valued community members who make a real difference in the church community. I call this a transformational issue—an issue that cuts to the very heart of our values, which then translates into behavior. As I've said, most congregants in the twenty-first-century church, not just seniors, are consumers. They attend the church that meets the greatest number of their needs. Over against this model of church is the community of believers where everyone's giftings are identified and utilized—the body of Christ in action.

Now we come to the senior contingent. You the pastor have heard their complaints. The church, beginning with you, ignores them. The music is too loud and contemporary. People don't dress the way they "should." On and on. But if you're patient with them and let them know that you're genuinely concerned about them and want to utilize them in service to the church, then you'll win the right to be heard.

Before entering this phase, make sure you have thought through a possible safety-net organization—what it would look like, who might lead it, what areas to begin to get volunteers to staff. Once you have your ideas and a potential leader in place, I suggest beginning with the seniors (chapter 19 will hopefully help in thinking specifically about this safety-net organization).

Let Them Help You Shape the Contours of the Solution

Buy-in emerges as people are able to wrestle with problems and solutions. Compliance is usually a result of people being told arbitrarily what to do. So, once you've framed up the contours of the problem(s) with the assistance of seniors, the next step is to begin to frame the solution(s). This cannot be an idle exercise. It must be meaningful both as to the nature of the problem(s) identified and the solutions proposed.

If you treat the seniors as a valuable resource for the church, they will respond in kind (a positive recursive pattern). This isn't just a one-time experience. This problem-identification-solution-generation needs to be held periodically, with seniors being solicited for their thinking and their potential assistance.

Turn Them Loose and Praise Them

Depending on the nature of the problems you're tackling, seniors may need some organization to get them moving in the right direction with the right people involved. Leadership will usually emerge within the senior ranks and that will greatly aid in motivating them to action. Finally, take every opportunity to recognize the efforts of the seniors and render them legitimate praise.

14

HOW TO EFFECTIVELY MANAGE YOUR CHURCH

Over and over again, people enter into positions of ministry with little or no idea as to what specific behaviors are necessary for successful management. Yes, ministry does involve management (remember, you're a business among other things). Often, it's the management of paid staff. Always it's the management of volunteers.

The only way to have a fully functioning church is to build the kind of work environment that attracts, aligns, focuses, and keeps talented employees on the staff and in the ranks of volunteers. Your job as a pastor manager is to help build such an environment. Below, we will look at the behaviors that support this kind of environment.

BAD MANAGEMENT PRACTICES

Let's begin with the negative. These are practices that I've seen multiple times in the church world—practices that indeed harm the life of the individual churches where they've occurred. Let's look at each one.

Failure to confront poor performance (i.e., hold people accountable). I have repeatedly seen the absence of accountability in the church world. People are just not held to a standard of conduct and performance. The first step in correcting this problem is to establish a clear set of performance guidelines for each person working at the church, be they paid staff or volunteers. As we saw in chapter 11, the three interlocking organizational models of the church make accountability somewhat more difficult than say managing at Walmart. But the need for clear guidelines that are universally enforced is no less critical.

Failure to empower subordinates. Again and again, clergy fail to help people identify their gifting, develop their gifting, and then turn that gifting lose to assist the church body in becoming all that God intended it to be. In some cases, this is due to the pastor's reluctance to cede power. In other cases, it's quality control. "How can I allow you to do X? You might make a mess of things. I'll just have to retain that function."

Failure to communicate clearly, or communicating to the wrong people, or communicating to the right people in the wrong way. Churches are rife with communication problems. People constantly complain that they don't know what's going on (and much of that is the fault of the individual congregants more than the church). But so often, pastor leaders are unclear in their communication, especially when it comes to communicating expectations. Surveys show that the majority of the workforce throughout the United States doesn't have a clear understanding of what's expected of them. This is true in secular as well as sacred organizations. Extra care must be given to clearly communicating your expectations of the staff and volunteers. Of course, this assumes that you the pastor are clear as to what you actually do expect; many are not. This is never a one-time occurrence. Expectations must be communicated over and over again. And when these expectations change, efforts must be redoubled to again communicate clearly.

Misunderstanding what "hat" you're wearing. This was discussed when we looked at the church organizational model in chapter 11, so take a moment to revisit that section.

Not taking into account the culture that embodies the organization. We discussed this in chapter 10. Remember, "Culture eats strategy for breakfast."

Treating certain people as special. This is particularly difficult in ministry. Just as parents foment sibling rivalry by treating one child specially over another, so too do ministers. Should you then not have any friends within the congregation? Some pastors, who have been burned a number of times, answer yes. I think friendships are possible, but they must be monitored closely to avoid as much as possible the appearance of special treatment (this is the parent "hat" you wear as a minister).

Avoiding conflict or getting triangled into conflict. We looked at this dynamic when we discussed conflict. Sufficient to say, many ministers are positively allergic to conflict, which is a trait that frequently lands them and their churches in trouble.

Failure to consider succession. Who will succeed you is a critical question, and one that points directly to the sustainability of the ministry you're now creating and perpetuating.

Allowing poor performers to absorb an inordinate amount of your time. I just spoke to a minister who told me he has spent literally hours with one of his staff members trying to bring his performance up to an acceptable level. I told him two things: first, he needed to move this staff member to a position where he can perform adequately and, if none exists, to move him off staff. Second, he needs to devote the lion's share of his staff time to his highest performers. In *First Break All the Rules*, Marcus Buckingham states that the preponderance of your time should be spent with your highest performers. Take heed!

MANAGING VOLUNTEERS

Just a few words at this point about managing volunteers (see chapter 11). Although this is a critical aspect of successful church ministry, it's often completely overlooked. (A more robust discussion can be found by researching "managing volunteers" on the internet.) Sufficient to say, most churches I'm aware of just sign volunteers up for Sunday school, youth ministry, the worship team, and so on, but then don't provide specific guidelines as to what's expected of these volunteers or for how long. "Sign here, and we'll expect you to teach the four-year-olds' Sunday school class until this first group of four-year-olds are grandparents!" Volunteer involvement in your church will only be as good as the attention you devote to it, so here are some suggestions to help you:

- Get clear on your philosophy of volunteers at your church: how do they specifically help fulfill the mission?
- As the numbers of volunteers grow, designate someone specifically responsible for overseeing all things volunteer.

- Establish written policies and procedures (if you have designated a volunteer overseer, they should have the central hand in creating this).
- Establish position descriptions for each volunteer role.
- Establish supervisors for each volunteer role.
- Establish specific training for each volunteer role and position.
- Periodically assess each volunteer area as to effectiveness.
- Make sure all volunteers are properly resourced to carry out their various functions.

MANAGING METRICS

Now let's look at how to get clear on exactly what you want people to do at your church. Hopefully by now, you're seeing that what is absolutely critical to alignment and ongoing good performance has to do with clear-cut expectations that are clearly communicated. Let's take a look.

The People Part: Managing Others

Undoubtedly, managing people is an important focus in your job, not an add-on. You therefore need to note the particular areas and possible ways to evaluate those for whom you are responsible. What follows are merely suggestions as to criteria for evaluations. Note that it's essential that each criterion is clear about a specific expected behavior. Much of the below criteria is for you in your role as pastor. If you were evaluating the worship leader in your church, then much of this would have to be altered.

To develop the list of competencies, have all staff members draw up a list of the specific tasks and behaviors they perform every week as part of their job. Make sure each item is specific ("If I turned a video camera on you here at your job for a week, what would it capture you doing?"). Then go over each job with the staff member to be sure the list is complete and clear. This now is the basis for the job description and evaluation.

Job evaluations can be done every six months or at least every year. You as the manager will score staff members on their evaluations, and they will also score themselves. When you sit down with them to do the evaluation, look for those areas where you and the staff member are in disagreement as to the priority of a particular task and/or the score you and that staff member have given a particular task.

Below you'll find a list of more generic behaviors that could be applied to practically everyone in staff leadership positions. Added to these are the specific behaviors that each department entails (music/arts director, youth director, family ministry director, etc.).

Scoring:

✓ Mark each behavior on the priority scale as to whether each behavior is an A behavior (Very Important), B (Important), or C (Less Important).

✓ Mark each behavior on the score scale as to your performance on each behavior from 1 (rarely occurs) to a 5 (constantly occurs).

Behavior	Priority A, B, C	Score 1 to 5
Builds Team		
Builds trust among team members		
Engages in healthy conflict		
Commits to decisions and actions		
Builds team where everyone holds each other accountable		
Focuses on collective results		

Behavior	Priority A, B, C	Score 1 to 5
Hires		
Understands the particular behaviors needed to fill vacant positions		
Understands the procedure to vet potential candidates to arrive at the optimum choice		
Orients new hires to the particular demands of the new position		
Trains and Develops		
Helps staff and congregants identify specific gifting		
Helps staff and congregants develop their unique gifts		
Helps congregants utilize their individual gifts appropriately		
Aligns		
Understands the unique culture of the church and how that culture influences the behavior of all members		
Understands the principles that are key to effectiveness and success		
Continually communicates a clear, compelling mission and vision of the organization to the church board and the congregation		
Continually orients each staff member and volunteer to team principles and the unfolding mission and vision		
Evaluates		
Orients new hires and volunteers to the church's mission, vision, and strategies		
Holds direct reports accountable to specific performance competencies by conducting periodic specific performance evaluations		

Behavior	Priority A, B, C	Score 1 to 5
When necessary, works in conjunction with direct reports to establish improvement plans and provides support in achieving goals		
Communicates clear consequences for performance deficiencies		
Mentor/Succession Planning		
Identifies top performers within the organization who can be developed		
Enters into mentoring (discipling) relationships with selected top performers		
Assists protégés with Individual Development Plans (IDP) to intentionally develop them for future leadership positions		
Communicates		
Direction: Clarifies the future for the workforce		
Order: Creates the norms and customs that determine how the organization behaves		
Protection: Exposes the staff and congregation, at a rate they can tolerate, to the internal and external threats that could potentially undermine the long-term well-being of the workforce		
Handles Conflict		
Encourages disagreements that focus on the fulfilling of the mission		
Refuses to become triangled into disagreements between subordinates		
Recognize and Reward		
Understands different recognition venues		
Understands each direct report vis-à-vis the particular recognition venue that best fits each person		

Behavior	Priority A, B, C	Score 1 to 5
Collaborates		
Regularly shares and contributes expertise, knowledge, and information		
Makes time available to assist others		
Creates positive relationships with critical outside organizations		
Serves Congregants		
Understands the particular needs of each congregant		
Works to fashion individual responses to the needs of each congregant		
Delegates		
Provides knowledge and resources to enable others to step into areas of giftedness		
Provides encouragement and feedback		
Encourages risk-taking		

The Non-People Part: Managing Tasks

While managing people is the primary task of management, it's not the only task. There are the non-people elements, though it's important that these non-people elements don't consume the lion's share of the manager's time.

Behavior	Priority A, B, C	Score 1 to 5
Manages resources		
Knows the particular resources within and without the organization that can best assist in mission fulfillment		

Behavior	Priority A, B, C	Score 1 to 5
Is able to apply appropriate resources to differing situations		
Develops/executes strategic vision plan		
Able to develop a strategic vision for the organization		
Able to execute the strategic vision		
Does lots of email/paper work (T&A, leave approval, etc.)		
Able to collect, process, organize, plan, and perform daily tasks effectively		
Handles email in such a way that it doesn't consume more time than necessary		
Outreach/Evangelism		
Understands the missional nature of the church		
Able to clearly message to outsiders the essence of the mission of the church		
Able to understand the particular needs of the targeted surrounding community		

The Personal Part: Managing Yourself

Personal awareness leads to personal management, which leads to social awareness, which leads to social management—all of which are critical prerequisites for effective management.

Behavior	Priority A, B, C	Score 1 to 5
Body		
Gets at least seven to eight hours of sleep		
Eats a healthy breakfast		

Behavior	Priority A, B, C	Score 1 to 5
Works out (meaning cardiovascular training at least three times a week and strength training at least once a week)		
Takes regular breaks during the day to truly renew and recharge		
Emotions		
Rarely feels irritable, impatient, or anxious at work, especially when work is demanding		
Savors accomplishments and blessings		
Has enough time with family and loved ones, and when with them is truly with them		
Has enough time for the activities that are deeply enjoyed		
Frequently expresses appreciation to others		
Mind		
Focuses on one thing at a time, and not easily distracted during the day		
Focuses on activities with longer-term value and high leverage rather than react to immediate crises		
Takes enough time for reflection, strategizing, and creative thinking		
Spirit		
Spends enough time at work doing what one does best and enjoys most		
What one claims to be of value matches how one actually allocates time and energy		
Decisions at work are influenced by a strong clear sense of one's own purpose		
Invests enough time and energy in making a positive difference to others or to the world		

15

DEALING WITH YOUR CHURCH'S GOVERNING BOARD

WHOSE JOB IS IT ANYWAY?

Are board meetings something to dread? Have you heard other pastors complain about how their board members grouch about their pastors? Maybe you've been a complainer yourself. Does it seem baffling that there's so much stress between pastors and their boards when everyone is supposed to be rooting for the same team? The following story may sound familiar.

John was the pastor of a church of some four hundred congregants. He'd been pastor for over five years, and the first year had been the quintessential honeymoon. He had succeeded a pastor who had been caught in a sexual scandal. When he arrived five years earlier, the church was hurting badly, feeling betrayed by their former pastor.

John got right to work, first concentrating on his staff (he had a dozen full- and part-time people working for him) and the church board (made up of a dozen lay folks from the congregation). John spent a lot of time building relationships, having lunch with various key leaders, and generally learning as much as he could about the congregation and its culture.

Initially, the board was pleased with all John was doing. Board meetings ran smoothly because the chair in charge discussed the agenda with John prior to each meeting.

There was some tension, however, especially around the K-5 church school that had been created twenty-five years ago and had grown in popularity with the congregation and the surrounding community. The school used the church educational wing during the week, and the headmaster along with half the school staff attended the church. A great deal of time and volunteer attention from the church was expended on the school—and it was here that the tension developed.

John, whose kids were older, was not as enthusiastic about diverting so many church resources toward the school. But the board chair—a woman who had two children in the school, often volunteered there, and had a social relationship with the headmaster and his wife—pushed back on any move John made to redirect resources. John knew that too much emphasis on the school was diminishing volunteers for other church programs, principally Sunday school.

As a result, tensions mounted between John, the chair, and several other board members who had children in the school and who were no less fervent about everything concerning the school. This tension began to affect all board meetings to the point that John and the chair could hardly have a civil conversation about the board agenda. An air of tension soon hung over every board gathering, affecting even the opening devotional time before each meeting, causing them to became strained and perfunctory.

Sound familiar, if not in the particulars at least in the general trajectory of the story? Church boards are notoriously sidetracked by member comments that distract from the overall forward path. Almost invariably, these comments have to do with personal preferences of a particular member. Depending on how these initial comments and discussions are handled, the situation can quickly spiral out of control.[1]

Often what happens is that the pastor and/or other board members are seen by the rest of the board members as irritants or as adversaries. The board agenda is then hijacked as precious time is absorbed to argue through whatever issues have been raised. Here are some that may seem familiar:

- "I want the new carpeting in the sanctuary to be red, but the pastor wants it to be blue."
- "I don't like the way the youth director's wife dresses. Can't one of you women speak to her?"
- "We need to think about changing the date of the spring cleanup day. It conflicts with the high school sports schedule."

---

1. See *Thriving through Ministry Conflict* for a full-blown board problem and the steps needed to address this kind of crisis.

- "The music at the late service is too loud and too fast. I don't want to come to church and mistake it for a nightclub."

Unhealthy boards emerge from unhealthy organizations—organizations that have a fuzzy sense of what their mission is (why they exist: their purpose), what's most important to them (their values), and where they see themselves going (their vision). Clear values, missions, and visions give a church a "pair of glasses" by which they can focus on what's important while filtering out the extraneous. Without these "glasses," boards are left to flounder—often sinking down into the weeds, focusing on issues that should be handled by staff.

Let's take a look at several critical issues that must be understood in order for boards to function properly.

WE'RE A BOARD: WHY ARE WE HERE?

Boards are critical to the overall functioning of churches. Understanding their purpose for your church is critical. Their main functions can be summarized as:

- Cradling the vision of the church: Where are we going?
- Guarding the church's values: What is truly important to us?
- Forcing an external focus: What is our role in the community?
- Separating large issues from small ones: What is the most important thing?
- Policy formation. This is an essential function for governing boards. Policy must be understood from two dimensions:

  1. The board must be proactive with regard to policy (not reacting to every little thing that goes wrong in the organization and making a policy to try to remedy it). Effective policy anticipates future needs.

  2. Those proactive policies need to focus on covering the broad issues as opposed to the multitude of details that could gum up the process.

From this list, you can see that boards should be dealing with broad, overarching questions. Unfortunately, many if not most people serving on church boards have little understanding on what they're supposed to focus. When they finally realize that their main focus should be on the "Big Picture"—broad, ethereal issues—they often aren't sure how to do this effectively. As a result, boards frequently get dragged down into the weeds, dealing with issues they generally have no business dealing with. To begin with, take a look at this diagram (this is obviously for a larger church; we discuss smaller churches below).

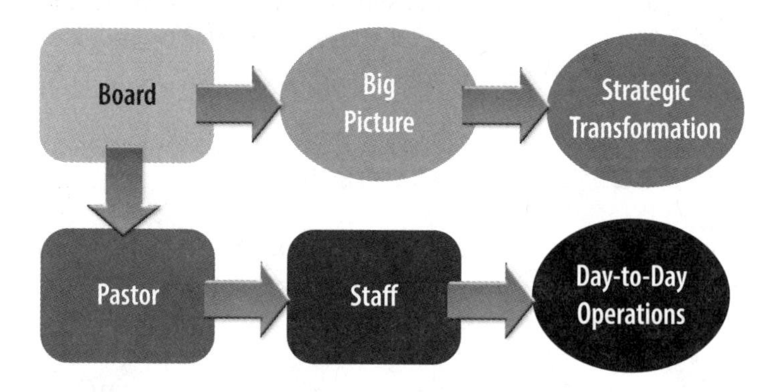

BOARD RESPONSIBILITIES

We've looked at the purpose of the board: why it exists. Now let's consider its specific responsibilities.

Spiritual support. Before any other responsibility, the church board should see itself as a spiritual support entity. As such, this spiritual component should infuse and inform everything the board does (not just an opening and closing prayer, which often functions as "a word from our sponsor").

Strategic planning. The board, in partnership with the pastor, is responsible for articulating the church's core values and mission, as well as a vision of its desired future and developing a plan to achieve that future. This plan is then delegated to specific departments of the church. For instance, if the church has an objective to create outreach programs for its community, the board should write actionable goals and delegate those responsibilities to someone, and then hold them accountable for getting them done.

Managing performance. The board is responsible for monitoring and holding leadership accountable for doing their job. This is done by developing annual *church goals*, delegating that responsibility to leadership, and then monitoring the progress. They show support by delegating decision-making and authoritative boundaries for achieving those goals. For example, executive pastors should understand the boundaries of their authority for making tactical decisions about the day-to-day operations of the ministry. This decision-making authority removes decision bottlenecks that can hinder progress toward achieving a goal

Financial oversight. The board oversees and ensures there is *responsible stewardship* of church resources and that it maintains financial accountability and solvency. This is done by approving and overseeing the annual *church budget*. The board provides input and direction into strategy and prioritizes spending to ensure that the strategy has the necessary financial resources to support it. Financial oversight includes identifying independent outside auditors to perform occasional audits to *safeguard against embezzlement*, ensure good business practices, and maintain compliance with state and federal laws.

Ensure legal compliance. Church boards are responsible for adhering to laws that govern nonprofit organizations. These include the duties of care, loyalty, and obedience. The board has a responsibility to ensure that the church stays true to its core mission by participating in decision-making, using good judgment, setting aside personal interests to ensure the best interest of the organization, and complying with governing laws.

Monitor conflicts of interest. The board is responsible for ensuring there are no conflicts of interest. It puts policies and systems in place to ensure full disclosure of any potential conflicts between outside organizations and church employees or the board. For instance, if a church board member owns a painting company, this could be a potential conflict if that company is given preferential treatment for outsourced painting jobs. The board should create a conflict-of-interest policy that requires employees and board members to disclose potential conflicts and sign a conflict-of-interest statement.

Maintain supporting documents and board records. This may not seem very spiritual, but well-run churches maintain good records of all aspects of the church. Church board minutes, board actions, and board/church policies are all curated for permanent record.

Board training. Help new board members by providing the appropriate orientation and training for their role.

AUTHORITY

Before any other considerations, you must be clear about the authority proposition. By this I mean, who is in charge and of what? Each denomination has polity that should set forth how this should work, at least on paper. Some churches are under no denominational authority. Often, they started as a small gathering in someone's living room and grew (one I've worked with started this way and grew to six thousand members!). Often in these churches, the pastor is the ultimate authority. The board may serve merely in an advisory capacity. The pastor's decisions are the last word in practically all decision-making. In other situations, the congregants have a great deal of power over decisions. In others, decision-making is relegated to committees. Let's first take a look at church polity to understand, at least as denominations state it, how your church is supposed to work.

Polity

Polity is the operational and governance structure of the church. First, consider these polity structures and note which of these your church falls into.

Representative. In this polity, people are elected by the congregation to represent them on the board. This follows the republican structure that guides the United States. The elected board makes most of the decisions for the church. Presbyterian churches along with Christian Reformed and many Baptist churches are examples of this polity. The pastor in this polity is the moderator when the board (the session for Presbyterians) is meeting.

Congregational. These churches tend to be characterized by the independence of the local congregation. In these churches, the congregations are empowered to make the decisions for the church (participatory democracy). Church business meetings are usually much longer than other polities, because the congregants themselves are tasked with primary decision-making. That said, often these churches have a board making many decisions that make them look like a representative church. Pastors can become confused as to where the power actually lies: Is it with the board or within the congregation during congregational meetings? Depending on how the culture of each individual church evolved over time, the power and thus decision-making process might be different from what the denomination says it should be.

Hierarchical. As a pastor, there is somebody above you (e.g., the bishop) who has the power. These churches historically have been top-down operations, although again (as time has passed) the hierarchy from church to church might, in practice, unfold quite differently.

Pastor led. These churches (such as megachurches, many of which follow this model) have a strong pastor (often the founder of the church) with a board of elders that provides accountability to the pastor. Often these boards serve in more of an advisory capacity.

Having said this, clarifying where the decision-making power resides in which domains is critical. I've worked with pastor after pastor who has stumbled into trouble with their ruling boards, misunderstanding who actually has the power to do what. Often conflict arises that can be devastating to a healthy ministry going forward.

Also, be advised that most denominations don't allow for the size of a congregation to determine how governance should unfold. One size fits all. But unfortunately, what might work for a church of twenty-five hundred won't be applicable to a church of seventy-five.

I would recommend first sitting down with the church by-laws to see what your individual church has set forth as to how the church should be run. Compare this document with denominational documents that should hopefully (but not necessarily) align with the bylaws). And then have an extended conversation with church board leadership to make sure everyone is on the same page as to whom has the power for what.[2]

Realize that possibly the majority of boards operate as a hybrid of one of the above polity structures. Because of this, there will be nuances to how things in your church actually run. And also, be advised, people within the congregation who exercise a great deal of influence may have no formal position of authority whatsoever. They are powerful because of how long they've been around, or how much they give to the church, or what their secular position in society happens to be. Everyone tacitly knows never to go against these people's wishes.

Power is an interesting and, in many cases, an elusive construct. Get clear on how things have worked in the past (if you are new). How have decisions been made? By whom? In what areas? Often ultimate authority doesn't rest at all with anyone in designated official roles of authority.

Church Size

In addition to polity, it's important to understand how the size of your church affects how its polity may be understood and practiced. Churches of differing sizes tend to function differently. As churches grow larger, the complexity of the organization also grows. This fact, among other things, exerts a great deal of influence on how the church is run and the time it takes to plan and execute. Lyle Schaller has written extensively on this issue of church size in the past.[3] Although the numbers used to describe each size church are arbitrary, he provides a rough estimate as to how each size functions.

The Small Church. A small church of fewer than a hundred and fifty members usually doesn't have the luxury of multiple committees to

---

2. This would be a good time to re-read chapter 13 on church politics. Dealing with your church board is shot through with politics that you must understand.

3. See Lyle E. Schaller's books: *The Very Large Church: New Rules for Leaders, The Middle-Sized Church: Problems and Prescriptions, The Multiple Staff and the Larger Church*, and *The Small Church Is Different.*

make decisions about particular areas of ministry. Actually, two-thirds of all churches in America have fewer than a hundred members, so the vast majority of churches are small. In some ways, these small churches look more like large extended families or Mom and Pop small businesses. Because the number of congregants is small, decision-making tends to be carried out by everyone in a participatory democracy or by the pastor who may have put the church on the map in the first place. Churchwide meetings involve many decision points about the overall trajectory of the church. Board members and church members are commonly incorporated into the various missions and functions of the church, and they operate as generalists (rather than staying within the realm of their individual giftedness). Distinctions between people are minimized as everyone pitches in to get the work done.

The smaller the church, the more likely that church is served by an inexperienced pastor. Pastors often don't stay that long in these churches but "move up" to larger churches as their experience grows, thus creating a great deal of instability in senior ordained leadership. As a result, lay leadership tends to be robust and may come into conflict with newly arrived and newly minted pastors.

The Middle-Sized Church. These can be described as churches between a hundred and fifty to four hundred members. More complexity is now introduced, beginning with the existence of a multiple staff that oversees the various ministries and functions of the church (e.g., youth director, worship leader, administrator, and so on). In these churches, most of the decisions are made in committees and then reviewed by the governing board before they ever reach the congregation. The annual meeting in these churches has a different focus. Rather than decision-making (since, more often than not, decisions have already been made and the congregation is merely being informed), the focus is on fellowship and the dispensing of information. Because of the growing size of the church, it becomes harder for everyone in the congregation to know everyone else; but this also means there are more volunteers from which to draw and that those volunteers tend to specialize within their giftedness.

The Large Church. Arbitrarily speaking, these are churches in excess of four hundred members, though arguably a four-hundred-member congregation will operate differently from a megachurch of five thousand, much less twenty thousand.[4] When a church has over a thousand members, one individual can't be expected to grasp its complexity. Often decisions defer to paid staff, who are able to see all that's occurring. Unfortunately, if the church isn't careful, the staff can over-function (see chapter 3) while the congregants under-function and fall into a consumer mentality, with the growing demand that paid staff do all the initiating. Also, the counterintuitive fact exists that it's usually harder to get good volunteers in a larger church. People naturally assume that if they don't teach this Sunday school class, there will be someone else who'll step up to do it.

One problem that arises is when pastors move from running a small or middle-sized church to a large church. Embedded in their minds is how that smaller church operated and especially how it was governed—participatory democracy. Unfortunately, the complexity of the large church works against this form of governance; and when new pastors try to force this different model onto their new calling, it causes untold difficulties. It's certainly a difficult task for these pastors to get their arms around all the complexity these churches represent.

BOARD TRANSITIONS

There are two important issues that most if not all boards must face include: first, the transitional nature of boards; and second (which is related to the first), the fuzzy understanding of the mission, vision, and values of the church.

Let's look at the first issue. Most church boards cycle membership. In other words, there is usually a certain number (often a third) of members that cycle off the board each year, with new members entering. Often these new members have never been on a board and have little to no idea as to what their role is. In the absence of clear guidelines, board members default to self-interest and to the familiar ("I don't know anything about organizational mission or vision, but I do know about procuring paperclips, so let's focus on that").

The second issue has to do with establishing and maintaining the organization's mission, vision, and values. Remember, boards exist to

4. These arguably are denominations unto themselves and do things pretty much as they see fit without outside interference.

protect the culture of the organization and to establish and monitor its trajectory. The first task of any church board is to establish a clear understanding as to why the organization exists, what its priorities are, and where it sees itself going in the next number of years. These understandings act as the organizational gyroscope guiding the organization in the proper direction.

As new board members are included, they must be first be given a clear understanding as to the mission, values, and vision of the organization. Current issues must be explained in light of these particular dimensions. When this is properly done, board members align with the staff in carrying forward the work of the church.

Once new members are schooled as to the what and especially the why of the organization, these folks must be carefully instructed as to what is expected of them: what is the role of the board in that particular church's polity, how each board member exists to maintain and forward the mission of the church, what items and issues will be discussed by the board, and which will not be discussed (because the board is not authorized to deal with these).

New board members must also be brought up to speed on current issues the board now faces, the context of those issues, and what is expected from each board member vis-à-vis those issues. In lieu of this, new board members (and indeed, many existing board members) will flounder around salient issues, attempting to not only understand the full context of the issue but also to determine how they should approach each issue when voting is elicited.

BOUNDARIES AND BALANCE MAKE IT WORK

In an article in *Christianity Today*, the Evangelical Council for Financial Accountability (ECFA) identified six top characteristics that seemed to point to a healthy board:

1. Board members were chosen by someone other than the lead pastor.
2. Policies were in place—and the board had the ability—to ask an underperforming staff member to resign.
3. The board was able to challenge and correct a lead pastor when necessary.

4. An active strategic planning process was in place.
5. Time and energy were devoted to assessing risks and opportunities.
6. The board guided the staff with strategic—but not tactical—input.[5]

In summary, the church board was more effective if it had more power.

Let's begin with this premise. Strong boards need strong leaders; strong leaders need strong boards. That's a balance that must always be held in tension, with each side understanding its own role and function. Whenever there is a strong board and a weak pastor, there's bound to be trouble. But even a strong pastor can be undermined by a board that fails to turn over enough authority to the pastor. In this situation, the board finds itself making day-to-day, tactical decisions that should be made by the pastor and staff. Just as good fences make good neighbors, good board/pastor boundaries make good churches. When the line between board and pastor is clear and their strengths are balanced, the church is well on its way to outstanding success.

I know of one situation where members of the congregation began calling various members of the board to complain about how the pastor was handling a particular and very popular staff member. When the board held their bimonthly meeting, various board members attacked the pastor on how poorly he was doing his job. They then offered suggestions as to how he should be dealing with the particular staff member. The situation continued to spiral until the denomination was called in to help in the dispute.

WHAT SHOULD THE MONTHLY AGENDA LOOK LIKE?

As already mentioned, boards notoriously spend an inordinate amount of time down in the weeds. It's usually clear that the board needs to figure out and approve budgets. But what about the operations of the church? What about conflicts in the staff? What about staffing and programming generally?

---

5. Sarah Eekhoff Zylstra, "Governing God's House: How 500 Churches Keep from Collapsing," *Christianity Today*, August 2, 2016.

There are three areas for boards to continually consider that should be on their agenda:

1. ***Tactical***. This is the operational aspect of organizational life, including budgeting and resource allocation.
2. ***Strategic***. This is the trajectory of the church into the future. Where do we see ourselves in five years? Ten years? How do we intend to reach these benchmarks?
3. ***Adaptive (transformational)***. These are the issues that touch deeply held beliefs and loyalties, that point to competing values that arise continually as church life unfolds (e.g., Do we stick with tradition, or are we innovative? Do we spend most of our time reaching out, or do we focus on building strong community within our church?). Note that transformational material may be hidden within tactical and strategic considerations. This often becomes evident when the solution appears to be simple, but the board goes round and round, unable to reach a decision to move forward.

Care should be given that each of these three areas is addressed and explored at each meeting, as well as ensuring that each meeting isn't dominated by tactical concerns. Although these are the most easily understood, they're arguably not the most important areas for the board to consider.

At the beginning of each board meeting, the purpose of the church should be stated and then the purpose of this board: "Our mission statement is [*insert description*]. In addition, these are our values—what we've said is most important to us. We as the ruling board are here primarily to guard this mission and align the church around this purpose."

Care must be taken to ensure that board meetings are spiritual events in addition to being business meetings. I know of one pastor who will stop board proceedings periodically to have everyone sing the doxology when a particular celebratory moment arrives.

As erroneous issues arise (e.g., Sunday hymn selections), the leader of the board should say, "I appreciate your concerns, but that issue is not what we are tasked to discuss in this forum."

WHERE BOARDS USUALLY GET INTO TROUBLE

Boards usually experience difficulties in the following areas:

- ***They spend their time on trivial issues.*** Boards must keep their focus on the broad issues that confront the organization.
- ***They focus on the short term.*** Boards must constantly peer into the future, taking the long view of things. The present is not their primary focus. And certainly, very little time should be spent on what happened in the past.
- ***They become reactive.*** They monitor day-to-day operations and react to what they see. In contrast, the high-functioning board actively sets policy according to the overall needs and direction of the organization.
- ***They become caught in rehashing, reviewing, and redoing things.*** Again, we're back to the details of the organization, where the board should not stray.
- ***Their accountability becomes leaky.*** Boards need to hold the pastor accountable. But if the board steps into the domain of the pastor and assumes the pastor's functions, it becomes impossible to effectively hold the pastor accountable.

HAVING A GREAT BOARD/PASTOR TEAM IN YOUR CHURCH

When I first consult with boards, it's helpful for me to hear what the pastor and the board members understand about their respective roles. There may be conflict within a board because various board members have different ideas about the ideal role for their board relative to the pastor.

My next step is to educate the board and pastor as to the roles that work best and are in the best interest of the church. This conversation provides a framework for resolving differences within the board and opening communication between the board and the pastor about appropriate boundaries between them. Then I assess the trust within the organization. Does the board trust the pastor? Does the pastor trust the board?

Often trust has been lost because boundaries were violated. Either the board, the pastor, or both have taken on responsibilities that belong to the other. Creating good, working boundaries and establishing an environment in which trust can grow become the primary agenda for the work that follows. Precious time and energy are saved when all parties involved have a clear sense of focus and responsibilities. Many are surprised to realize that board meetings can be efficient and sometimes even fun to attend.

Effective organizational functioning demands strong boards working in conjunction with strong pastors. Unfortunately, history and the landscape are littered with the remains of churches where boards and pastors have had difficulty dealing effectively with one another. It is essential that boards understand clearly what their functions are. They must also realize that the tendency of board members is to slide from a strategic focus (overall values and mission of the organization) to a tactical focus (monitoring day-to-day operations).

Board orientation is crucial. All new board members should be educated on what governance is and the role of a director. It's vital that they understand the conflicting roles they have as director, beneficiary, and perhaps even program volunteer. Help your directors to be good governors right from the start.

Board development must be continuous. Every board meeting should have time to learn about some aspect of governance or board service. Every board should have the goal that they will produce the very best board members possible by the end of their terms. Based on the number of regular board meetings you have per year, and the number of years in a single board term, develop a learning plan for the board that a director will cycle through once per term.

Both pastor and board must work hard to ensure that everyone truly sees church leadership as a partnership between staff and board. While you must follow your denominational practices, legislation and trust law require the board to exercise its authority in civil matters. Pastors and directors must never fall into the trap of thinking it's "us versus them." I like the way Charles Olsen describes the board:

> *The board of a* Christian organization is the people of God in community, the body of Christ, with members having differing gifts, wisdom and functions. The group's life should be formed by scripture, prayer, silent waiting, witnessing and serving. *Their meeting is not a gathering of individual people with business to transact, but is the functioning body of Christ.*[6]

Wow! That puts church governance into proper perspective.

---

6. Charles M. Olsen, *Transforming Church Boards into Communities of Spiritual Leaders* (Herndon, VA: Alban Institute, 1995).

16

WHEN YOUR CHURCH HITS THE GROWTH CEILING

"Why has my church has reached a certain size and we're unable to increase that number?" This is a central question I've heard from small churches everywhere. Studies show that numbers plateau rather predictably—two hundred, five hundred, a thousand, and so on. The most important plateau—and the biggest barrier—is the two-hundred membership plateau (some put the number at a hundred and fifty).

The average church in the United States has sixty-six people in Sunday school attendance with eighty-seven in worship attendance. That's across the board out of the 350,000 churches in America. That means if you run more than eighty-seven people on Sunday morning, you're already above average in America. Eighty-five percent of all churches in America average less than two hundred in worship attendance. If you run more than two hundred in worship attendance, then you're in the top 15 percent of churches in the United States.

Why is it that churches reach this critical plateau and so often are unable to exceed it? The answer is simple but with complex implications. Breaking the two hundred plateau requires a different way of doing church, and a different way of doing church requires a different way of doing leadership. The role of the pastor must change as the role of the congregation changes.

A pastor of a small church and the congregation that makes up the small church have a settled sense of what church life should be all about. In these small churches, the pastor personally ministers to virtually everyone in the congregation. This is precisely the reason that two hundred is the magic number. It's the number of people one person can reasonably pastor.[1]

So, what's the usual pattern to increase church attendance numbers? The pastor or someone in the church starts talking about growth: "We need to grow in order to fulfill the great commission." A committee is then formed with those who seem interested, suggestions are generated as to next steps, and possibly a standard outreach program is adopted. The committee excites certain members of the congregation who are gung-ho—for about six months. Then, when everyone begins to sense that nothing new is happening, the church settles back into its usual patterns with all the usual suspects.

Since this is a common pattern, let's take a closer look, beginning with the pastor.

PROCESSES FOR HEALTHY CHURCH GROWTH

Remember what I said about process: it surrounds us and usually remains unseen. But processes also dictate and guide virtually every action that unfolds in life. There are many processes that dictate the healthy growth of a church. I say *healthy* because in the last generation, some churches found a formula for growth that may not prove particularly healthy and sustainable.[2] Concentrating on processes rather than goals is a more productive pursuit.

---

1. This number is a suggested cognitive limit to the number of people with whom one can maintain stable social relationships. These are relationships in which an individual knows who each person is and how each person relates to every other person. This number was first proposed by British anthropologist Robin Dunbar. By using the average human brain size and extrapolating from the results of primates, he proposed that humans can comfortably maintain only a hundred and fifty stable relationships. Proponents assert that numbers larger than this generally require more restrictive rules, laws, and enforced norms to maintain a stable, cohesive group. It has been proposed to lie between a hundred and two hundred and fifty, with a commonly used value of a hundred and fifty. From *Wikipedia*.

2. In our competitive number-obsessed culture, be careful of comparing your church and its health with other churches around you on this one dimension of numbers. Your church, as one megachurch leader confessed, can be a mile wide and an inch deep.

What are those processes that will ultimately lead to healthy growth? While different people will include different elements in answering this question, here is my list:

1. ***An effective leader.*** The lead pastor is self-aware, and constantly and consistently growing spiritually, emotionally, mentally, and physically. All four of these elements are interrelated. In other words, if you're emotionally unhealthy, this will be reflected in your physical, mental, and spiritual life. This first trait, as I mentioned back in chapter 1, is the most critical element.
2. ***A clear congregational identity.*** Who are we? What's most important to us? Where are we going? How are we going to get there?
3. ***An understanding of the new complexity in the organization.*** Staff members clearly understand their roles and responsibilities and are held accountable to these; and the staff is aligned with the church's mission and values. Once the staff clearly understands their roles and responsibilities, they must be aligned with the mission; otherwise, they'll default to self-interest.
4. ***A developing congregation.*** A congregation that's developing into kingdom citizens is all of the following:
   - ✓ Emotionally healthy
   - ✓ Growing spiritually
   - ✓ Identifies giftedness
   - ✓ Develops giftedness
   - ✓ Deploys giftedness

THE STARTING POINT

Changing from Minister-Centric to Minister-Leader

People go into the ministry because they want to be helpful to other people. They don't necessarily see themselves as leading large congregations or managing complex multifunctional staffs. As they begin their ministries (by planting churches, taking over smaller churches, or serving on staffs of larger churches), their energies usually focus on ministering to people.

More often than not, they've had little or no training in the best practices of leadership. Then when problems and issues arise within their congregations, they handle them in an intuitive manner. Unfortunately, these intuitive actions are often the wrong actions. Intuitive actions are almost universally tactical actions

As an example, a pastor sees how much is being spent on printed bulletins each week. He researches the cost of a slide projection system and realizes he can recoup the cost in a year by discontinuing printed bulletins. When he offers this alternative to the congregation, people become angry and push back, startling him. Another pastor notes that the Sunday school class attendance for young couples now exceeds class attendance for the seniors. The only problem is that the seniors are in a bigger classroom. The next Sunday, the pastor announces to the senior and couples classes that they will switch rooms the following week—which outrages the seniors. Both pastors took the tactical, intuitive action—and both met with strong resistance, much to their surprise and dismay.

Congregational issues that arise within a church require quite different responses from pastors—their roles must change depending on what's being faced. Unfortunately, most pastors (and leaders generally) have no idea when the situation has actually changed, let alone what new role they must assume because of it. But as the saying going: If you have only a hammer in your toolbox, then everything looks like a nail!

Revisiting the "Leadership Triangle"

Consider once again this graph taken from Ford and Tucker's *The Leadership Triangle* that we first discussed in chapter 2.

Tactical. When the problem is *tactical*, the leader's role is that of an expert or an expert-finder and their tone is confident: "We can apply our current base of knowledge to solve this problem." The key is to find out what's wrong and the evident problems that need to be solved. As leaders interact with their people, they function as a trainer, bringing knowledge to bear. They also function in the present tense, asking, "How can we solve this problem right away so our today can be better?"

	Tactical	Strategic	Transformational (Adaptive)
Role	Expert	Synthesizer	Facilitator
Tone	Confident	Vision-casting	Creative
Key Question	What's wrong?	What's the focus?	What's the question?
Problems are to be . . .	Solved	Planned	Reframed
Interaction	Training	Inspiring	Free-flowing and robust
Tense	Present	Future	Past, present, future

Here's a simple tactical issue: It snowed last night, and someone needs to remove the snow from the church sidewalks and parking lot.

Unfortunately, we all like to function in the role of expert. We like people to turn to us for answers and, worst of all, we're more than happy to fuel the belief that we are the go-to person in everything dealing with the church.

Strategic. When the problem is *strategic*, the leader's role is that of a synthesizer, bringing together knowledge of the internal organization, the external constituency, and the broader climate. The appropriate tone now is that of casting vision, introducing an inspiring picture of the future that takes advantage of and confronts the changing landscape. The key here is to find out what their focus should be. These leaders realize that the main way to tackle problems is through innovation and integration. Their interaction with their followers is best described as inspirational, and they focus on the future tense: the imagined and aspired-to results of careful adherence to a clearly articulated strategy.

Strategic issues involve the future direction of the church and the resource allocation that must follow.

Transformational (Adaptive). When the problem is *transformational (adaptive)*, the leader's role is that of a facilitator, inviting dialogue and discovery, particularly in the areas of values and beliefs. The tone struck here is one of creativity, whether in problem-solving or in conflict! These leaders know that the key question now is itself: "What's the question?" These are problems that aren't so much to be solved or planned for as much as reframed—that is, considered in an entirely new way. They know that group interaction at this level of leadership needs to be free-flowing and robust—everything on the table—and that their focus is not only on the present but also on the past and the future.

Transformational challenges are the very stuff of leadership and require someone operating at full creative capacity.

In the above two examples—the slide presentation replacing printed bulletins and the switching of classrooms—both issues appeared on the surface to be purely tactical. But judging from the reaction of the congregations (both examples actually happened), there was a great deal of transformational material in the two responses.

Take the issue of growing beyond the two-hundred-person plateau. If pastors are operating as transformational leaders, then they will call a town meeting and say something like the following:

> Several in leadership in the church, along with myself, have considered a concerted effort to reach out into our community and grow our numbers. The value of reaching out is clear to all of us, I believe. But competing with that reaching-out value is the competing value of maintaining a solid community here at the church, which will inevitably be disrupted as new people enter our doors.
>
> My role as your pastor will also need to change. I will no longer be available for hospital visits, etc., when the need arises. That means you all will need to exercise your various gifts more intentionally. This will be exciting and disruptive, all at the same time.
>
> So I've called you together to discuss this issue of growth. I can't make this decision alone. It will affect all of us, so let's discuss our options and the possible consequences of each one.

The pastor then becomes a facilitator. This can be difficult for some ministers, because they want to direct the conversation and supply the answers. But the conversation must take on a life of its own as the stakeholders wrestle with the implications of growth and what they need to do. It should be noted that as pastors move into the facilitator role when they recognize the issue is transformational, there will be substantial pushback from many in the congregation. The demand will be for the pastor to "take charge" and do the hard decision-making ("Isn't that your job?"). But pastors must realize that transformational work is actually the work of the stakeholders who will have to navigate the conflicting values and ultimately live with the resulting conclusions.

During this discussion, anxiety will usually grow (the pastor must carefully regulate this). As anxiety grows, there will be an effort on the part of the congregation to have the pastor step in and "apply strong leadership" (i.e., "Tell us what to do and take the burden of this decision off us!"). This seduction must be resisted because the work must be carried on by the congregation. They must wrestle with the implications, even though the struggle is painful.

Pastors must also realize that they can't solve this problem. In fact, no one can solve this problem. It can only be navigated. It will be an ongoing problem (as it is for all churches): the problem of growth versus building a strong community.

FOCUSING ON IDENTITY, NOT OUTCOMES

Pastor leaders, when they think about growth, tend to think of outcomes. "I'd like to exceed two hundred members in five years." Or "I want ours to be a megachurch." These outcomes are the results of other actions and shouldn't be the focus when a pastor is considering exceeding a growth ceiling.

Rather, the focus needs to be on identity—the beliefs and values surrounding the mission that underlies all desired outcomes. In other words, if you've decided you want a larger church, no matter what the size, then why is this number important to you? Does having a larger church mean you'll more significant than if your church remains smaller? Are you comparing your church size to other churches around you? If the answer to these questions is yes, then there's a good possibility that a large church has become an idol.

I would argue that the main focus of the pastor should never be on the size of the congregation. I have worked with extremely effective and healthy pastors whose churches numbered around a hundred members. I have known other pastors with megachurches numbering in the thousands that are completely unhealthy. Numbers should never be the focus.

Then, what is the identity of the church? So many church leaders I've worked with set goals for their church but never focused on the church's identity. And identity begins with the following questions: Why are we here? Why has God placed us at this time and in this place? What is our unique contribution to building his kingdom? Arguably, these are the questions leadership must continually ask, and every church board meeting should begin with answering them. Every new program, every new staff member, every new building should be considered in light of these questions. "Let's remember, as we begin this board meeting . . ."

Another way of saying this is that your focus should not be on outcomes (in this case, how to break the two hundred attendance ceiling). It should be on your identity: Who are we? Then from that: What is our mission here in this community? And from that: Where do we understand God to be leading us in the next year or two?

My business partner Kevin Ford has led hundreds of churches through a process that helps them first identify their unique identity—what we call "Code." Code is the DNA of any organization. Code is the underlying fertile ground of an organization from which the culture of that organization grows. Culture shapes the beliefs, customs, and practices of an organization. These culture-shaped practices can be seen in everything from the shape and décor of the church building to the form worship takes and the programs emphasized. But most people focus only on these outward practices, never bothering to look beneath to see the informing culture, much less even deeper to the identity or code of the church.

PAIN AND RESISTANCE

One of the hardest concepts to grasp for those who wish to grow is that fact that growth brings pain—pain from the loss of important things valued by the pastor and the congregation. What losses am I talking about? Growth looks like a good thing, right?

The first loss for pastors is the loss of their role as the sole minister in the congregation's life. Pastors of small churches are jacks of all trades. Their responsibilities extend from administration, to public speaking, to hospital visitation. They are the go-to people for practically everything. And many ministers truly cherish this aspect of their lives. In addition to this, having all of these functions gives the pastor a great deal of control—control that's often hard to relinquish. But failing to relinquish this can-do-everything role means pastors become the bottleneck to growth.

There's also pain for the whole congregation—pain from the loss of a small, tight community, and from the loss of their familiar role as a congregant as they've known it.

Pain, or the anticipation of pain, causes anxiety and anxiety creates resistance. I don't want the pain, so I'll resist whatever creates it, which in this case is change. Here's an important concept to keep in mind: Resistance is not a foe but an ally. It's an ally because it gives you information, nothing more, nothing less—information as to where certain member(s) are vis-à-vis your initiatives. But resistance also tends to mess up plans for moving forward, so most people don't think of it as an ally.

A better way to understand resistance, however, is to consider it as merely the force that exists within each of us that struggle against change and the pain that change creates. Our brains are structured in such a way that makes us feel most comfortable during a steady state when nothing is altered. Introduce the hint of change, though, and our brains tend to react and resist.

The first signal resistance sends is, "I don't like this change. In fact, I don't like *any* change." The second is, "Okay, I can tolerate some change, but you're going too fast!" When the signal inside of us (or from our protégés or direct reports) activates, it's up to us to figure out what it means. It's like when your smoke detector goes off in your house late at night. You can curse it while you rip it off the wall and stomp on it. Or you can try to figure out what it's signaling to you. If there's a fire, you sure want to know about it!

COMPETING VALUES: CONTINUALLY MANUFACTURING *NON*-CHANGE

Let's review what we discussed in chapter 6 about competing values. These concepts are critical in understanding how we can be our own worst enemy as we seek to grown our congregations.

Just because you become a facilitator when the issue is transformational, don't think that you're unimportant. The key element in growth still defaults to you as the pastor. Your leadership role changes depending on the demands of the situation, but you're still the leader and central to success. Remember that arguably the most important characteristic of any successful leader is self-awareness. Self-aware leaders understand their own hard-wired personality (those elements that are God-given) and their own story (those people and factors that molded them as they grew up), and how their surrounding culture impacts their thoughts and behavior. Such self-aware leaders are able then to regulate their own anxiety as situations become disquieting.

Let's start with how we resist change—how we even tend to resist the very changes we *ourselves* say we want to make. Remember our discussion of values. Values are those things that matter most to us. The majority of us hope that our values are always aligned and consistent. Unfortunately, that is rarely the case. Life in general, and organizational life in particular, has a nasty habit of offering up choices based on values that aren't always aligned.

Every organization—business, government agency, church, club—holds numerous challenges as they go about conducting their missions. That will always be true. But what is it within us that these myriad challenges elicit? It may be nearly impossible for us to effect any important change in an organization without first understanding who we are and then working to change ourselves.

Notice that much of what we've talked about involves delegation (aka empowerment). Delegation is extremely important for pastors, although too many pastors get into micromanaging. There is undoubtedly a competing value at work inside them, unless they simply believe that micromanaging is the absolute best way to do kingdom work and lead their people (which flies in the face of all best management practices, much less kingdom values).

It's important for you to begin to see how one value (i.e., delegation) gets trumped by another value (competence). Think for a moment of what that competing value lies inside of those micromanaging pastors. There's a good chance their need to be competent may be the competing value. After all, what happens when you delegate? You cede quality control. You know how you would perform, but what about your congregants? Will they do an equally good job? The only way to know is to constantly look over their shoulders.

You might want to fill in the chart below to see where you might be defeating yourself because of internal competing values.

What do you want to see in your church? What do you value?	What are you doing/not doing that defeats column 1?	What competing values in column 2 drive your actions?
I want to see my church grow. This requires distributing leadership duties to others.	Whenever I try to turn over leadership, I become anxious and jump in and take back leadership.	I must do everything perfectly, and ceding leadership to others is too uncertain as to quality.

This graph will give you a good start in understanding your own internal inconsistencies that may be sabotaging your best intentions.

NOW WHAT? LEADING CHANGE

For an excellent look at how an organizational culture can change, take a look at the movie *Moneyball.* In this movie (based on the true story of the Oakland As baseball team in the early 1990s), general manager Billie Beane comes to a harsh reality: they had no money to buy quality players to win against the big money cities, so they fundamentally had to rethink how they selected players. Sound familiar? In our case, how can we compete against the megachurch when it's nearly impossible to close the gap between us?

With the help of Pete James, who had looked at the game and its statistics from a different paradigm, Beane began to rethink how he should "do" baseball. Right away, of course, he received massive resistance from his scouts, then his manager, and finally the players. They immediately realize the losses they'll personally suffer if they implement this new program. Their anxiety peaks and so they push back, hard. But Beane continues his program, first getting a few early adapters and then demonstrating how his plan can work (though the pushback remains fierce).

The church world is no different. If you decide you want to break the two-hundred-person barrier and grow, then the pushback will be massive. The stakeholders (congregation) will need to wrestle through the implications. The journey will be difficult. But if you stick to it, the results can be rewarding.

I think John Kotter's work is helpful here. In *Leading Change*, he describes how the change process goes through a series of phases that, in total, usually require a considerable length of time. Skipping the steps below creates only the illusion of speed and never produces satisfactory results. Making critical mistakes in any of the phases can have a devastating impact, slowing momentum and negating hard-won gains. Let's look at the stages he outlines for change:

1. Establish a sense of urgency
2. Form a powerful guiding coalition
3. Create a vision
4. Communicate that vision
5. Empower others to act on the vision
6. Plan for and create short-term wins
7. Make improvements and keep the momentum for change moving
8. Institutionalize the new approaches[3]

For a detailed discussion on these steps, see Kotter's book *Leading Change* and revisit chapter 11 where I talked about these steps in greater detail.

---

3. John Kotter, *Leading Change* (Cambridge, MA: Harvard Business School, 1996).

What's critical for you the pastor to understand is that *you* may in fact be the single most serious impediment to change. Change won't always involve growth, though we as Americans tend to see it in these terms. If this is the case, then you'll need to do a great deal of soul-searching so you can begin the change process within yourself. This process almost never occurs in a vacuum. In other words, you need other pastors whom you trust and with whom you can take this journey. The ability of each of us to deceive ourselves while our own competing values run rampant is unlimited.

17

SURVIVING AND THRIVING IN CHURCH CONFLICT

Life can be dangerous—especially church life! In all my years of coaching ministers, most of them have implicated conflict as the top culprit that makes church leadership such a challenge.

As I've said to countless ministers through these years, ministry doesn't involve conflict: ministry *is* conflict. Consider the life of Jesus as depicted in the Gospels. Nearly every interaction of his involved conflict that he needed to successfully negotiate. Several, such as when he was confronted with whether to pay taxes, were actually life threatening.

Now consider this. The healthiest churches are loaded with conflict, as are the least healthy. It's not the conflict per se; it's the very nature of the conflict that counts. It's therefore critical to understand how that conflict works.

CONFLICT: FRIEND OR FOE?

Most ministers I've worked with run from conflict. Yet conflict has an annoying habit of continually showing up, even though every possible measure is taken to prevent it. Here's the truth of the matter:

- You can't escape conflict. The issues on which we can disagree are endless.
- Conflict isn't really the problem. The problem is how people relate to one another when they are in conflict. Conflict is not only *not* a bad thing, it's good and necessary.

The Faces of Conflict

Understanding conflict and its place in your life and ministry is absolutely critical to successful ministry. I'm not going to unpack all of this issue, however; I'll just hit the highlights (you can learn more on this from my book, *Thriving through Ministry Conflict*).

I realize that the word *conflict* is emotionally loaded. Many people associate conflict with destructive images: people shouting at one another, gangs shooting at each other, countries bombing one another, and so on. Certainly, those are conflicted situations. But conflict, at its core, involves disagreement, differing ideas and opinions, and discrepant evaluations and judgments. People are different. Each person walking this earth has a different slant on things, different ways of seeing what's unfolding, differing priorities, and different strategies for dealing with all the situations life throws at us. Issues regarding conflict are also confusing. Is conflict good or bad? How do I manage it? Let's put one proposition on the table right up front: Conflict is necessary and beneficial, at least conflict that is focused properly (i.e., the Blue Zone, which we will discuss later in this chapter). As conflict strays away from issues and accesses personal stories instead (i.e., the Red Zone), conflict becomes unmanageable and destructive.

Let's make some distinctions that will help us understand conflict and the way it can be helpful or destructive. I like to divide conflict into two classes: Red Zone conflict, which is personal and destructive; and Blue Zone conflict, which is professional and helpful. Take a look at the chart on the following page.

THE RED ZONE

The Red Zone is where the atmosphere is characterized by a lack of professionalism and emotional heat. When we talk of Blue Zone conflict, we're not talking about conflict that has no emotion. That's absurd. But in the Blue Zone, the emotion is in the service of the intellect, because the primary source of the conflict is not emerging from your personal story but from the mission of the organization. The Red Zone emerges from the emotional centers within the brain, meaning that the conflict revolves around you, your story, neediness, and personal issues.

Red Zone	Blue Zone
• This conflict is personal • It's about me! • Emotions rule without being acknowledged • I must protect myself, because I'm feeling weak • Emotions are denied in myself, therefore "projected" onto others • I allow the situation to escalate	• This conflict is professional • It's about the church • The mission of the church rules despite what I feel • I must protect the staff team and the church • I understand and acknowledge my emotions, but my intellect rules • I reframe the situation into a more useful construct
Behaviors	**Behaviors**
✓ I disengage ✓ I become easily annoyed ✓ I'm resentful toward people or circumstances ✓ I procrastinate ✓ I attack the other personally ✓ I use alcohol as medication ✓ I avoid people or situations	✓ I'm thoughtful ✓ I'm reflective ✓ I listen deeply for what the underlying issue might be ✓ I don't see negative intentions in other people

When I sink into the Red Zone, my personal story begins to emerge. That story has a central theme or premise: Will I survive? Am I acceptable? Am I competent? Am I in control? When people begin to sink into their Red Zone, the same core theme usually emerges. Consequently, you'll hear people repeat the same general theme over and over again: *You're trying to control me*! (control) *Don't you think I can do this?* (competence). This Red Zone theme can color every interaction unless you become aware of this and able to manage it appropriately.

In the Red Zone, the focus becomes personal. Even though we might verbally be still disagreeing about an issue involving the organization, the real energy is coming from that personal, emotional place. The main focus isn't furthering the mission of the organization but self-protection. As I sink into the Red Zone, I disengage, becoming distracted and easily annoyed. As I become more resentful, I may attack others or avoid them, or I might turn to alcohol or other artificial means to distract myself.

RED ZONE THEMES

The Red Zone tends to elicit one of four themes:[1] survival, acceptance, competence, or control. As a Red Zone core theme is activated, the feelings associated with that issue are also activated. We then sink down deeper into a morass of feelings, many of which come from stories long ago completely unrelated to the current story that provoked the Red Zone response. These feelings then become more prominent than the ability to think clearly. As a result, we carry on the conflict immersed in our own stories and our feelings associated with it. This obviously colors our actions and reactions, and the ability to clearly understand the issues involved in the conflict are compromised.

Survival

"I must take care of myself. The world is full of peril, so I must enjoy the moment."

Those who think this often grew up in dysfunctional homes where their caregivers (usually parents) were inconsistent, unavailable, or abusive. Because of this, these people at an early age were thrown to their own resources rather than find help from others. They have traits of competence, self-reliance, and responsibility; but they also lack the ability to trust others (their initial caregivers were untrustworthy) and tend to be wary and troubled in relationships. They may have little interest in anything but what's of practical benefit to them. They become angry and panicky (Red Zone) whenever they feel their survival has been threatened.

Acceptance

"I will do anything to be loved and accepted by others. I am a people-pleaser."

---

1. We began this discussion in chapter 1: security involves the themes of survival and control, and significance involves the themes of acceptance and competence.

These people have a heart for serving others and are attentive to the needs and feelings of others. They can be overly compliant and self-effacing, and they tend to be rescuers. They become angry and carry personal grudges (Red Zone) whenever they feel rejected, but they can also read people and situations very well.

Control

"The world is a threatening place, and the only way I can feel safe is if I can control every situation and all the people around me."

These people tend to have strong leadership qualities. They are vigilant, highly organized, and have high expectations of themselves. They also often wall themselves off emotionally and don't let others get too close. They can be overly controlling toward others—bossy, directive, demanding, rigid, and nit-picking. They impose perfectionist demands on others. They become anxious and angry (Red Zone) whenever anyone or anything threatens their control. Often, though they make good leaders, they can make poor followers.

Competence

"I am loved only on the basis of my performance. My performance is never good enough, so I never feel worthy of being loved."

These people tend to be high achievers. If you're a leader, you want them on your team, because they'll work hard to achieve a great performance. They're never satisfied with their achievements. They have a hard time receiving from others, and they impose perfectionist demands on themselves. They are defensive and easily angered (Red Zone) whenever they perceive that their competence has been questioned.

POSTURES WE ASSUME IN THE RED ZONE

Understand that not everyone appears and acts the same way as they descend into the Red Zone. Some people become overly angry and shout and scream. Then it's obvious they're in the Red Zone. But others remain cool on the surface and quite possibly even sound intellectual. Yet underneath, they too have descended into their own stories and the issue has turned emotional and personal for them as well. Sufficient to say, if the disagreement around an issue is too intense, and the disagreement lasts much longer than we'd consider reasonable under the circumstances, this usually means that the conflict has entered the Red Zone for one or more of those involved.

ACTIVATING THE RED ZONE

How does the Red Zone become activated? Say I'm in a disagreement with a church board member about the color of the new carpet in the sanctuary. All of a sudden, I feel a whole load of energy rising up inside that makes me feel contempt for the board member. This energy apparently springs from nowhere. If I'm not careful, I'll begin speaking to the board member contemptuously (my usual MO when I'm provoked this way).

At this point, I'd argue that you're no longer talking about carpet. Quite probably the board member's manner and the fact that she disagreed with me (and as I see it, this was an affront to my authority or saying I'm not competent enough to pick a good color) was the activator.

Our brains have a structure that culls through incoming messages and stimuli and determines where those stimuli should go. If the message is sent to the intellectual centers of the brain, then we'll be able to think through the situation rationally (Blue Zone). But if the message is sent to our emotional centers, then our response will be quite different (Red Zone). Oh yes, I might sound quite rational, but underneath my response will actually be shaped by emotion (*How dare she*!), not by rational contemplation (*Let's see, does her suggestion of red carpet make more sense than my preference for green*?).

Those emotional centers deep within our brains are also where our stories are kept. By this, I mean that every life situation you've experienced and every person you've encountered are still there. Not only are these people and experiences there, but the meaning attached to each of these situations is also there, as well as the reactions you had to all of these people and situations. So, as these stories are evoked by present-day circumstances, the emotions surrounding those stories are elicited.

THE SAME PEOPLE KEEP SHOWING UP IN OUR LIVES

These concepts may be hard to grasp, so let's dig a little deeper. When we're growing up, certain people, beginning with our primary caregivers, carve an indelible impression on our brains—into our personal stories. Each of these important people has distinct characteristics that influenced us. These can be positive and negative. The kindly grandmother imprints the characteristics of love, acceptance, and nurturance. The overbearing father imprints control, disapproval, and non-acceptability. These characteristics remain buried in our stories in the emotional centers of our brains, until later in life we encounter people who remind us in some way of that primary person who first influenced us. And what it takes in another person to remind us of the primary character is often minimal (e.g., a boss is nothing like my overbearing father, but he is in a position of authority over me, and that's enough to activate Dad's characteristics).

So, as I meet a person later in life who reminds me of the primary person who imprinted my brain, I place on that person (i.e., project) the characteristics of the primary person. I meet an older woman with a certain smile, and I place on her the characteristics of my loving grandmother and then expect her to act in a similar way (transference). I meet the boss who can be gruff at times. I place on him all of the characteristics of my overbearing father and act toward him in similar ways (or in ways I would've liked to have acted) toward my father, all the while expecting him to be that father person I so disliked.

Our minds also play tricks on us. Once the primary characteristics have been projected, our minds see in the other person only those actions and behaviors that confirm our suspicions they're just like the primary person. In other words, when my "overbearing" boss acts kindly toward me, I just might dismiss or ignore that behavior. I filter out the good in my boss and see only those behaviors that confirm who I've already made him out to be.

These primary people, the good ones and the bad ones, keep showing up in our lives. If you're thinking this sounds a lot like prejudice, you're right. Prejudice has to do with prejudging people before we really get to know them. And once the judgment is made, it's often difficult to disconfirm how we've already judged that other person. This is because, as I said, our minds censor out disconfirming data and allow only that data that confirms our prejudgment.

Let me give you an example. A pastor told me he was having disagreements with his board chair and getting nowhere with him. After praying that God would give him discernment, he realized that this board chair was pushing all of his "Daddy buttons," reminding him of his father's arbitrary nature. This minister told me, "It was like putting on sun glasses. All of a sudden, I could see the situation without all of the glare." He was able to move into the Blue Zone, own his part of the conflict, and move the relationship to a much better and more productive place.

Take some time to fill out the graph below. Note those who had the most influence in shaping who you are (for good or ill) when you were growing up. Pay special attention to the fourth column, where you have to discern the characteristics that you tend to miss about each person.

People who were initially influential in your life	Most important characteristics	People in your life today who exhibit the same characteristics	Ways you react when you're around this person
My mother and grandfather	Warm, loving, accepting, nonjudgmental	Susie, Mr. Jones, Mrs. Smith	I feel close, accepted, and more open

THE BLUE ZONE AS OUR LIFE'S WORK

People who are well defined (as discussed in chapter 1) are those who tend to stay in the Blue Zone most of the time. That's because they have a much firmer grasp of who they are—their values, beliefs, talents, gifts, and abilities. Intellect (the primary domain of the Blue Zone) rules over emotions (the primary domain of the Red Zone). The Blue Zone allows them to have conflict (even heated conflict) around ideas, values, mission, and strategy, without seeing the conflict as personal (about me). Blue Zone conflict moves us toward a common purpose.

The Blue Zone allows us to deal with conflict, because our thought process takes place in the brain's frontal lobes where rational thought is conducted. Oh yes, there might be emotion, but that emotion is controlled by the intellect.

The Blue Zone begins when we become aware of our own Red Zone and acknowledges this. This is precisely why I emphasized self-awareness in chapter 1. If we don't have a deepening sense of who we are, then we'll be at the mercy of internal promptings that often prove not only unhelpful but quite possibly destructive.

Creating the Blue Zone is essentially the life work of everyone who aspires to lead a deeply meaningful life. The first step is, of course, the most difficult. It requires us to be completely honest with ourselves in identifying our core issues—and by extension, honest with those around us. The Blue Zone is the willingness to accept responsibility for all our behavior and the consequences of our behavior. It is the continual refusal to shift responsibility for our actions to anyone or to any institution or to any system.

Take Action!

Awareness of our response sequences helps us consciously decide about our thoughts, feelings, and actions. Note that each of these steps activates the rational brain center, thus moving the message out of the emotional brain center. You can become better aware of your feelings in a conflict by asking yourself these three questions:

1. What is your reaction in the conflict?
2. What core issues in you are being triggered?
3. What is an alternative constructive response?

Although we can't control what happens to us, we can certainly choose how to respond. Accepting responsibility for our behavior allows us to change the behavior that's inconsistent with our most personal values. And the inverse is also true! Accepting responsibility for our own behavior protects us from accepting responsibility for others' behavior.

When disagreements arise, those who disagree need to keep their focus on the mission of the organization and what's ultimately in the best interest of their organization. You'll know you're in the Blue Zone if you respond with the following behaviors:

- You're thoughtful
- You're reflective
- You're listening deeply for what the underlying issue might be
- You don't see negative intent in those who are disagreeing with you

When you're in the Blue Zone, you'll no doubt provide a non-anxious presence.

BOUNDARIES

As mentioned in an earlier chapter, healthy boundaries identify and separate the self from others and consequently are the foundation of the Blue Zone. Boundaries are the fences, both physical and emotional, that mark off our world creating zones of safety, authority, privacy, and territoriality.

Boundary difficulties go hand-in-hand with Red Zone issues. As I sink deeper into the morass of the Red Zone, my personal boundaries invariably become involved and compromised, and I engage others in my emotional drama in unhealthy ways.

For some people, their boundaries become too rigid while for others, their boundaries become too porous or ambiguous. In such cases, the integrity and cohesion of the person is threatened by a lack of definition, and we may end up asking, "Who am I, other than an extension of you?"

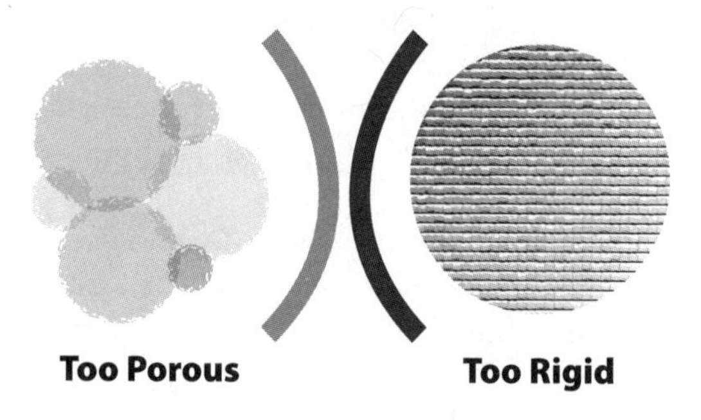

Those with porous boundaries are usually the ones most noticeably in the Red Zone. They're the ones who seem to be constantly influenced by what others do, say, and think. But those with too rigid boundaries can be just as influenced by the Red Zone. They've just constructed higher and denser walls to keep out external influences, because of their feelings (Red Zone) of vulnerability.

Boundaries are critical in understanding the Red Zone, because (as already said) sinking into the Red Zone represents a boundary violation. When I'm in conflict with someone, it's critical that I focus my thoughts and emotions on staying present to the issues on which we disagree. When I permit old storylines to creep into the equation and color my feelings, I've violated a boundary and I compromised my thinking. When I begin to see a person as someone other than they truly are (to be discussed below), I violate a boundary. For those who have poor boundaries (too rigid or too porous), the dangers of Red Zoning are all the more prominent.

Take Action!

Write down your core Red Zone issues as you understand them and how they affect you personally. Note that although everyone can experience all four themes, usually one stands out as the dominant or signature theme, with the other three subordinating to it.

Your Core Issue	Your thoughts and behaviors that flow from this issue	The result of these thoughts and behaviors	Impact this has on other people
Acceptance	I want to be loved, so I'm always nice	I'm afraid people won't like me, so I never hold them accountable	They see me as nice but wishy-washy

NOW CONSIDER YOUR BOUNDARIES

Boundaries Questionnaire

See if you agree (Yes) or disagree (No) with the following statements:

YES NO

☐ ☐ You have difficulty making up your mind.

☐ ☐ You have difficulty saying no to people.

☐ ☐ You feel your happiness depends on other people.

☐ ☐ You'd rather attend to others than to yourself.

☐ ☐ Others' opinions are more important than yours.

☐ ☐ People take and use your things without asking you.

☐ ☐ You have difficulty asking for what you want or need.

☐ ☐ You'd rather go along than express what you really want to do.

- ☐ ☐ It's hard for you to know what you think and believe.
- ☐ ☐ You have a hard time determining what you really feel.
- ☐ ☐ You don't get to spend much time alone.
- ☐ ☐ You have a hard time keeping a confidence.
- ☐ ☐ You're very sensitive to criticism.
- ☐ ☐ You tend to stay in relationships that are harmful to you.
- ☐ ☐ You tend to take on or feel what others are feeling.
- ☐ ☐ You feel responsible for other people's feelings.

If you answered yes to even two or three of these statements, then you have at least some issues with porous boundaries. The more statements you agreed with, the greater your tendency in that direction. If this is the case, then you have trouble knowing where your story ends and others' stories begin.

Now let's see if your boundaries might be too rigid.

YES NO

- ☐ ☐ Your mind is always made up.
- ☐ ☐ It's much easier for you to say no than to say yes to people.
- ☐ ☐ Your happiness never depends on others.
- ☐ ☐ You'd rather attend to yourself than to others.
- ☐ ☐ Your opinion is more important than others.'
- ☐ ☐ You rarely if ever lend your things to other people.
- ☐ ☐ Most issues appear black and white to you.
- ☐ ☐ You know exactly what you think and believe on almost every issue.
- ☐ ☐ You have a hard time determining what you really feel.
- ☐ ☐ You spend much time alone.

- ❐ ❐ You keep most of your thoughts to yourself.
- ❐ ❐ You're immune to criticism.
- ❐ ❐ You find it difficult to make and maintain close relationships.
- ❐ ❐ You never feel responsible for other people's feelings.

If you agreed with two or three of these statements, then your boundaries are probably too rigid. As a result, you may find that you're walled off from information and relationships that could prove helpful to you.

Remember, conflict is possibly the best arena in which you can understand yourself, your triggers, and how well-defined and non-anxious you truly are. Pay attention to your responses when people around you push back, disagree, and draw you into conflict. Conflict in and of itself is never the problem. The problem, if conflict tracks into negative territory, will lie with you and your responses.

18

BUILDING A LAY PASTORAL CARE MINISTRY FOR YOUR CHURCH

In *Transforming Church*, Kevin Ford points out that the consumer is the center of our culture. Since the founding of the United States, individualism has been present. Not surprisingly, this sense of the individual and the consumer mindset that accompanies it have found their way into the church.

In the Christian world, we're constantly called to a life in community, and yet we reside in a culture that pulls us decidedly in the opposite direction. When people are connected, they tend to see themselves as partners in the life, ministry, people, and mission of the church. When they don't feel connected, they tend to have a consumer mindset. A healthy community is one where people experience deep relationships and feel personally connected to the church's purpose.

So, how do we go about building community? Bearing each other's burdens? Becoming intentionally involved in one another's lives? Churches are filled with people with many needs: spiritual, psychological, relational, and physical. Churches are also filled with people who are uniquely gifted and resourced to meet those needs. An excellent strategy for building community, while at the same time bearing one another's burdens and exercising the gifts in each member, is to develop a Lay Pastoral Care Ministry (LPCM).

Let's build on what we've already said about church culture, how to change it, and especially how to help congregants recognize, develop, and deploy their gifts.

Below is a chart to show you the various roles within the LPCM.

EXPECTATIONS

Organizational life is about expectations—setting expectations, monitoring expectations, and recalibrating expectations. Before you proceed further with this chapter, I recommend you sit down with your church staff (and/or lay leadership) and discuss the expectations congregants have regarding lay involvement. How do congregants view their own involvement in the ongoing ministries of the church? Do congregants feel they're adequately prepared for participation in church ministry? Do congregants know of their unique gifting? Do congregants know in which church ministries they could usefully participate? Does the staff support lay folks in developing and participating in church ministries, or does the staff inadvertently thwart lay efforts at involvement?

Prior to this discussion, and as an aid in this discussion, it would be beneficial for you to administer the Transforming Church Index (TCI) to the congregation (see leightonfordministries.org). This survey will render a great deal of information as to the church's functioning and the expectations of the congregants. This instrument will point up five key indicators for healthy church functioning as listed below:

1. ***How church members relate to each other***. Unhealthy churches are a collection of individuals, while healthy churches relate as a community.
2. ***The church's genetic "code."*** Unhealthy churches lack a clear identity, while healthy churches have a clear sense of their DNA and take steps to align their ministries and culture with their code.
3. ***The church's leadership***. Unhealthy churches tend to be overly autocratic or bureaucratic (all decisions and initiatives must flow from the top down), while healthy churches view leadership as a shared function and a ministry.
4. ***How the church relates to the local community***. Unhealthy churches disengage from the world around them, while healthy churches focus on their mission and have an outward orientation that starts with their own locale.
5. ***How church members think about the future***. Unhealthy churches resist change and fear or deny the future, while healthy churches embrace change, even when it's painful.

PRACTICAL ISSUES THAT MATTER

The Lay Pastoral Care Ministry is designed to organize the practical resources of your congregation to assist in the various needs that arise within the church. It's one of the first caregiving ministries that needs to be put in place. It's also a ministry in which virtually everyone in the congregation can become involved. The larger the church, the more of these particular subunits you can develop with its own leadership. Small churches, of course, won't need all of the hierarchy.

There are four committees that are part of this ministry: The Compassion Ministry, Household Services, General Churchwide Ministries, and Professional Services. If you're in a smaller church, you might want to scan through the list of services presented below and pick out those that would be most practical and manageable (undoubtedly, you'll find that you're already doing several of these ministries). There is also the Duty Caregiver who's on call during the week (on a weekly rotating schedule) as special needs arise.

As your church develops the LPCM, it's important to construct a database that can be accessed and used by everyone involved in this ministry. An IT specialist within the congregation should be able to assist in the construction of this database. I'm not including specific instructions here, because each church will find tit has different needs it wants to include in this database.

COMPASSION MINISTRY

The Compassion Ministry is specifically designed to express compassion when people have particular needs.

Funerals. This is a time when grieving families are particularly vulnerable and in need of care. This care usually begins with the pastoral staff, but the needs of the family can quickly outstrip the resources the average pastor(s) can provide. This ministry will help bereaved families make arrangements for an organized and comforting funeral or memorial service. The following elements would be most helpful in the process:

- The leader of this committee is the person who contacts the family to discuss their needs and wishes (done in conjunction with the minister).
- A reception is organized through this committee for the family as desired. It's important to determine the number of people the family anticipates will attend.
- A telephone tree should be in place to alert committee members of impending funerals, along with attendant receptions so that members can perform predetermined functions.
- If the family chooses a reception at home, the committee can deliver cookies or a deli tray (though they won't be expected to set it up or serve).
- Church receptions usually require at least an hour prior to the service for setup.

- A procedural manual would help provide details for each responsibility. This would be kept at the church and passed on to each new chairperson of this committee.

Cards and sympathy plants. The purpose of this committee is to express love and concern to members of the church family in time of illness, discouragement, or loss of an immediate family member. A supply of appropriate greeting cards is kept at the church. Receptionists, small group leaders, and others involved in the LPCM are alerted to forward information as they receive it concerning those in the church who should receive a card. The card can be combined with the delivery of plants when a death occurs in a church family (it's important to coordinate this with the funeral ministry above).

Hospital visitation. Designed to provide support and encouragement to persons in the church community who are in the hospital. It's important that those involved in this ministry keep in close contact with the church staff regarding who is ill and what their special needs are. Coordination with the Duty Caregiver is important in the following ways:

- The Duty Caregiver (see definition below) must be kept informed as to needs of the hospitalized person and their family while the person remains in the hospital. It's also important to alert the Duty Caregiver as to what needs the hospitalized person will face when released.
- As soon as a release date is known, the person ministering to the hospitalized patient should alert the Duty Caregiver and ask for arrangements to be made for meals and, if necessary, discuss other services the LPCM can provide.
- In cases of permanent need, the Duty Caregiver should be asked to call the Friendship Calling Coordinator.

Nursing home ministry. Provides worship services to local nursing homes. The coordinator of this ministry should contact the Activities Director of each institution, give them the person's name, and ask for any suggestions they might have.

Volunteers need to be scheduled to do the worship services. On Monday before the scheduled worship service, confirmation needs to be obtained that all volunteers are in place. Following the service, thank you notes should be sent to volunteers.

Tele-care. A way to periodically contact every visitor and church member via telephone to express support, gather prayer requests, and disseminate information. All Sunday visitors should be called on Monday evening. It would be good to call every member every six to eight weeks. The following items can be attended to during calls for members and nonmembers:

MEMBERS

- Offer love and encouragement
- Find out ways the church can help them
- Take prayer requests—pray with them
- Work at getting them into small groups
- Work at getting them into one of the caregiving ministries

NONMEMBERS

- Offer love and encouragement
- Answer any questions about the church
- Take prayer requests—pray with them
- Look for evangelism opportunities
- Encourage them to get involved in a small group

Friendship calling. Designed to express the love and concern of the church family for individuals in times of illness, divorce, death of a spouse, or loneliness and old age. Also, this ministry will determine if these individuals have other needs. If so, arrangements will be made for meeting these needs. An up-to-date list of members and friends needing the support of the church family should be kept. There are three categories:

1. Elderly
2. Chronically ill, divorced, widowed, and lonely
3. Temporarily ill

Discretion needs to be used for the type and frequency of visits. Some people need a personal visit, while others need only a phone call of support and concern. The Duty Caregiver will apprise this committee as people in the hospital are in need of services. Typical needs that arise include:

- Pastoral call
- Home administration of Communion
- Tape of sermon or inspirational tape
- Transportation
- Meals
- Home aid
- Financial counseling

Also under the purview of this committee are the holiday deliveries, which delivers food and/or presents at Thanksgiving and Christmas. A list of families to receive these deliveries, along with addresses and phone numbers, should be kept in the database.

HOUSEHOLD SERVICES

Meals. Designed to prepare and have on hand meals for members of the congregation and others whenever the need arises. People who volunteer in the LPCM need to know that meals are available as they come across needs within the congregation. When there is a a need exists, it's strongly suggested that volunteers don't ask if a meal is wanted, as it's usually declined. Instead, assure those being helped that the caregivers already have a meal and want to deliver it. The database should include a listing of people who are willing to make and/or deliver meals. Check to determine food preferences and allergies, the number of people in the family, their address, and preferred time of delivery. Regarding storage, if the church has adequate storage facilities for frozen meals, a number can be stored for future use. It's important to label each meal as to date prepared, contents, and cooking instructions (meals should be used within three months). If the church doesn't have adequate storage, then volunteers can be asked to store a meal at their homes.

Transportation. Provides transportation for those unable to drive themselves to worship services, medical appointments, or on routine errands. It's important for the lead of this ministry to have a roster of volunteers with a designation as to when each volunteer is available.

New mothers aid. Offers love and support to new mothers and babies. The lead of this ministry should contact them to ascertain their needs. The lead can then contact the various other ministry heads for assistance (e.g., often meals will be needed when a new mother has just returned from the hospital).

Childcare. Provides childcare for those who don't have the resources or personnel to provide for their children. A roster should be kept of volunteers, complete with times of availability.

Extended family. Provides an opportunity for church families to "adopt" a single, widowed, or international church member, or a single-parent family by including them in family activities (e.g., dinners, outings, holiday gathers).

GENERAL CHURCHWIDE MINISTRIES

Except for the altar guild, these are areas of ministry that are more seasonal in nature.

Altar guild. The altar guild is made up of people who assist in the weekly preparation of the church for services. Duties include the arranging of flowers and preparation for Communion. Duties may also include the servicing of pew racks with visitor cards and so on.

Caregiver fair. The purpose of the annual (or semiannual or quarterly as may be deemed appropriate) caregivers fair is to provide the congregation with current information regarding the LPCM and to elicit their support and participation. Tables should be set up in a conspicuous place for people entering and leaving the sanctuary for Sunday services. These tables should be manned by caregivers who can explain the various ministries and provide opportunities for people to add their names to the appropriate volunteer rosters.

Caregiver fund. This is a fund established to meet the short-term requirements of the needy and those in distress who come to the attention of the LPCM. Priority can be based on physical needs such as food, medical care, childcare, and emergency housing. Needs other than financial can be channeled to another ministry within the LPCM (e.g., financial counseling, home aid, emotional support). It's best to form a committee out of the various ministry leaders within the LPCM. This committee should meet regularly to consider requests and on an ad hoc basis when emergency needs arise.

All active caregivers, members of the church staff, and other designated leaders in the church can be allowed to spend up to $50 if supported by proper documentation and receipts. Expenditures over $50 need to be submitted to the fund committee for approval. Funds may be distributed in one of two ways:

1. An outright gift to the party requesting funds
2. A no-interest loan that will be repaid at whatever schedule can be worked out between the borrowing party and the committee

It's important to maintain contact with other area churches in order to be able to coordinate assistance (if necessary) as needs arise. This will also help prevent abuses to church funds (e.g., someone going from church to church seeking assistance). Funds can be obtained in several ways:

1. United Way (application to this nonprofit organization can be made through the local chapter)
2. Monthly special offerings during or after worship services
3. Direct, designated donations from the congregation
4. Monies set aside from the general operating budget

Needs and blessings. Provides the congregation with a means of communication whereby specific needs as well as blessings can be shared. People from the congregation submit needs and blessings to the church office weekly, which are then screened and published in the church newsletter (and/or posted on a bulletin board). Requests need to be dated when received and removed after a set period of time. A decision must be made whether to include items and services for which these is a charge.

Senior citizen services. Provides a number of ministries to the senior population within the congregation, such as the following:

- *Dinner.* An annual dinner with entertainment for the elderly in the community.
- *Day program.* A half- or full-day program once a week (or month or quarterly) for seniors in the community at the church for programs, crafts, meals, and so on.
- *Family services.* Many families find themselves in positions where they must care for aging parents. This puts strain on the family, and often family caregivers feel isolated. In addition to the other LPCM services, a support group for family caregivers is provided each month where they can come together, voice common concerns, and gain support from one another.

Blood bank. Provides blood replacement as necessary for members, their families, and others in the community. The chair of this service will be responsible for organizing the blood donor program and contacting mobile units to be available twice a year at the church. A list needs to be maintained of names and numbers for contacts at the blood bank and agencies that have a high need for blood replacement

PROFESSIONAL SERVICES

These are areas of ministry that utilize the particular professional expertise that resides within the congregation.

Financial counseling. Offers free financial counseling by qualified volunteers for acute problems of financial crisis, including the special needs of widows/widowers, those divorced, and the unemployed. All matters involving financial counseling, including names and circumstances, are to be held in strict confidence between the counselor and the individual or family being counseled. Counselors should have a designated amount (see Care Fund notes) they can use at their own discretion. Higher amounts of loans/grants must be submitted to the fund committee.

Legal counseling. Qualified legal volunteers offer legal counseling. All matters involving legal counseling are to be held in strict confidence.

Unemployment services. Provides resources for those seeking employment. Volunteers for this service will:

- Instruct job seekers on the technical aspects of the job search.
- Stay in contact with job seekers during their search, either by telephone or meeting face-to-face.
- Build a job search library and loan job search books to job seekers.
- Encourage job seekers to help each other through the exchange of information. This is usually done by holding monthly meetings.
- Send information to job seekers to broaden their awareness of resources that would further their job search.
- Seek out suitable speakers who are qualified to provide information that would enhance effectiveness of job seekers.
- Request a copy of every job seeker's résumé and post on a designated board in the church or on the church website for those who would like interested parties to know their qualifications.

Auto maintenance. Assist in car maintenance and repair for those unable to do the work themselves or pay for the services. The chair of this service will organize help to perform the work needed. As an example, a team of church mechanics could be available at the church once a month to assist members with car problems. Bills of reasonable expenses are then presented to the Caregiver Fund committee for approval.

Home maintenance. Provide assistance in home maintenance and repair for those unable to do the work themselves or pay for the services. The chair will organize volunteers to perform work as needed. Bills of reasonable expenses are presented to the Caregiver Fund committee for approval.

DUTY CAREGIVER

This is a rotating position with a new person fulfilling the duties each week. The Duty Caregiver roster contains the names of the leaders of each of the various caregiving ministries (e.g., Compassion, Household Services). The Duty Caregiver needs to be reachable at all times (via a cell phone or a pager). The church phone system needs to have an extension that is dedicated to the Duty Caregiver. As people call the church requesting assistance, calls are routed to the Duty Caregiver. It is the responsibility of this person to take the vital information from the requester and then route the request to the proper ministry. A secure site on the church's website should be created to contain resources either within the church or outside that might be needed in the event of a crisis.

The Duty Caregiver will:

1. Call the church office in the early afternoon each day to see if anyone has gone to the hospital, needs transportation, needs food, and so on. The receptionist will call if something urgent comes up.
2. Contact the person or family to ascertain particulars and then call the Caregiver responsible for that area of ministry. This may involve many different committees for each situation. If this appears to be a permanent need, then advise the chair of the Friendship Calling committee.

3. Call the Hospital Visitation Committee on Monday morning for an update on people listed in the Sunday bulletin.
4. Ask the chair of the cards and plants committee to send greeting cards appropriate for the event (e.g., sympathy, get well soon).
5. Notify the church secretary of any illness, hospitalization, or other problems reported.
6. Confer with another caregiver or one of the pastors if there are any questions about how to meet a need.
7. Make note of all information received and the disposition of services. This can be done on a secure dedicated site on the church's website, or in a Duty Caregiver notebook.
8. If a notebook is kept, this needs to be taken back to the office on Sunday morning to be picked up by the next Duty Caregiver.

CREATING A MARRIAGE SAFETY NET

Premarital Assistance

Every church has some procedures in place to assist couples seeking to be married in the church. Here are some suggestions that will also provide couples with information and services that would strengthen their bond.

A premarital flowchart needs to be created for the church so couples can move through the marriage process and receive the help and information necessary at each juncture. There is a need to decide which parts of this are optional or mandatory.

Education for Married Couples

New married class. Provide a Sunday school class just for couples married under two or three years. Those married in a particular year could be formed into a group covenanted to meet for that year. A dinner could be held at the end of the year to commemorate their first year of marriage. *Implementation:* The Wedding Coordinator could be directed to organize this class, select a teacher for a year, and see to it that all newly married couples are notified as to time and place of meeting.

Preaching series on marriage. Emphasis could be on commitment and ongoing accountability. *Implementation:* Clergy needs to draw up a list of times/topics.

Strong teaching on singleness. Include encouragement of those who choose to remain single. Could be part of the marriage sermon series.

Couples' discipleship. Create a list of strong couples who could take on a newly married couple to help them along for a year.

Intensive marriage workshops. Provide several levels of workshops and seminars on a variety of marital topics with different levels of participation (one day, intensive week away, PAIRS, etc.). These could be arranged in a progression, beginning with a half-day presentation that would lead into a more intensive workshop format. *Implementation:* A task force of those involved in teaching/counseling couples at the church should convene to determine a series of programs to be offered to the congregation. Planning needs to be coordinated between everyone involved in marital assistance. This is especially true with the educational side. After the task force has organized the series of couples' programs, those who have, or who plan to do any teachings—seminars, workshops, Wednesday night adult classes, etc., need to meet on a regular basis to plan strategically as to what's working and what needs to be added/subtracted from the program.

Marital issues class. A class for married couples that would meet on a weeknight, emphasizing various topics such as the following:

- Communication
- Conflict resolution
- Intimacy
- Budgeting
- In-laws
- Leadership

One-day intensive workshop. How to make the most of your marriage (topics from above could be expanded at this time).

Marriage Encounter Weekend. This requires a strong church representative to be successful. For more information, visit the Worldwide Marriage Encounter website (www.wwme.org).

Marriage Alpha. This is a program offered through the auspices of Alpha International. For more information, visit their website (www.alphausa.org).

Marriage Groups

- Groups of couples could be organized to come together (therapist or lay led) to discuss common concerns, support each other, and so on.
- Groups for those married to unbelieving spouses to provide support to one another (lay led).
- Groups of only men or only women to discuss common concerns.

Additional Marriage Considerations

Church newsletter. Include a page each month in the church newsletter or on the website titled, "Marriage Enrichment Activities" (this would coincide with a singles page of activities). Include all upcoming events for couples (seminars, classes, retreats, etc.) for that month, as well as any pertinent articles. In case anyone is having marriage trouble, include contact details for someone to help provide an assessment and possible referral.

Therapist list. Develop a list of couples' therapists list in the area, including those who can provide intensive therapy at special rates for parishioners in financial difficulties.

Counseling fund. Establish a fund as part of the church budget to be used for counseling for couples who cannot afford it.

Annual couples retreat. Provide weekend retreats featuring a special speaker. Can begin on Friday night and run through Sunday, or Friday night and all day Saturday, ending Saturday evening.

Honor fifty-year anniversaries. Mention all fifty-plus wedding anniversaries during announcements Sunday mornings. A nice idea is to present a bouquet of roses to these couples.

Date nights with childcare. Once a month, allow couples to go out on a Friday or Saturday night. Couples can go out in groups or by themselves.

Men's/women's night out. A time when people can go out without their spouses to enjoy activities at the church. This could involve a time of singing, testimonies, and a teaching from clergy. They could be encouraged in their roles as husbands and/or fathers or wives and/or mothers. It would provide an opportunity for them to meet new people or become better acquainted with one another.

Childcare. Create a list of those willing to provide childcare so a couple could go away for a weekend or few days.

WHO'S GOING TO LEAD ALL OF THIS?

Organizing your Lay Pastoral Care Ministry (LPCM) will take time and thought, though you can start slowly. Then, as ministries and people are added, the need for more organizational levels will become apparent.

Getting Started

Bring together several key lay leaders and possibly staff from the church who have expressed particular interest in pastoral care. All small group leaders must be included at this time. Also involve people from the ruling board of the church. At least four hours should be set aside for this meeting, and it should be introduced as a strategic conversation with a view toward organizing a Lay Pastoral Care Network within the church.

In Presbyterian and several other traditions, the deacons perform in the LPCM. This body is often elected to a set term (e.g., three years) at the same time the ruling board is elected. The benefit of this system is in the clarity of expectations (see below).[1]

Leadership

It would be best, before having the strategic conversation with key church leaders, to already have appointed a person who will serve as the overall leader of this LPCM and who will be appointed for a designated amount of time (two to three years would be best). They would then work closely with a designated staff person (lay or clergy) who would coordinate with them and the staff.

The LPCM leader and the staff representative first decide which ministries will be instituted initially. Then they'll develop a leadership list of people in the congregation who could serve in the LPCM. This will be relatively easy if a Church Resource Data Bank (see below) has been developed. Potential lead caregivers should be brought together for an introduction to the program. It should be made clear from the beginning that this meeting is regarding the program, that it's not a time for sign-ups. This is when you present your overall vision for the ministry, along with the various ministry areas. Attendees should be told that they will be individually contacted within two weeks to determine interest in the program.

It would be good to have an idea, looking at the list of attendees at this introductory meeting, as to who would best serve as lead for each of the areas you've decided to open initially as part of the LPCM. Then, in contacting the attendees, each person can be offered one or two possible lead opportunities within the LPCM. Each new lead can then be supplied with a list of those who signed up to be volunteers, so that each lead can begin to fill in their areas with volunteers to do the work.

---

1. Much of what I've written in this chapter comes from my involvement with the deacons at Community Presbyterian Church in Danville, California. These folks are incredibly organized in providing for the needs of the church and surrounding community.

EXPECTATIONS

There are two critical expectations that must be specified up front with each leader and volunteer who subsequently joins the LPCM:

1. What is the task they're being asked to do? Begin with the main lead for the whole LPCM, then with leads for each area, and then with each volunteer recruited for specific areas.
2. How long are they being asked to perform this duty? All lay caregivers should be given a specific length of service that's understood from the beginning. (e.g., three years).

Commissioning

At the start of the term for these people, there should be a formal time of commissioning at which time church leaders can have the opportunity to lay hands on them and pray. In this way, the whole congregation can observe and participate and be reminded that these people have been set apart to serve.

Decommissioning

Some churches find it helpful to have a formal decommissioning, whereby people can be thanked and then dismissed from service. At this time, they could be given a certificate of appreciation to clearly mark the end of their particular role in this ministry.

HOW DO WE GET PEOPLE TO SIGN UP?

A perennial problem in churches is motivating people to get involved. This problem needs to be seen from two perspectives: mission and expectations.

Mission

Here's the first question your leadership must ask: "Is the mission of our church clear?" People fail to volunteer when they're uncertain about the mission of the church (and the code of the church generally). Then, building on this first question, you should ask: "How does the task for which the people are being asked to volunteer fit into the church's mission?" When people have a clear sense of the code and mission of the church, and how each ministry fits into that mission, they will much more readily volunteer.

Expectations

The second difficulty I find in congregants getting involved has to do with expectations. Many churches inadvertently communicate a message of consumerism: "Come to our church. We're the best show in town. We'll meet all your needs." These consumer messages provide no expectation that we're a community and that we expect all who come here to be involved in the ongoing ministries of the church. To combat this impression, some churches say to newcomers, "Welcome, we're glad you're here! Should you choose to affiliate with us, we expect that you will become involved in one or more of our ministries here. That's because we believe this is what church membership is all about." Not only is this message given to newcomers, but it's also reinforced constantly from the pulpit and throughout the formal and informal communications of the church. These churches then provide gifting surveys or listings of the ongoing ministries in which they can volunteer.

A sign-up sheet should also be provided for new members so they can become involved in one or more of the ongoing ministries of the church. The nature of the LPCM is such that people can participate as much as they want. They can become loosely involved (through calling or card sending) or greatly involved.

Church Resource Data Bank

- The norm is set as new members arrive: "You are expected to use your gifts to help one another. So, we will help you identify your gifts, and then we will channel you into our various ministry options."
- A form is distributed that lists different practical areas, many of which are covered in the LPCM, within the church where

service can be rendered (e.g., transportation, meals, carpentry, etc.).

- Data from these forms is transferred to the computer where it can be tapped by various ministry teams.

Community Resource Data Bank

Put together a file (or webpage) of outside resources available from the following:

- Other churches
- Parachurch resources (e.g., Salvation Army)
- Community nonprofit resources (e.g., Red Cross)
- Governmental resources
- County social services
- Mental health centers
- Hotlines
- Shelters

PART FIVE

Finishing Well

Your ministry at your current church is drawing to a close. You are either retiring from ministry, or you've been called to a new place of ministry. You have led the people of your current church for some time, and as a result, you have become important to them in many ways. You've married them, buried them, baptized their children, and walked with them through the ups and downs of life. Let's now turn our attention to finishing well.

19

HOW TO SUCCESSFULLY LEAVE A CONGREGATION

There comes a time for pastors when they must say goodbye to a congregation.[1] In certain situations, this is due to the pastor's retirement. In other instances, the pastor has accepted another call. Each departure involves a transition that causes distress within the congregation. How these departures are handled by pastors will greatly enhance or diminish the congregation's ability to move forward successfully.[2]

The following discussion begins with the end in view and what you can do to ensure a successful departure from your church when the time comes.

Honor the Church

When you honor something, you show it respect. This can be an easy task when the church has proved honorable toward you during your tenure. It's much more difficult, however, when you've had to battle through certain issues, receive unwarranted criticism, and been generally second-guessed along the way. Whatever has happened along the way, it's important now to recognize what specifically has been honorable and then honor those aspects.

Since honoring something that isn't honorable is a pointless exercise, you might want to take some time and list those aspects of your tenure of which you're proud. This could form the basis of your farewell message to the congregation.

---

1. This chapter was cowritten with my dear friend John Holm who, before he was an effective consultant, was an equally effective pastor for many years.

2. In certain situations, pastors are asked to step down because of particular failings. This latter situation is beyond the scope of this chapter.

Honoring the Staff and Key Leaders

Again, showing respect to those who have walked the journey along with you is much easier when those staff and leaders have been truly helpful. As with the church collectively, think of each staff member and key leader as to their particular attributes, behaviors, and contributions that you now wish to honor. Share this with each of them in private meetings. It's not recommended that you do this publicly as this may lead to jealousy and suspicion with the others.

Not Doing Any Damage on the Way Out or After You Leave

"Do damage?" you might be thinking. "I would never dream of it." Perhaps not, but ministers can do damage inadvertently, even with the motivation of helping. Let's look at an example.

Mary leaves her church after a successful fifteen-year head pastorate. Although things haven't always been perfect in the church, she's seen growth overall in the members and an intentional outreach to the community. Now retired, she moves to a new community far from her old congregation. But she begins to receive emails and other communication from former congregants. Some ask her advice, some criticize the new minister, some ask her to perform weddings and funerals. Not wanting to disappoint anyone (she was always a people pleaser), she says yes to almost all requests, gives advice on church matters, and entertains criticisms of the pastor who replaced her.

PREPARING THE CHURCH FOR THEIR NEXT PHASE

There are usually two parts to the next phase in a church's life: the period when an interim pastor fills in until a new pastor is called and takes up office.

Interim

When a church is between installed pastors, many members become highly anxious. One reason for the anxiety is at least a perceived loss of stability and continuity. After all, the community has lost a key leader. Another reason for the anxiety is the fear factor. Members are afraid that attendance will drop, contributions will decrease, and no one will join the community while this position is vacant. A vital key to a church's healthy movement through this anxious time is to engage someone specifically trained to lead congregations in transition. Often due diligence is not undertaken by the congregation (they're solely focused on the next pastor) to select a competently trained individual to fill the interim role. A transitional interim ministry specialist significantly increases the possibilities for a congregation to establish and maintain their positive, forward motion. The departing pastor needs to be aware of this and offer advice to those authorized with the transition.

Coming of the New Pastor

Though it's wise to stay out of any direct involvement in the selection of the next pastor, there are several areas where the departing pastor's expertise may be helpful.

- *Pastor search resources.* These resources (beginning with the denomination) are available to the Pulpit/Search Committee.
- *Denominational requirements for searches.* Each denomination, depending on polity, has slightly different requirements regarding searches, beginning with how much the denomination expects to be involved in the search.
- *Preparation for the arrival of the new minister.* Work with the board and staff to make any needed adjustments for staff responsibilities during the interim.

Technical Issues

What frequently occurs is the departing pastor thinks that an issue is purely technical, and goes about a step-by-step process of solving a problem or moving in a particular direction, only to be surprised by a disproportionate push-back from some faction within the congregation. Often the departing pastor reads these signals incorrectly, takes the push-back personally, and responds in ways that escalates the problem.

Realize that for many within your congregation, the experience of your departure is similar (especially those who are more emotionally needy) as abandonment of a parent. Those people who have been the most emotionally dependent on you will be the ones who are most affected, and the ones who will 'act out' (i.e., translate their emotions into action that is usually negative). These negative actions, though unconscious, are designed to draw you closer to the hurting congregant.

Strategic Challenges

Because you are departing the congregation, strategic questions about going forward will now be largely left to others to decide. And this might very well be painful for you, as you see your own pet projects, dreams and visions discarded, or greatly modified. Your temptation may be to jump back in to redirect discussions back in to the path you had designated. But this would be a mistake. In stepping away from this particular pulpit, you are handing over the mantle of leadership to others. And they now must set the course and accept the challenges that course demands.

DO THINGS IN THE PROPER ORDER

The Process

Here is the order in which the leaving process must unfold (unless of course there is a particular polity in your denomination that dictates differently). Depending on what audience you are addressing, you need to have lined up your talking points as to why you have decided on this particular course of action at this time (e.g., the board chair will need a more thorough explanation than the average weekly attender congregant). To try to think of how to respond in the moment is a bad idea, and will lead to faltering explanations that contain the wrong information to the wrong audience.

Inform the Board Chairperson. The chairperson of your leadership board is the very first person who needs to know of your decision to terminate. S/he holds the place of authority within the congregation, and therefore must be the first to be informed. Be prepared (unless you've been working toward this termination moment for a long time with many discussions).

Inform the Board. Next comes the board. You and the chairperson can determine the timing of this. Do not drop this announcement at the end of a board meeting. People will need to discuss this thoroughly with you.

Immediately inform key staff. Understand that this information will spread like wild fire throughout the congregation and then to the surrounding community. It would be best that, following close on the heels of the announcement to the board, a meeting of the staff is held when the announcement is made to them. You do not want them learning of this from a secondary source. They need to hear it from you.

Inform congregation by letter. Next comes the congregation. Think carefully as to how you wish to word this letter. This letter should contain dates of your last Sunday in the pulpit and, if known, what the future is (next call, retirement, leaving the profession, etc.). Recount the process by which you have come to this decision.

- On Monday or Tuesday leading up to the Sunday announcement, send snail mail letter to the membership.
- Friday of that same week, send an email of same letter.
- Make a verbal announcement at the following Sunday services.

THE TIMING

Consider having at least six weeks between your announcement and your departure. This will give people time to say their good-byes and arrange celebrations of your tenure. If you shorten this timeframe, you won't allow enough time for any of this. To have too long an interval, however, will turn you into a "lame duck" leader that could leave the congregation directionless.

During Those Six Weeks

Preach a sermon series that will help people with your departure and their transition to an interim pastor and the eventual call of a new pastor. This will let them know that everything will be okay and that they have everything they need to transition well. Here are some points you can make:

- "You are the church (thanks for being the church)."
- "God has a plan for you."
- "Seek forgiveness and reconciliation as needed and where appropriate."
- "I'm leaving and can no longer do pastoral acts (weddings, baptisms, funerals, and so on), and I can't and won't comment on what the interim pastor or the new pastor do."
- "Trust the call/search committee and their work by trusting your new pastor."

For Your Last Service

- "This church isn't mine or yours; it belongs to Jesus."
- "I know along the way I must have irritated, offended, and/or disappointed you." *[Have a period of silence.]* "It's important now for you to say to me that you forgive me for whatever is was. This is for my sake, your sake, and the sake of the next pastor."
- Tell them (and make sure it's true) that you went through the parish director and talked with each one of them.
- Then tell them, "The best way for you to continue a relationship with me after I leave is to get along with the next pastor."

It would be best, if you do not already do this, to keep a journal of this whole process. This will give you a good place to write down your thoughts and feelings as the process unfolds. All being well, you shouldn't experience too many disorienting twists and turns.

Wherever the Lord takes you, may he bless you in your future ministry journey!

20

SUMMING UP

To sum up, I thought it might be helpful to enumerate what we've talked about by providing a checklist for success.

For you to be truly successful in ministry for the long haul, I think there are several essentials to which you must attend by asking yourself the following questions:

- ✓ Who am I as a person and as a leader? What are my strengths? What are my challenges? How do others perceive me?
- ✓ What are the processes that surround me in which I participate? And how do these processes affect my success?
- ✓ How is my thinking distorted? When? By whom?
- ✓ What are the competing values that confront me personally? That confront the congregation I'm attempting to lead?
- ✓ Given all of my responsibilities, what do I do really well? Not so well? And what/who can I use to help with those not-so-good areas?
- ✓ Do I have a sufficient grasp of the interpersonal skills I need to establish and maintain appropriate relationships?
- ✓ How am I managing my time?
- ✓ Have I done due diligence when considering a new call?
- ✓ Do I know how to go about the first ninety days in a new ministry to set the proper tone going forward?
- ✓ Do I have a firm grasp on how to build trust?

- ✓ Do I know how to build a culture in this church that's moving the congregation toward authentic kingdom living?
- ✓ Do I understand the complexities of the church organizational model? How to best utilize it? How this model can also sabotage me?
- ✓ Can I navigate effectively the tricky political landscape within the church? The denomination? This community?
- ✓ Am I mastering the leadership skills I need to make me successful?
- ✓ Do I know how to effectively manage my staff?
- ✓ Do I know how to successfully interface with my ruling board?
- ✓ Do I understand what elements might impede the growth of this church?
- ✓ Do I know how to build a safety net for this church?
- ✓ Do I know how to leave this congregation well?

That's a tall order to consider. And because it's a tall order, I think it's important you and your key staff and lay leaders revisit this checklist each year to get a good read on how you're doing. This list is much like a golf swing. In my basically marginal golfing abilities, I've decided that at any given moment about two dozen things can go wrong with my swing. That's why those who take the game seriously visit golf pros periodically to have them evaluate their swing to see which elements might be deteriorating and in need of attention.

In this book, I've intentionally not included the steps you need to establish and maintain a robust spiritual life. Others much more qualified than I have done this, and there are many excellent resources available. But I do think it's imperative that you become involved in several of the following key helpful relationships:

- ✓ *Spiritual direction.* This concept has slowly gained traction in the Protestant world, having been a key element of the Catholic tradition for years. Every area now has spiritual directors. Finding one with whom you have rapport would be well worth while.

✓ *Coaching.* This is something I've done for years, coaching ministers from many different traditions. A good coach will help you gain immeasurable insights into yourself and how your church is functioning.

✓ *Mentoring groups.* The organization for which I now work, Leighton Ford Ministries, is involved in establishing and supporting mentoring groups for pastors around the world. Several denominations also provide for mentoring groups. This will give you a safe place where you can "bear your soul" and find invaluable fellowship and direction.

✓ *Counseling.* You may benefit from a competent counselor who can assist you with personal and relationship struggles you're facing. There are also several retreat centers established around the country where you can go for an extended period of time when you sense that you're overwhelmed and have reached a threshold where continuing on in ministry is threatened.

As you've read this book, I hope you've noticed critical issues that you must face as your ministry unfolds—and that you've also seen a way forward with each of them. If you've found significant areas that need attention, then I encourage you not to launch into a wholesale reordering of your life and your church's life at this point. Pick one or two issues you can begin to address. If possible, see if you can enlist a coach, or at the very least a friend on the journey, to help you walk through the various transitions you might need to make. Also, see if you can connect with a cohort of like-minded ministers with whom you can be honest vis-à-vis your struggles.

God bless you as you continue your journey.

FURTHER READING

Allen, David. *Getting Things Done: The Art of Stress-Free Productivity*. New York: Penguin, 2015.

Arbinger Institute. *Leadership and Self-Deception: Getting Out of the Box*. San Francisco: Berrett-Koehler, 2018.

Ariely, Dan. *The Honest Truth about Dishonesty: How We Lie to Everyone—Especially Ourselves*. New York: Harper Perennial, 2013.

Bennis, Warren. *On Becoming a Leader*. New York: Basic Books, 2009.

Blanchard, Ken, and Spencer Johnson. *The New One Minute Manager*. New York: William Morrow, 2015.

Brooks, David. *The Road to Character*. New York: Random House, 2016.

———. *The Second Mountain: The Quest for a Moral Life*. New York: Random House, 2019.

Buckingham, Marcus, and Curt Coffman. *First, Break All the Rules: What the World's Greatest Managers Do Differently*. New York: Simon & Schuster, 2016.

Buckingham, Marcus. *The One Thing You Need to Know . . . About Great Managing, Great Leading, and Sustained Individual Success*. New York: Free Press, 2005.

Chait, Richard P., William P. Ryan, and Barbara E. Taylor. *Governance as Leadership: Reframing the Works of Nonprofit Boards*. Hoboken, NJ: Wiley, 2004.

Collins, Jim. *Good to Great: Why Some Companies Make the Leap and Others Don't*. New York: Harper Business, 2001.

Covey, Steven M. R. *The Speed of Trust: The One Thing That Changes Everything*. New York: Free Press, 2008.

Crouch, Andy. *Strong and Weak: Embracing a Life of Love, Risk and True Flourishing*. Downers Grove, IL: IVP, 2016.

De Pree, Max. *Leadership Is an Art.* New York: Currency, 2004.

———. *Leadership Jazz: The Essential Elements of a Great Leader.* New York: Currency, 2008.

DeYoung, Rebecca Konyndyk. *Glittering Vices: A New Look at the Seven Deadly Sins and Their Remedies.* Grand Rapids: Brazos Press, 2009.

Drucker, Peter F. *The Effective Executive: The Definitive Guide to Getting the Rights Things Done.* New York: Harper Business, 2006.

Ford, Kevin, and Ken Tucker. *The Leadership Triangle: The Three Options That Will Make You a Strong Leader.* New York: Morgan James, 2014.

Ford, Kevin Graham, and James P. Osterhaus. *The Secret Sauce: Creating a Winning Culture.* New York: Palgrave Macmillan, 2015.

Ford, Kevin. *Transforming Church: Brining out the Good to Get to Great.* Colorado Springs: David C. Cook, 2008.

Ford, Leighton. *The Attentive Life: Discerning God's Presence in All Things.* Downers Grove, IL: IVP, 2014.

———. *Transforming Leadership: Jesus' Way of Creating Vision, Shaping Values, and Empowering Change.* Downers Grove, IL: IVP, 1993.

Friedman, Edwin H. *A Failure of Nerve: Leadership in the Age of the Quick Fix.* New York: Church Publishing, 2017.

Gilbert, Roberta M. *Extraordinary Relationships: A New Way of Thinking about Human Interactions.* Lake Frederick, VA: Leading Systems Press, 2021.

Goulston, Mark. *Just Listen: Discover the Secret to Getting through to Absolutely Anyone.* New York: AMACOM, 2015.

Grenny, Joseph, Kerry Patterson, Ron McMillan, Al Switzler, and Emily Gregory. *Crucial Conversations: Tools for Talking When Stakes Are High.* New York: McGraw-Hill Education, 2021.

Handy, Charles. *The Age of Paradox.* Boston: Harvard Business School Press, 1995.

———. *The Age of Unreason.* Boston: Harvard Business School Press, 1991.

———. *Beyond Certainty: The Changing Worlds of Organizations.* Boston: Harvard Business School Press, 1998.

Hanson, Rick, with Richard Mendius. *Buddha's Brain: The Practical Neuroscience of Happiness, Love, and Wisdom.* Oakland, CA: New Harbinger, 2009.

Headlee, Celeste. *We Need to Talk: How to Have Conversations That Matter*. New York: Harper Wave, 2018.

Heifetz, Ronald A., and Marty Linsky. *Leadership on the Line: Staying Alive through the Dangers of Change*. Boston: Harvard Business Review Press, 2017.

Heifetz, Ronald A. *Leadership without Easy Answers*. Cambridge, MA: The Belknap Press of University Press, 1998.

Heifetz, Ronald, Alexander Grashow, and Marty Linsky. *The Practice of Adaptive Leadership: Tools and Tactics for Changing Your Organization and the World*. Boston: Harvard Business Press, 2009.

Kegan, Robert, and Lisa Laskow Lahey. *How the Way We Talk Can Change the Way We Work: Seven Languages for Transformation*. San Francisco: Jossey-Bass, 2002.

Kerr, Michael E., and Murray Bowen. *Family Evaluation: The Role of the Family as an Emotional Unit That Governs Individual Behavior and Development*. New York: W. W. Norton, 1988.

Kotter, John. *Leading Change*. Cambridge, MA: Harvard Business School, 1996.

Lawler III, Edward E. *From the Ground Up: Six Principles for Building the New Logic Corporation*. San Francisco: Jossey-Bass, 1996.

Lencioni, Patrick. *The Advantage: Why Organizational Health Trumps Everything Else in Business*. San Francisco: Jossey-Bass, 2012.

———. The *Five Dysfunctions of a Team: A Leadership Fable*. San Francisco: Jossey-Bass, 2002.

Loehr, Jim. *The Only Way to Win: How Building Character Drives Higher Achievement and Greater Fulfillment in Business and Life*. New York: Hachette, 2012.

Miller, Rex, Mabel Casey, and Mark Konchar. *Change Your Space, Change Your Culture: How Engaging Workspaces Lead to Transformation and Growth*. Hoboken, NJ: Wiley, 2014.

Osterhaus, James P. *Family Tales: Rewriting the Stories That Made You Who You Are*. Downers Grove, IL: IVP, 1997.

Osterhaus, James P., Joseph M. Jurkowski, and Todd A. Hahn. *Thriving through Ministry Conflict: A Parable on How Resistance Can Be Your Ally*. Grand Rapids: Zondervan, 2010.

Schaller, Lyle E. *The Middle-Sized Church: Problems and Prescriptions*. Nashville: Abingdon Press, 1985.

———. *The Multiple Staff and the Larger Church*. Nashville: Abingdon Press, 1980.

———. *The Small Church Is Different.* Nashville: Abingdon Press, 1982.

———. *The Very Large Church: New Rules for Leaders.* Nashville: Abingdon Press, 2000.

Scazzero, Peter. *The Emotionally Healthy Church: A Strategy for Discipleship That Actually Changes Lives.* Grand Rapids: Zondervan, 2015.

———. *Emotionally Healthy Spirituality: It's Impossible to Be Spiritually Mature, While Remaining Emotionally Immature.* Grand Rapids: Zondervan, 2017.

Senge, Peter. *The Fifth Discipline: The Art and Practice of the Learning Organization.* New York: Doubleday, 2006.

Sinek, Simon. *Start with Why: How Great Leaders Inspire Everyone to Take Action.* New York: Portfolio / Penguin, 2009.

Sloman, Steven, and Phillip Fernbach. *The Knowledge Illusion: Why We Never Think Alone.* New York: Riverhead, 2018.

Stanovich, Keith E. *The Bias That Divides Us: The Science and Politics of Myside Thinking.* Boston: The MIT Press, 2021.

Tavris, Carol, and Elliot Aronson. *Mistakes Were Made (but Not by Me): Why We Justify Foolish Beliefs, Bad Decisions, and Hurtful Acts.* Boston: Mariner, 2020.

Ten Elshof, Gregg A. *I Told Me So: Self-Deception and the Christian Life.* Grand Rapids: Eerdmans, 2009.

Toon, Peter, L. Roy Taylor, Page Patterson, and Samuel E. Waldron. *Who Runs the Church? Four Views on Church Government.* Grand Rapids: Zondervan, 2004.

Wheatley, Margaret J. *Leadership and the New Science: Discovering Order in a Chaotic World* San Francisco: Berrett-Koehler, 2006.